THIS
GOLDEN
FLEECE

*A Journey Through
Britain's Knitted History*

ESTHER RUTTER

GRANTA

Granta Publications, 12 Addison Avenue, London W11 4QR

First published in Great Britain by Granta Books, 2019

A CIP catalogue record for this book
is available from the British Library.

1 3 5 7 9 10 8 6 4 2

ISBN 978 1 78378 435 6
eISBN 978 1 78378 437 0

www.granta.com

Typeset by M Rules

Printed and bound by CPI Group (UK) Ltd,
Croydon, CR0 4YY

MIX
Paper from
responsible sources
FSC® C020471

THIS
GOLDEN
FLEECE

For Tom and Rose –
chief recipients of my knitting

In Memoriam
Walford Arnold Griffiths
14.11.1932–01.05.2019

Contents

List of Illustrations   ix

Prologue   3

1   Dentdale Gloves   9
2   Proper Ganseys   37
3   Revolutionary Knitting   61
4   Highland Kilts and Stockings   85
5   A Not-So-Itsy-Bitsy Bikini   105
6   Carding, Combing and Cricket   129
7   Vikings, Socks and the Great Yorkshire Llama   155
8   Knit-frocks, Guernseys and Jerseys   177
9   Shetland Stitches   205
10 Monmouth Caps and Funeral Stockings   235
11 Haps, Shawls and New Arrivals   255
12 A Time of Gifts   277

Notes   293
Select Bibliography   309
Acknowledgements   320
Illustration Notes and Credits   325
Index   328

List of Illustrations

PLATE SECTION

1 Completed Dentdale gloves, January 2017
2 Fisher lassies at Yarmouth, knitting in front of a pile of 'Yarmouth swills'
3 Author wears her Pussyhat at anti-Trump protest, March 2017
4 *Virginia Woolf* by Vanessa Bell, 1912
5 Temperature and knitting yarn chart, Marsha Willey
6 Gairloch stockings, Gairloch Museum
7 Uist Wool's Canach yarn
8 Yarn in production at Uist Wool
9 Military hose, Highland Folk Museum
10 Knitting frame, Ruddington, Framework Knitters Museum
11 Dubied hand-flat machine, Heriot-Watt School of Textiles and Design
12 Author in handmade bikini, Northumberland, June 2017
13 Completed child's cricket slipover, August 2017
14 Author and friend Elly Murrell with raw fleece
15 Nålebound Jorvik sock, 2017
16 Jersey spinning wheel, Hamptonne Country Life Museum, Jersey

17 'Grey-belly' and navy sleeves knitted with Jersey
     patterns, Hamptonne Country Life Museum, Jersey
18 1920s knitwear display, Shetland Museum, Lerwick
19 Jumper knitted from handspun yarn dyed with
     ground elder, Shetland Wool Week, September 2017
20 Madder dyeing, Julia Billings's Workshop, Shetland
     Wool Week, 2017
21 Fair Isle fisherman's kep, Shetland Museum, Lerwick
22 Rib and loop of replica Monmouth cap, October 2017
23 Detail from *Woolcraft: A Practical Guide to Knitting
     & Crochet with Beehive & White Heather
     Knitting Wools*, November 2017
24 Eliza Lewis's funeral stockings, St Fagans National
     Museum of History, Cardiff
25 Lace shawl knitted by Betsy Williamson, Ollaberry,
     September 2017, Shetland
26 Border and edging of baby hap, 2017
27 Completed gansey detail, January 2018
28 Author's father, Michael Rutter, in his gansey,
     January 2018

ILLUSTRATIONS IN TEXT

1 Fleece on a wire fence, Heald Brow, Cumbria   2
2 Knitting fingers of Dentdale gloves   8
3 H. Inglis gloves   17
4 Rib of Dad's gansey with needles   36
5 Robertson family of Buckhaven, Fife, knitting,
    baiting lines and mending nets   43
6 Murray brothers and crew, Cellardyke, c. 1900   51
7 A Pussyhat   60
8 *Les Tricoteuses Jacobines*   77
9 Gairloch stocking with Glenfeshie behind   84

10   Gairloch, looking south   91
11   A not-so-itsy-bitsy bikini   104
12   Jedburgh Abbey   106
13   Pattern from *Practical Knitting Illustrated* for an Easy
     to Wear Beach Suit   124
14   Cotswold sheep   128
15   Carders, niddy-noddy, raw fleece, bobbins   137
16   'The Cathedral of the Cotswolds', the Church of St
     Peter and St Paul, Northleach, Gloucestershire   141
17   Scarborough Cricket Club   149
18   Cricket jumper pattern by *Wendy, c.* 1980   150
19   Starting a Jorvik sock   154
20   Nålebinding needle and Léttlopi yarn   160
21   Detail of latched needle, Imperia knitting machine   168
22   Jersey spinning wheel, Hamptonne Country
     Life Museum   176
23   Polperro harbour, Cornwall   181
24   *The Docker*, statue by Colin Miller, Jersey   186
25   Detail of an undyed Guernsey   197
26   Shetland scarf detail   204
27   Hay's Dock, Lerwick, Shetland   208
28   Anderson & Co. advertisement in *Manson's Shetland
     Almanac and Directory*, 1892   212
29   Oliver Henry and Shetland fleeces at Jamieson &
     Smith, Lerwick, Shetland   218
30   A skein of Garthenor Ryeland yarn   234
31   Male Welsh stocking knitter, Bala   247
32   Completed miniature hap   254
33   Chrissie Cheyne, Brig o' Wass, Shetland   265
34   Lace hap knitted by Betsy Williamson, Ollaberry   267
35   Knitting needles laid down beside yarn   276
36   Preston North End fans, 1954   281

THIS
GOLDEN
FLEECE

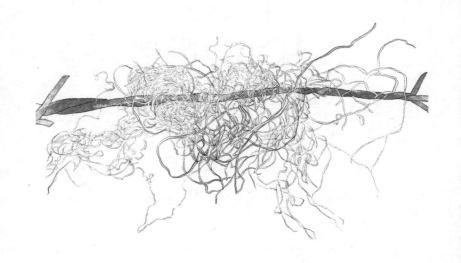

Prologue

'Biographies of things can make salient what might otherwise remain obscure.'

IGOR KOPYTOFF, *The Cultural Biography of Things*[1]

It was December, the dog-end of the year. Across the country, offices hit their annual administrative climax. Work piled up: reports to finish, invoices to issue, Christmas cards to send. I scribbled my signature on letters to people I had never met, compiled spreadsheets, printed out an acreage of labels. I hated not only the grind of endless meetings and stuffing envelopes, but also the secondary nature of this job, centred on assisting someone else's working life. At home in the evening, I sat and stewed as I knitted a soft blue scarf, a Christmas present for my mother-in-law. Knitting normally soothes me, but the repetitive knit, purl, knit of the scarf did not occupy enough of my mind to wrest away my frustration with work. My mind turned to January, with its promise of newness. I did not want to spend another year in that office. I wanted out.

Christmas arrived, and I headed south to pay my respects to parents, siblings, friends. After a week squashed into a small house whilst rain thrummed on the windows, I travelled with my husband to visit his family in Grasmere, Cumbria. New Year's Day dawned clear and cold, and we strode out to shake off the old year's languor. The frost-nipped air blew in chilly celebration as we stepped from the car at Rusland Cross and took our first year's steps towards High Ickenthwaite.

Bundled into coats, with scarves wrapping us like untidy parcels, we were pushed along by brisk winter winds. After an hour, we reached the wood at Heald Brow, which was ringed with a wooden fence topped with rusting wire. Caught in the fence's barbs were tufts of wool, silver in winter's weak sun. Sheep, at the bounds of their territory, scratched their itches here, leaving traces of themselves on the wire. I pulled away some fibres and rolled them on my palm. Grey, black and white, the strands curled in my hand. They felt waxy against my fingers, soft and greasy with lanolin. I balled the fibres in my pocket, carrying them with me like a charm.

Cumbria is a landscape shaped by sheep. The county's hilly slopes require a particular type of farming: upland shepherding, quite different from its lowland cousin. Old Westmorland and Cumberland's drystone walls enclose the more fertile land around farms, keeping sheep away from the valleys' cultivated fields to graze on the fells. This higher pasture is common land: sheep are free to graze as far as their feet can take them. Native Herdwick sheep need no fences: they are 'heafed' or 'hefted', equipped with internal compasses calibrated to their own acreage.

By half-past three, the gloaming began to gather in, driving us indoors. Warm and weary, I let the weather pin me to the sofa, where I looked again through my Christmas presents. Inside a paper bag with the tag 'love from Mum' were four balls of wool – peaty black, charcoal, dove grey, white. Banded with paper round the middle, this was Shetland Heritage yarn from Jamieson & Smith. Printed on the band was a line of tiny symbols: a shepherd's crook, a hand dipped in water, an iron crossed through, and – my favourite – three tiny Shetland sheep with horns and curling fleeces, staring down the crook. Three renegades from Britain's north-east edge, their horns a proud trumpet and a warning.

I took a sniff. A strong outdoor smell, rich and greasy, caught my nostrils. It was an unmistakably sheepy funk, the same scent from Heald Brow wood. Woolly fibres waved and snaked away from the yarn's central strand, black flecked with white, cream specks on brown. This was soft and sturdy Shetland *oo*, the *w* and *l* clipped off the English word. Familiar yet strange; the wool had come from among some seven hundred crofts and farms in Shetland's scattered archipelago, caught between the Atlantic Ocean and the North Sea. My four balls of yarn, fading dark to light, yielded to the pressure in my palm then bounced back, comfortable in their shape. My fingers prickled with the urge to knit them up. What would I make from this hardy wool?

I am not new to knitting. Gloves, hats, jumpers, cardigans and bootees: for more than twenty years I've made clothes for everyone from baby cousins to grandparents. Like many knitters, I began with a simple scarf. Herald of a lifelong love affair or a short, frustrated passion, making a scarf is a new knitter's rite of passage. Cast on by Mum, Grandma, friend or neighbour, we are handed down crafty DNA in DK yarn. 'DK' is our first shibboleth, an abbreviation for 'double knitting', the weight of yarn light enough for inexpert fingers to handle easily but sufficiently thick to soon show progress. Needles looped with a row of simple stitches are placed in eager hands like magic wands. Hands whose muscles must learn new lessons.

At first we hold too firmly, stabbing and pulling stitches in excitement. Faced with knitting now bunched tight as tweed, we loosen our stitches, which swell, drop and increase in number outside of our control. With its row upon row of knit stitches, the scarf is a teacher in tension. When presented with a hole, a bulge, an unexpected widening, the other knitter is momentarily dismayed. 'How did you do that?' comes the question; 'I don't know,' wailed in answer.

Quotidian yet extraordinary, wool has been worn for millennia on every part of the human body. Coated with lanolin, its fibres are waterproof and absorb odour. Wool draws moisture away from the skin, keeping us warmer and dryer than most synthetic fabrics. For several thousand years humans have spun the hair from sheep, goats and llamas using spindles or a spinning wheel, or matted it to form felt. Once twisted into thread, wool fibres can be knitted, or woven into cloth then draped across the floors, walls and windows of our homes, blocking drafts and damp. Wool cocoons our families in its warmth.

I love the magic of turning yarn into a garment, but I felt stumped by the sheepiness of these small, strongly scented cobs. Would anyone I know want something made with this rich-smelling wool in its proud natural shades? The symbols on the yarn band told me it could not be machine-washed, or ironed, and that its fibres needed hand-washing. It was too full of personality to be subdued into an ordinary knit. This Shetland wool demanded more of its knitter, issuing a challenge and an invitation: that I find a pattern that allowed it to be itself. To do this, I needed to understand its genesis, and its story.

A woollen thread runs back several thousand years through British history. Long before the Romans, Stone Age Britons used the fleece and hide of sheep for clothes and bedding; spindle whorls found from Shetland to Jersey show that these islands' people have spun yarn from wool for millennia. Yorkshire's mill towns swelled on the wealth of wool; the stone churches of the

Cotswolds raised spires to their skies in thanks for its abundance. Without wool, Britain would not be itself, and yet it is a history that I barely knew.

I decide to unpick Britain's woolly story. This will be my new year's quest, starting with 440 metres of fine Shetland wool. I will leave my office job to knit my way across the British Isles. Wool will be my compass and my guidebook – to Fair Isle, Yorkshire, the Cotswolds, and beyond – as I work my way from north to south and east to west. I will write about the wool I find and what I knit with it: why we do it, how we do it, who has done it.

Knitting will shape my journey through the coming year.

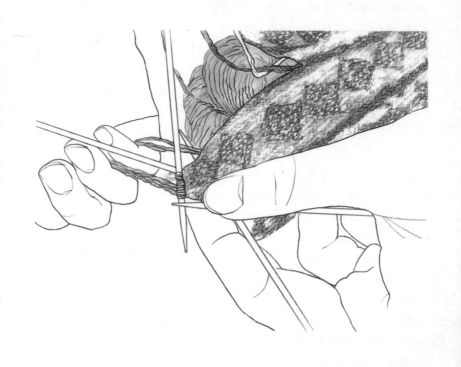

I

Dentdale Gloves

The thought of spending a year with wool feels like a homecoming. From the age of five until I was a teenager, I lived beside a sheep farm in Suffolk. My family had ended up there by mistake: my father's bankruptcy had snatched away our house, and this cottage was the only place available to rent. With newspaper stuffed under the floorboards for insulation and a bathroom in a lean-to out the back, Farm Cottage was a messy, working house, its dark-brown acrylic carpet chosen to resist stains from muddy boots. Once a dairy, the cottage was the width of a single room, ensuring that at least two walls in every room were kept cool by the outside air. Opposite was a muddle of barns and farm buildings, where rats hid in feed bins and swallows nested in the rafters. The air was ripe with the smell of mud and muck and straw.

'If I see a sheep, I have to have it.' These words have been a family joke since we first heard them on the doorstep of our new cottage, the greeting of a stocky middle-aged man in corduroy trousers and checked shirt liberally spattered with brown matter, who farmed the fields around our home. Walford Arnold Griffiths – the Celtic syllables of his name gave away his Welsh border roots – was a man obsessed by sheep.

My parents were not farmers, and we had never lived on a farm before, but I soon fell in love with living there. The farm was an escape from the house, from money worries and unvoiced guilt and disappointment. As soon as we arrived, I began volunteering to 'help' on the farm as much as I could, a handy retreat from the times when my parents let their anger bloom into shouting.

Sheep were simple in their needs. They wanted food, water, the occasional helping hand with lambing. In the farmyard uniform of wellies, grubby trousers and an old jacket, I trudged out to the fields early on dark spring mornings to stick my small hands inside lambing ewes, reaching for heads and slimy ankles to guide new life into the world. I blew warm breath into ovine lungs, got covered in ticks during shearing, and lugged around cracked buckets of mineral lick. My younger brothers and I rode on the hay wagon in high summer and scrambled up the sides of slippery straw bales. Sheep nibbled at the edges of our garden and sometimes strayed inside it, panicking back into the fields when we ran towards them. Lamby, an orphan whom no ewe would mother, came to live on a pile of newspapers in our kitchen. Penned in by cardboard boxes and my baby brother's stairgate, Lamby was fed from a bottle, sucking the long orange teat with lusty vigour. His urine stained the kitchen lino yellow but I loved Lamby with a child's unchecked passion. I am not sure my parents felt the same.

Farming was the stuff of life for Mr Griffiths, as we always called him, a passion surpassing even his love of church and song. His attachment to sheep was lifelong, his knowledge and skill connected through the generations to an ancient culture of sheep farming in Britain.

Since the Bronze Age, much of Britain's wealth has come from sheep's fleece. The Roman historian St Dionysius Alexandrinus remarked that spun British wool could only be matched in fineness by a spider's silken thread.[1] There had been sheep in the

British Isles for at least two millennia when the Romans arrived, but these Continental colonists brought their own sheep with them, some of which seem to have been a short-fleeced, self-shedding Cretan type suited to the Mediterranean climate, perhaps precursors of today's Wiltshire Horn breed.[2] They had been bred to have fleece with fibres shorter and paler than those of Britain's native sheep. Selective animal husbandry tends to breed out natural pigments, and pure white wool will take a coloured dye, whereas naturally pigmented fibres are far harder to colour reliably. Wherever the Romans colonized, their sheep came too. And they were well-protected: sources speak of Roman sheep wearing jackets made of skin to keep their fleece free of burrs and twigs.

The Romans found that the fleece of British flocks was thick and waterproof, with a long staple (the natural length of a lock of fleece), which could turn the rain. They bred their Continental sheep with native stock to create the forebears of many of the breeds we know today, and as the Roman world stretched across Europe, so too did the trade in British wool. Diocletian's *Edict on Maximum Prices*, issued in 301 CE, notes that 'British woollen rugs are priced above all others.'

In the Middle Ages, British wool spun on looms in northern Europe still fetched the highest prices in the Western world. During the fourteenth century, intricate and skilful ways of weaving wool were introduced to Britain by Flemish weavers; what followed was a boom in weaving cloth, bringing wealth to wool-producing counties from the Cotswolds to East Anglia, Devon to Yorkshire. The economic importance of wool was such that it was placed at the very heart of government: Edward III (1327–77) proclaimed that the Lord Chancellor should sit on a bale of wool in Parliament. This Woolsack is still in use in the House of Lords, albeit in a newer form – it is now filled with wool from across the Commonwealth. In front of it is the Judges' Woolsack, the huge cushion occupied during the State Opening of Parliament by the most senior members of the judiciary.

Successive monarchs and parliaments were keen to maintain the buoyancy of the wool trade and its associated industries. In 1571, Elizabeth I had Parliament decree that everyone older than six ('except Maydens, Ladyes and Gentlewomen [and] al Noble Personages') should 'use and weare upon the Saboth and Holy Daye, onles in the tyme of their travel [...] upon their head one Cappe of Woll Knytt, thicked [felted] and dressed in England [...] and onely dressed and finished by some of the Trade or Science of Cappers'.[3] Failure to do so incurred a fine of 3*s*. 4*d*. per day, which represented five days' wages for a skilled tradesman.[4] A sumptuary law not for the wealthy but the ordinary, the Cappers' Act had been introduced to protect the livelihood of members of the Guild of Cappers and their dependants; unpopular and difficult to regulate, it was repealed in 1597.

Regulations on wearing wool were not just for the living. Responding to a depression in the wool trade in the following century, Charles II's Parliament passed an Act in 1666 making it illegal to bury 'any corpse in any shirt, shift, sheet or shroud [...] in any thing other than what is made of sheep's wool only';[5] framed as a statute in 1667, it was only repealed in 1814.[6] Upholding the regulation required the swearing of affidavits by 'two credible persons' in front of a Justice of the Peace or a priest within eight days of the burial. As with the earlier Cappers' Act, however, it was often ignored: by 1735, Pope's satirical *Moral Essays* indicates that the practice of burying in wool had become if not obsolete, at least unfashionable. Narcissa, believed to be a representation of either the Duchess of Hamilton or the popular actress Anne Oldfield, ends her life with the words, 'Odious! in woollen! 'twould a Saint provoke!', instead requesting,

'No, let a charming chintz and Brussels lace
Wrap my cold limbs and shade my lifeless face:
One would not, sure, be frightful when one's dead.'[7]

North of the border, sheep reshaped Scotland's landscape and history; money from the wool trade built the monasteries in the twelfth century and, six hundred years later, was responsible for tearing down the Highland townships[8] as landowners replaced the human population with an ovine one. In Yorkshire, wool built the great mill towns of Halifax, Bradford and Leeds in the eighteenth and nineteenth centuries, where British fleece was combined with imported fibres from across the world – silk, alpaca, cotton – to produce textiles such as grosgrain, princetta and parramatta.[9] The increase in labour costs and the ready supply of cotton from Britain's colonies finally caused the decline of these industries by the beginning of the twentieth century.

Turning raw wool to spun yarn has a magic charm. As a free-range child on the farm, I pulled tufts of wool from wire fences, stuffing them into my pocket. My mum had a wooden spinning wheel and from time to time would spin her own yarn. Using a huge pair of carders – broad brushes with hard, sharp spines – she untangled the clots of dirty wool I brought in from the fields. The carders tugged at each other like burrs, separating the wool into smooth strands. By pushing the spiny paddles towards each other, a smooth rolag of wool would magically appear between their spikes. Then Mum set the spinning wheel whirring with her foot to coax this fat cigar of carded wool into yarn.

If this sounds like a fairy tale, it's no coincidence. Images of transformation at the spinning wheel pepper the world's folk stories. Think of *Rumpelstiltskin*, spinning gold from straw. Or Sleeping Beauty, pricking her finger on a spinning wheel and falling into a slumber so deep naught but one can wake her. From

Greek mythology comes Jason and the Argonauts' quest for the Golden Fleece. Jason, eager to reclaim his father Aeson's stolen throne, was tasked to bring back a golden fleece from Colchis, part of present-day Georgia. There Phrixus, after escaping death on the back of a winged ram, had sacrificed his unusual steed and gave its golden fleece in thanks to Colchis's ruler, Aeëtes. Hanging the fleece in a tree, Aeëtes instructed that it should be guarded by a never-sleeping dragon, lest a prophecy should come true that his kingdom would fall if it left. With his crew aboard the Argo, Jason set off to claim the fleece, enduring numerous tribulations before passing through the Bosphorus, the straits at the edge of the Greek world. In Colchis, Aeëtes, loath to lose the fleece, set Jason further trials: he must yoke fire-breathing bulls to a plough and sow dragon's teeth into its tilled furrows. From these sprang soldiers, to be slain by Jason. Assisted by Aeëtes's daughter Medea, Jason won back the fleece, aureate symbol of wealth and power.

Women who spin, knit and weave are legend, from Homer's Penelope, unravelling and reweaving a shroud as she waits for Odysseus's return, to mythic Ariadne, saving Theseus in the Cretan labyrinth with her ball of yarn. In Greek mythology, the three Fates, the Moirai, hold the mother thread of life – Clotho spins it, her sister Lachesis measures it, and Atropos clips it short. In Norse mythology, the Norns, goddesses wielding shears and spindles, do likewise. Women with their spinning wheels have long been agents for change and enchantment.

It's not only the tales we tell, but how we tell them. Wool has left its mark on our speech. When we want to recount a story, we spin a yarn. If we deceive, we pull the wool over people's eyes. For centuries, female spinsters (the masculine form is 'spinner') spun wool to earn their livelihood, and the word gradually became synonymous with 'unmarried woman', one not dependent on a husband for her keep. We weave narratives as we weave cloth, and our words for them are bound together: 'text' and 'textile' share the same Latin root, *textere*, to weave. Our terms for working wool and words intertwine.

In Cumbria, amid the debris of Christmas, I plan this year's adventure. Shetland yarn beside me, I think through the months ahead, plotting a knitter's course around the British Isles and planning visits to places shaped or built by wool. In Scotland, there are the islands of Shetland and the Hebrides, the settlements of Brora, Gairloch, Hawick. Down through the dales and mill towns of Cumbria, Northumberland and Yorkshire and past the knitting-machine clatter of the Midlands, I could then head east to the wool towns of Suffolk, thence west to Wales to unpick the Welsh love of sheep. Where should I start, and what shall I knit first?

A confession. *Mea culpa*, I am a messy and disobedient knitter. I can't stick to patterns, baulking at their prescription for specific needle sizes and yarn types, and instead experiment by changing colours, adding stripes and meddling with stitch counts. Recipients of this knitwear have been known to hide my handiwork discreetly in drawers whilst their babies outgrow it. Three times I have made hats so misshapen as to be unwearable, sometimes needing hot-washing to shrink them down to a suitable size. Once this resulted in a dense Rastafarian-style cap with a crown so tight I had to cut it open to fit my head inside, my face then framed by two unintentional earflaps.

I've had better luck with hands than heads, working from the Victoria and Albert Museum's archive of historic patterns to knit several pairs of 1940s Fair Isle mitts. With stiff and sturdy DK-knit fingers, these are gloves thick enough to keep you warm in a North Sea gale. When I wear them, people say, 'I'd pay money for those,' but, though I'm flattered, I have no intention of going into business. It would be false economy: weeks of knitting in exchange for a few pounds and the heartbreak of letting go.

Gloves are, then, the perfect place for me to start. After all, this will be a journey of the hands, knitting fingers acting as my guide. To become more skilful, I must learn to trust them. A knitter's hands are those of an artist, deft and often quicker-thinking than the conscious mind. Knitwear designer Karie Westermann first experienced this when her desire to knit revived after many years' absence. Recovering from a serious illness in her twenties, unable to read, watch television or listen to the radio, she amassed yarn and needles in her lap and asked her partner to find instructions for casting on. 'Look at your hands,' he responded, and Westermann found that her fingers were already casting on: 'my hands' memories of carefully forming stitches were still inside my body.'[10] With muscle memory hardwired, our bodies are palimpsests of our experience. Memory exists in the body as well as the mind.

With gloves as my talisman, I now need a pattern to suit the Shetland yarn given to me, one that will work in tones of black and white. Seeing me searching for patterns on Ravelry, the knitter's social network, my father-in-law asks me what I am doing. When I explain, he reminds me that the Wordsworth Museum, where he has worked all his adult life, holds a small collection of black and white gloves hand-knitted in the nineteenth and twentieth centuries. The museum lies across the lane from this house, metres from where I sit. Though its doors are now shut for winter, Jeff, as the curator, always has the keys to hand.

As well as displaying original manuscripts and Wordsworthian ephemera, the museum tells the story of the Lakeland world that inspired the Romantic poets William Wordsworth, Samuel Taylor Coleridge and Robert Southey. Jeff unlocks the door, silencing alarms and flooding display cabinets with light. Here, in an old wooden case perched in the museum's darkest corner, hang three pairs of exquisitely patterned gloves, made by Dentdale knitters. Thirty miles to the south-east of Grasmere, Dentdale anomalously falls within both the Yorkshire Dales National Park and the county of Cumbria – and, in the nineteenth century, became famous for its 'Terrible Knitters', immortalized as 'the Terrible Knitters e' Dent', in Southey's tale of the same name.[11] Two sisters from Grasmere were apprenticed to a knitter in Dent and Southey tells of their unsuccessful attempt to learn this trade. Dentdale's knitters were known for their speed and skill – 'terrible', like 'awful', then denoting impressiveness.

The gloves made by such 'Terrible Knitters' show few signs of wear, though the oldest was knitted around 170 years ago. Protected from curious hands in their curatorial vitrine, their slender fingers droop in checkerboard black and white, palms and backs patterned with diamonds. The cuffs are ribbed and tasselled, girdled with letters and numbers. I lean forward to get a closer look and see a set of minute names and dates knitted into the gloves: *G. Walton, 1846*; *A. Pearson, 1885*; *H. Inglis, 1924.*

For me, these gloves have a time-travelling draw, both enthralling and repellent. The people who worked and wore these gloves are long dead, but a trace of them lives on in the museum. Thousands of poetry pilgrims, searching for Wordsworth, Coleridge and Southey, glance at the names George Walton, Mrs Inglis and A. Pearson as they pass by. Caught in the woollen fibres of their gloves are their skin particles, their sweat, the remaining mortal traces of themselves. This thought causes me to shiver as Jeff opens the case to let me briefly hold the gloves in my cotton-wrapped hands.

Jeff leads me through the half-lit museum to the archives. Disappearing into underground store rooms, his assistant returns with a stack of buff boxes and blue-grey folders. Placing them reverently on long wooden tables in the research room, she leaves me with a pile of tools: a magnifying glass, two foam book rests, and a pencil.

I open the first box, and get another shiver. Inside a nest of tissue are four needles, two tiny balls of wool, and a loop of black-and-white knitting. The needles are rusted and three of them still hold loops of yarn. This is the beginning of someone else's glove, but one which only got as far as its wristband. No palm or back or fingers have been knitted. The knitter has, however, worked their name, and a date into the cuff: E. Rawnsley, 1926.

Eleanor Rawnsley, born Eleanor Simpson, was the wife of Canon Hardwicke Rawnsley, co-founder of the National Trust and campaigner for the Lake District to become a national park. Born in Grasmere, Eleanor became the canon's secretary and later his second wife, outliving him by thirty years. Known half in jest as 'Mrs Grasmere', Eleanor took an active role in village life and, among her many activities, directed Grasmere's Dialect Plays, compiled scrapbooks of stories from local life, and stockpiled boxes of Westmorland ephemera. Mary Allen, the knitter of the museum's Inglis gloves, had died two years before Eleanor began hers. Looking at Eleanor's needles, I can imagine her plying them decisively, urging herself to carry on in Mary's stead, determined to keep up this dying Westmorland tradition. Yet the redoubtable Mrs Grasmere gave up at the cuff, and for ninety years these needles have sat idle, waiting to be picked up and the work completed.

But not by me: this half-finished glove has now become a relic in its own right. I will make my own replica Dentdale gloves – and I am not the first. Beside these gloves in their acid-free archive box is a copy of *Knitting Traditions* magazine, one page clearly marked. Turning to it, I find the pattern that I need. In 2011, knitting expert Sue Leighton-White painstakingly worked out pattern charts for Mary Allen's gloves, and here they are, ready for me to use. This black-and-white glove design is typical of the Dales, specifically of Yorkshire's West Riding. In these sheep-farming valleys, many families supplemented their household income with proceeds from the sale of their hand-knitting; indeed, the marketplace at the nearby town of Kirkby Stephen goes by the name of Stocking Square. Mary Allen was one of the last in a five-hundred-year tradition to earn her living by hand-knitting.

Over time, a special style of Dales knitting developed to maximize speed whilst maintaining quality. Leighton-White described how Dales knitters of old moved to and fro with a swaying loll, known as swaving,[12] caused by lifting the right arm to strike the loop on the left needle quickly and accurately before slipping the wool over and the stitch off. Dales knitters sang as they plied the needles, repeating rhymes and ditties that, like rope-hauling seamen's shanties, helped them to concentrate on their monotonous work. So effective was this particular style of knitting that, from the seventeenth century until the nineteenth, schools were set up to teach impoverished and orphaned children to earn a living by their pins.

Back in my in-laws' cottage, I set to work, using Leighton-White's charts to plot my name and the year. The graph squares are minute, and although my name isn't long, I struggle to squeeze it into the space given. I've not used graph paper since school maths lessons; my eyes ache and shoulders tense as I count the tiny squares, each one about a twelfth of my littlest finger. The letter E followed by a four-square flower, then R u t t e r. The year I have to shrink, shortening the gaps between the numerals to fit the wristband. I also check the amount of yarn the pattern requires, and realize that, to complete the pair, I will need to use not only my black and white skeins, but also the light and dark shades of grey. I decide to use black and white for the back of the gloves and the grey for the mostly unseen palms, where the fibres will felt and blur through use, working the front and back back and forth, then joining them into the round before knitting the fingers. Knitting is often as much a matter of necessary thrift as carefully considered design.

Next I need the right needles: fine pins, 2 mm thick, and double-pointed. I only have single-pointed 2.75 mm needles with me, and wonder if I could get away with using these instead. But patterns are exact and often unforgiving, and first I must knit up a tension square. Doing so tests my own natural tension against that of the pattern; I work a small square of stocking stitch before beginning the gloves in earnest. The pattern says eleven rows of thirteen stitches should make a square inch of knitting: on my larger needles, the square comes up too large by half. I fish out a pair of single-pointed 2 mm needles and try again; this time the square is perfect. I order the requisite set of five double-pointed needles; soon I will begin this challenge in four strands.

The new needles have arrived by the time I'm back at home in Fife after Scotland's Hogmanay bank holidays. Reading the pattern, I see I need to use both pale and dark yarn to cast on each stitch. Casting on is the start of every knitted item, securely looping the first row of stitches around the needle, though novice knitters often do not learn how to cast on until they have mastered the *in, round, over and off* of the knit stitch, relying on someone else to make their first row of loops. Though I am accomplished with a cable or thumb cast-on, this two-strand method is new to me, and I carefully reread the instructions. 'Form a loop with the background yarn by looping yarn over index finger.' I awkwardly crook my finger and wrap the wool around it, then drop the stitch as I turn back to consult the pattern. Next comes the command to 'purl into the yarn at the rear of the finger using the second yarn to form the stitch'. Purling is the knitter's second stitch, the inverse of a knit stitch. Putting one needle into the front of each cast-on loop held on my finger, I wrap the yarn in front of both needles before slipping one pin under the other, moving the new stitch from left to right. Using one yarn I can purl with aplomb, but purling with two strands is tricky.

After a few false starts I have one wobbly stitch, so loose it barely holds together. I need to tighten both strands, 'first with the left hand, and then with the right', and, like magic, the two-yarn tangle transforms into a neat black loop, held in place with a white twist. I start another stitch; this falls in place beside its sister. Eight stitches later I count back to check my work and see a pleasingly smart lower line of porcelain-white stitches topped with a row of black loops: a parade of neat black sheep with small white feet.

I continue casting on up to the required seventy-eight stitches. It's easier to do with the right needle hooked under my arm so that I am working onto its point. Dent's Terrible Knitters held their pins in place with wooden needle guards, which had a circular hole at the top and were tucked into the waistbands of their skirts or tied round their waists. I wish for one of these to hold the needle steady at my waist. Often made from a single piece of wood as a lover's token, the needle guards could be straight, curved like a goose's wing, or articulated into several looped sections. Some were ornately carved, often with initials, dates and heart motifs; others were completely plain, little more than a stick. A few survive that have been made from busks, the wooden stays used to stiffen a woman's corset.[13]

Casting on has taken me nearly an hour. There are ninety more rounds to knit to complete the cuffs and palms, twenty-five for the little finger, thirty-three for the ring and index, and thirty-seven for the long middle digit. The thumb needs fifty-six short rounds, and everything needs to be doubled for the other hand. In total that's 548 rounds. At my current speed, I'll be knitting twenty-four hours a day for three weeks before these gloves are done.

As I alternate the black and white yarn for the knit one, purl one rib, I notice that neither colour is exactly true. Against a piece of plain paper, 'Natural White' is really a creamy porcelain, a warm shade without a hint of blue. 'Shetland Black' isn't black, but deepest brown, a dark chocolate flecked with coffee. Wiry fibres reach out from each yarn, connecting cream to carob. the Shetland Heritage wool was developed to mirror the homespun wool found in the Shetland Museum and Archives in Lerwick, echoing an era when every element of a garment could be grown, spun and knit at home.

How far back does Britain's love affair with wool go? It's hard to tell; textiles degrade quickly and pre-Roman written sources about them are few, but bone remains show that by the Bronze Age (c. 2500–800 BCE) sheep were being farmed in Britain. At first, they weren't kept for their wool or meat, although both were likely used by those who kept them. It was the sheep's unparalleled prowess in fertilizing the land that made them such a boon to early Britons.

The Soay is Britain's oldest native sheep breed. Farmed in the British Isles since at least the Iron Age (800 BCE–100 CE), Soay sheep are small, brown, slender and agile. Today most of the world's population of Soay sheep live on the island in the St Kilda archipelago from which they take their name. 'A most attractive little animal, by nature a great wanderer,'[14] Soay have medium-fine fleece, made of two types of wool. The first, closest to their skin, is fine and short, with each follicle measuring 15–25 microns, (thousandths of a millimetre). The primary, or outer, layer is usually 30–50 microns thick. This fleece is rougher and includes coarse hairs, and is gathered for combing and spinning.

I say 'gathered' because Soay evolved to shear themselves. Since the Bronze Age, sheep have had their fleece removed by hand, either by rooing – where the shedding fleece is gently pulled away from the body in spring – or by shearing. Left to their own devices, Soay sheep moult their coats each summer, the outer layer falling away in time to keep the sheep cool on the hottest days. They can manage themselves, and need to – St Kilda now has no permanent human population to shepherd them. This natural moulting process, known as the 'rise', causes much of the wool to be lost, carried away on the Atlantic winds that buffet the island.

Today's Soay sheep are what the archaeologist J. P. Wild calls 'living fossils': they remain genetically near-identical to Britain's Iron Age sheep. They are one of the Northern European short-tailed breeds, hardy sheep from Europe's Arctic edge evolved for cold, wet climates. Many direct descendants of these sheep still live in Britain, the most numerous being the Shetland. Shetland sheep are very like Soay, but their wool has been thickened through selective breeding. Where a Soay fleece typically weighs around half a kilo, a Shetland fleece tips the scales at two or three times that.

Shetland, administratively part of Norway until 1472, retains Old Norse words in its farming and knitting vocabulary. As well as using a rainbow of specific terms for fleece colour, Shetlanders also name the markings on their flocks. To me it is an alien litany, the words exotically unfamiliar. *Bersugget* means 'irregularly variegated'; *bielset* refers to a sheep with a differently coloured band around the neck. Animals that are dark with white patches at their head are *smirlset*; pale beasts with snow-white faces are *snaelit*, and those with lower legs a different colour to their bodies are, fittingly, *sokket*.

Each of us dwells in a polyglot house. Even if we have only a smattering of schoolgirl French, within our mother tongue lie multiple modes of language, each special and specific. Some are simple theft: Latin plant names, unapologetically untranslated, imported wholesale. Gardeners know and love them, scattering them like seeds. To the rest of us, they can be at best incomprehensible, at worst exclusive. But many subtle tongues are spoken every day, idiolects particular to a place, people and skill. Consider the builders' weighty kentledge and the printers' colophon. The vibrato of a violinist, the meteorologist's anemometer, the painter's gomme and gouache. Selvedge is the strengthened edge of a piece of fabric, kemps the coarse hairs that crop up in wool.

Some words pop up in many places with different meanings, seemingly unconnected. The rider's tack is a world away from the seamstress's. Compare the cable and cast off of the knitter with the sailor's. Each special skill offers the acolyte a new tongue – how do Latinists voice Melpomene and Calliope, horticulturalists pronounce corymbs?

Knitting is no different. The tools of the trade are simple: wool and needles. But even those terms are complex: wool is fleece when raw and becomes yarn once spun. Needles can be pins or wires. Each weight and thickness of wool has its own nomenclature: four-ply or two-ply, sport, double knit, Aran, bulky. Needles are double-pointed, circular, sized differently in different countries, modernly measured in quarter-millimetre increments. The language of knitting is also regionally diverse: whilst most know purl and plain, cast on and cast off, Dent's Terrible Knitters called their ball of wool a clew, and wound it around the thropple – a goose's windpipe filled with dried peas. Should a ball of wool fall to the floor, the sound of the thropple could be followed even in the dark of a candlelit cottage.

As I work the gloves' second row I muse on the words knit and purl, the building blocks of knitting. These one-syllable words, as everyday as food and light and cup, have meanings difficult to describe to those who do not knit. Both are stitches, secure loops of wool made by looping yarn around two sticks. Noun and verb, knit is 'the plainest stitch in knitting', its roots in the Old English *cnyttan*, 'to knot': joining by knotting. The Old English word was first written down in the tenth century in Abbot Aelfric of Eynsham's Latin *Grammar*: '*Ic nytte*', glossed with the Latin '*necto*', I bind. To knit means to bring together. When broken bones regrow, they knit. Furrowed brows knit too, and have done so at least since Chaucer wrote his *Knight's Tale* some eight hundred years ago: 'This Palamon gan knytte his browes tweye.'[15]

If knit is the plainest stitch, purl is more complicated, both in its formation and etymology. *Pirl, purl, pearl* – all three refer to a technique of twisting, winding or spinning thread. A purl is a 'thread or cord made of twisted loops'. The earliest record of purling when knitting is from 1655; the use of purl as a verb meaning 'to twist' goes back three centuries further.

Although I'm a native English speaker who spent three years at university studying English and eight years teaching its literature, knitting patterns use words I've never used before. Armscye, steeking, raglan: they offer shibboleths, but I don't yet know the code. There's knitting's curious shorthand too: 'k1, p1' seems simple enough, but 'cdd' and 'p2tog tbl' send me straight to Google. I can be completely fluent in my own language and not be able to understand instructions in a knitting pattern.

As I inch my way around this glove's wrist, I am reminded that knitting is fundamentally about binding together. Not only binding wool to wool, but wool to sheep and sheep to place. Wool comes from sheep grazed on specific plots of land, and land gives wool particular properties. In Shetland, two layers of fibres are necessary to protect sheep from the wet and windy weather. In contrast, the fleece from a mountain breed such as Herdwick is coarse, wiry and thick, evolved to protect the animal from the cold of the hills. It makes for dense tweed, rough cloth, hardwearing carpet – and is not often knitted.

This localism is mirrored in the nomenclature of sheep: the Cheviot, Suffolk, Black Welsh Mountain, Romney, Bluefaced Leicester, Cotswold, Swaledale – all breeds displaying their origins in their names. Spun yarns are the same. The word 'worsted', used to describe smooth, tightly spun yarn and the textiles woven from it, appears to come from Worstead, a Norfolk village buried deep in East Anglia.[16] Today Worstead is a scattering of houses hard to find on a road map, but 'worsted' is a term recognized worldwide. Cardigans, jerseys, Aran sweaters; Harris tweed, Fair Isle knitwear; fishermen's guernseys, Welsh-weave blankets: all are seemingly named for the places that made them, garments often particular to the wool that makes them and the lifestyles that needed them. Wool can always tie us to a place.

I have now knitted as far as the gloves' name band, which sits like a watch-strap above the ribbed cuff. Working two different-coloured yarns at the same time is known as 'stranded colourwork' and is found in traditional patterns across knitting communities of the North Atlantic. I check the chart: nine rows of stitches to spell out my name. Mary Allen's gloves have *H. Inglis* worked into them – they were made for money so bore their intended owner's name, not the knitter's. Comparatively wealthy H. Inglis, a visitor to the dale, drawn there perhaps by the grouse shoot, has become history's placeholder, obscuring the maker, Mary Allen. Mine will have my name knitted into them, the manufacturing chain between maker and wearer pulled as short as it can be.

As I work my name in stocking stitch, alternating strands of black and white, I wonder: What was Mary Allen's story? Who really were the knitters of Dent, terrible and otherwise? I turn to textile historian and writer Penelope Lister Hemingway. Could there be a better name for one dedicated to uncovering knitting's history? The Penelope of Homer's *Odyssey* spent long years weaving and then unpicking a shroud for Laertes, Odysseus's father, delaying her suitors as they vie for her hand in marriage in her husband's long absence. Hemingway is a West Yorkshire name from the heart of the county's woollen industry. To hem is to stitch closed the edges of a textile with your needle, making it fast. Hemingway stitches together history through textiles and knitwear, bringing back to life the knitters and the wearers of those garments.

One story she traced is that of Margaret Thwaite, a nineteenth-century Dentdale knitter incarcerated in York's Quaker-run asylum, The Retreat. Trawling through the admission books, Hemingway discovered that Margaret, admitted as a teenager in 1836, was a Dales farmer's daughter. Although Margaret was one of several siblings, she and her mother, Ann, lived together in an isolated cottage, away from their family and the world. When Margaret was admitted to The Retreat, Ann is described as being 'in a state of mental excitement chiefly connected with religious subjects'; Margaret herself is diagnosed as 'frantic'.[17]

As the years passed, Margaret remained in The Retreat, save for one brief release. Her doctor's notes of 1838 say, 'Now and then she does a little needlework, but it is so badly done, as to be of little use.' Hemingway, with her expert eye for knitting turns of phrase, suspects this 'needlework' is knitting. By the time

Margaret was in her fifties, knitting had become a fixation: 'She has been induced to employ herself at knitting, but the work she performs is more a tangled web, which, like Penelope of old, she pulls out as fast as she does it.' Fourteen years later, there was no change: 'She still knits away with a piece of string and pieces of wool and needles producing only a tangle.' But more than this: 'If she cannot get anything to employ herself in this manner she rubs her hands together all day long till she rubs the skin off. Then she rubs away at the sore.'[18]

By 1882, Margaret was nearing seventy and often 'has a piece of tape or string and bit of wood in her hands, with which she goes through the manoeuvre of making a stitch in knitting, immediately dropping the stitch, this is incessantly repeated'. Five years later, she still 'sits all day long playing with a piece of string and wood'. She died in 1900, at the age of eighty-five, having spent sixty-four years trying to knit in The Retreat. Hemingway reckons that the piece of wood she held was a substitute for the Dales knitter's stick to hold her needle.[19]

As I work these gloves, I think about someone else who uses knitting as a psychic guide to help them when their mind races then grinds to a halt – a modern-day Margaret, a knitter navigating her way through life's storms. The person who taught me to knit is the mother of my childhood best friend, more aunt than acquaintance. My mother preferred spinning and weaving, so it was Suzanne who showed me how to wield a pair of needles and a crochet hook. The daughter of a German woman who moved to Britain after the war, Suzanne's house was filled with fabrics, books and pictures with a glamorous European flavour. She had lived in Hamburg and travelled in Scandinavia, and made my best friend beautiful coats, jumpers and dresses patterned with Nordic colourwork. Rather thrillingly, she once took us out of school for a day to haul her family's treasured trinkets to a nearby stately home to be valued on *The Antiques Roadshow*. Alas, nothing was found to be of great financial worth, but her status as a connoisseur of culture was firmly established in our minds.

Suzanne also has bipolar disorder. As a child, I was confused by her changes in mood; sometimes she was frantic, mind racing and hands reaching for her needles. Other times, months would pass when she could hardly leave the house. In making these gloves, I am minded to thank Suzanne for teaching me how to knit over twenty years ago. Knitting is a skill passed down, most often from woman to woman. It connects us: Suzanne learned to knit from Omi, her grandmother, born at the end of the nineteenth century. I never met Omi, but Suzanne has passed on her craft to me.

After seven days of knitting, I reach the base of the fingers, having broadened the palm by two stitches in the thirty-third row and another two in the forty-first row. Measuring the glove against my palm, I slide my hand inside to check the length. Short-palmed and long-fingered, my hands are too short for this pattern. I go off-piste. Beginning the fingers two diamonds short, I decide to continue the diamonds up the back of each finger, keeping the chequerboard pattern on the palm and underside of the fingers. Now I work quickly – the first finger now only twenty-nine rounds and I swiftly knit my way up its length. I keep checking the length – four diamonds for the first and third fingers, five for the middle, three for the pinkie. The pattern is known as 'adder-back', and I plot this clutch of adders along my own hand's length.

I want to know more about Dent's latter-day Terrible Knitters, and head to the National Library of Scotland to read *The Old Hand-Knitters of the Dales*. Published in 1951, the book came about when the editor of the *Dalesman* magazine suggested that Marie Hartley and Joan Ingilby, who both went on to receive MBEs for their services to the heritage of Yorkshire, should write a pamphlet on the region's hand-knitting industry. Hartley and Ingilby were chronicling an industry in its death-throes, and they knew it. In the book's foreword, they note with both pride and sorrow:

'We stand back and admire the knitters' frugal lives. In the end the long-time threat of machine-made goods triumphed, and the industry finished.'[20]

I collect the book from the desk, and in the library's silence tear open a pack of brand-new pencils with their petrol scent of graphite. This grand library leaves me feeling disconnected from the knitters and their world – I need to mentally relocate myself into their landscape. The book includes a hand-drawn map, sketched before new county boundaries created Cumbria and North Yorkshire from Westmorland and Yorkshire's West Riding. Scanning the chart, the place names seem to come from Middle-earth, but then Tolkien stole from Britain's early tongues. Ravenstonedale and Wild Boar Fell; Mallerstang, Yockenthwaite, Garsdale; Aysgarth and Wharfedale. Names with wild, seductive magic and, like Shetland's fleece terms, Norse in origin. The *garth* and *stang* and *thwaite* and *dale* give it away.

On the second page I meet my first Dent knitter face-to-face. Wearing a heavy blouse and thick dark skirt, her keen eyes glance down to her ball of yarn, disappearing at the picture's corner. Her hands hold a set of needles, *pricks* in the dialect, with a needle guard at her waist. Pale hair in a chignon, her mouth curls into a smile. To her right sits another knitter, dressed in black bombazine from head to foot – including a pie-tin hat perched on her head and a high starched collar – and around her shoulders is a knitted sleeveless jacket. The two women sit out-doors on high-backed wooden chairs, their eyes intent upon their work. Our knitter has a huge piece of knitted work before her; its curves look like those of sock – but what a sock! It takes up her entire lap. Such pieces would have been felted, agitated with hot water and elbow grease, to create a dense boot of wool to be worn inside a sailor's wader.

Next is Mary Kirkbride, nicknamed 'Molly i' t' Wynd', sit-ting on a padded chair outside her home in Gayle. At Mary's feet is a huge whorl of yarn, sitting in its own dish, a strand linked to her fingers. Molly was famed for her knitting of those same dense 'bump' stockings for sailors. Living to the age of ninety-three, she was so adept at knitting that the clicking of her needles could be heard across the unlit street at night. Fixed in sepia, her gaze rests on something unseen and distant, dark brows furrowed. That unconscious sternness, the concentrating brow, is an expression I am told I assume when knitting and reading. I cannot see myself, but my mother and my husband tell me I frown at my books and my needles in equal measure. 'I'm not cross,' I rejoin, but I cannot deny that I look it – the sharp and now indelible crease between my eyebrows gives tacit witness. I recognize this fold of skin: it is on long-term loan from my mother, along with a rounded nose and high hairline.

After Mary come Kit and Betty Metcalfe, a husband and wife who sit knitting on either side of their door like guarding lions, proffering their knitwear to passers-by. The Metcalfes were known for knitting cycling stockings with distinctive decorative tops made especially by Kit, with Betty knitting the rest. Kit sits in his shirtsleeves and waistcoat, his large white beard almost brushing the top of his starched white apron. Their yarn spools from a large floral-patterned box at his feet. In the Dales, it wasn't just the women who knitted – they were joined by men and children to boost the family's coffers, and a good Dentdale woman could sing and knit whilst lugging her milking pail as she herded her cows – or so the old rhyme goes:

> *She knaws how to sing and knit,*
> *And she knaws how to carry the kit,*
> *When she drives her kye to pasture.*[21]

'Keep short needles.' Three wise words from these Dales-women, urging folk to work as close to the tips of their pins as possible. Their language is as distinct as their knitting: stitches were counted using the old sheep-telling numbers *yan, tan, tethera* for one, two, three. The thick undyed yarn they called 'bump'; a common praising simile of the time was for a person to be 'as open as bump knitting'. 'Striving needles' competed to see who could finish their row first.

On another page, Martha Dinsdale plies her needles in Apper-sett. One of the last to earn her living through hand-knitting, she made sailors' long-sleeved jerseys and 'popped jackets', with banded blue-and-white bodies. A thin woman with grey-white hair, bent over her needles and a ball of dark wool, she has a woven shawl round her shoulders and a knitted blanket on the chair behind her. At her waist is the needle guard for her curv-ing pin. When Hartley and Ingilby met Martha, they told her that their knitting, on straight needles, was slower than hers. She responded with a laugh: 'They aught to 'a' learned ye better.'

Knitting and laughter go together like cakes and ale. The geologist Adam Sedgwick, born in Dent in 1785, remembers from his childhood the women gathering for evening 'sittings' round their fires and knitting 'with a speed that cheated the eye'. Gloves and worsted stockings were conjured whilst the 'heart-cheering sound of the human tongue' told stories and jokes and riddles and 'ancient songs of enormous length'.[22] Sometimes a younger woman would be asked to read, and, 'apparently without inter-rupting her work by more than a single stitch', would rip through some popular novel such as *Robinson Crusoe*, the reading of which 'would charm all tongues to silence'. The historian William Howitt, travelling to Dent in the 1830s, attended one such sit-ting. Like Sedgwick, he hears an evening full of tales, and 'all this time their knitting goes on with unremitting speed. They sit rocking to and fro like so many weird wizards.'[23]

Near the back of *The Old Hand-Knitters of the Dales,* I pick up the trail of 'my' gloves. Here is a small oval photograph of their maker, Mary Allen, born in 1857, her rounded cheeks framed by wavy hair. She wears a smart dark dress, with a white frill at the neck and a cameo brooch at her throat. Hartley and Ingilby note that Mary's work is 'a last flowering of the art of the old knitters – those people to whom skill in the craft was a birth-right from past generations'.[24]

I leave the library long after dark and, as the train rattles north to Fife, finally finish the first of my Dent gloves. The trouble with gloves is the need to knit a pair, identical in nearly every stitch. I baulk at starting the second, but as the night hurtles by in alternate flashes of neon and black, I can't bear to be *haund idle*, the Scots phrase for a woman sitting with her hands lazy in her lap. Seventy-eight stitches took me a whole evening to cast on last time. But this time my fingers bypass my flitting conscious brain and seem to remember the knack. In minutes, I've made a row of black loops tethered with white. These are neater too – even as the train jinks, they form neatly and with ease, though the engine vibrations shake my writing as I tally the stitches to keep my work on track. Back at home, I work my way swiftly up the second wrist, ribbing in black and white, and knit my name again.

As January draws to a close, I begin the second glove's thumb. On the first I employed the easiest technique I know, shifting the thumb stitches onto a holder and returning later to knit these stitches and pick up those behind to form the thumb. But this time I use the method suggested in the pattern. At the base of the thumb joint I start creating a gusset, working it at the same time as the palm, adding stitches with each row. The result is usable but lumpy, a rough Frankensteinian digit that irks me. I pull my eyebrows down in frustration and work through my mistake.

I knit on, up and away to the top of the palm, and divide for the fingers. The fingers knit up quickly, and as I near the tip of the final finger a buzz of excitement builds in me, and I pause to photograph these last stitches. In my hand, I hold a pair of Dentdale gloves, made from Shetland yarn, with my name at the wrist. I wriggle my hands inside, delighted to find that each glove fits. I hope Mary Allen, Eleanor Rawnsley and Margaret Thwaite would be pleased – I am.

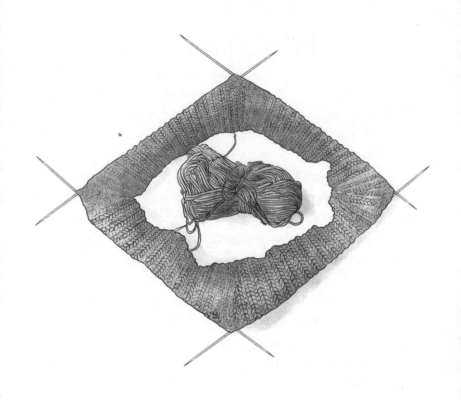

2

Proper Ganseys

I do not agree with T. S. Eliot: February is the cruellest month. Twenty-eight days of rain upon hail, frost upon fog. Two dour Scots words, *snell* and *dreich*, sum up this cold and bitter weather. Car journeys lengthen as we creep along country roads, watching for black ice and standing water. Power cuts plunge us into darkness and we keep an eye on the forecast. After the dark days of December and January, February is the last full month of winter we endure. Our reserves, buoyed up by Christmas and New Year, are now at their lowest ebb. Above the fifty-sixth parallel, we've not seen sun since the clocks changed in October. There's another month to thole until March springs us forward. We hunker down at home, gorge on television, keep up our winter weight.

What better time of year to begin a gansey? Heavy and dense, these traditional fishermen's jerseys are tightly knitted to repel water, encasing the wearer in a woolly cocoon from neck to waist and wrist. From the Pentland Firth to the Yarmouth Roads, ganseys were the *de facto* uniform of Britain's fishing fleet from the early nineteenth century until after the advent of waterproof PVC in 1913. Even if we do not recognize the word, most of us have seen a gansey. Under his yellow foulies, the old seaman on my tin of Fisherman's Friend cough drops wears a navy one, and Captain Birdseye sports a cream gansey with his dark blue blazer. One famous photograph of Ernest Shackleton shows the explorer gazing into the distance under furrowed brows, clad in a gansey with a pair of thick fur mittens dangling from a leather strap.

Usually dark blue, but occasionally grey, cream, or even red, ganseys were worn up and down the UK's coast and along Britain's inland waterways. Before inexpensive mass production, most were knitted at home by the wives, mothers, daughters, sisters and grandmothers of the men who wore them. Knitting a gansey will be my challenge for this dark and enervating month.

How did the gansey get its name? Used interchangeably with 'guernsey', the gansey's roots are uncertain and debated. Jersey and Guernsey, two of the Channel Islands, are both bywords for woollens. The island of Guernsey has long been known for its fine hand-spinning, but the gansey jumper is found as far north as Shetland, without apparent connection to the Channel Islands' style of knitting. Scotland's ganseys are knitted all in one piece, but historically, jumpers from Guernsey have been knitted as separate pieces that are then stitched together. Some believe that 'gansey' is not a bastardized form of 'guernsey' but instead the offspring of *garn*, or 'yarn': the hard Germanic *g* kept on the eastern seaboard but softened to a *y* elsewhere. As we say 'woollies' for 'woollens', a gansey might really be a 'yarnsey'. There's good evidence for this: in Norwegian and Danish 'yarn' is *garn*, and a Norwegian jumper is a *genser*. The *Oxford English Dictionary* doesn't agree, but its entry for 'gansey' is thin. In Irish Gaelic, *geansaí* is the generic word for 'jumper', the sister of the Scottish Gaelic *geansaidh*: two Gaelicizations of 'guernsey', parallel to the English appropriation of 'jersey'.

I begin to follow the gansey trail in Fife, at the Scottish Fisheries Museum. Ganseys are firmly associated with the coast, with the fishing communities that wore them. People have fished along Scotland's coast for at least nine millennia. For most of this, fishing was for subsistence; the aim survival, not commerce. By the fourteenth century, trade in fish for export to the Continent had been established on Scotland's east coast, but the scale was small.

Then came the Highland Clearances. Prior to the eighteenth century, Highland townships, or *bailes*, were run as communal concerns, the land shared and farmed between households.[1] Fertile land was divided into 'rigs' of roughly equal size – around 240 paces long and six paces wide – and reallocated every two to three years among community members.[2] This 'runrig' system, divided between the fertile infield ('croft-land' or 'mucked land') and the outfield (the 'folds' or *faughs*), supported perhaps only four or five households, with *bere* (barley), small oats (*Avena strigosa*), flax and kale grown in the infield, and a mix of grazing and turf and oat on the outfield.[3] Beyond this was moorland for rough grazing, providing further turf and peat to the steading. Stock, mostly small dark sheep and cattle of an ancient native type, would be moved to graze on the summer pasture and back to the 'winter-town' each year, with much of the township's population moving with them.[4] This type of subsistence farming was managed by the tacksman (from the Old Norse *taka*, 'tenure of land'), a key figure operating between the clan chief, who owned the land, and the (often related) tenant farmers. By farming small herds in this way, each township could produce much of the fleece for domestic use. From at least the twelfth until the sixteenth century, this was the primary method of farming across Highland Scotland.[5]

Further south, the agricultural landscape altered fundamentally with the enclosure of common land. With the Union of the Crowns in 1603 and the Union of the Parliaments in 1707, the old Highland system of clan-based tenancies started to change. Land began to be enclosed and divided between households, developing into what we now recognize as crofting: single-household husbandry, which combined traditional farming with fishing and other essential crafts to support each family. The old clan system with the tacksman at its heart was dissolving, as the chiefs changed from paternal figures inspiring fealty to landlords, many eager to sell lands they now saw as unprofitable.

By the eighteenth century, farmers in Scotland's south and England's north (in particular Ayrshire, the Borders, and Northumberland) were developing new techniques for large-scale farming, along with new breeds of sheep to maximize wool yield. Cheviot and Blackface sheep (also known as Lammermoor, Tweeddale, Galloway and Linton) were brought onto the grazing lands in great numbers. They displaced not only the ancient Highland sheep, small and fine-fleeced, and producing perhaps only half as much wool as the improved breed,[6] but also those who farmed them. By around 1760, the first large-scale sheep farmers from southern Scotland were established in Argyll and Dunbartonshire.[7] So came the Clearances, seen in microcosm in the parish records of Assynt in Sutherland. Between 1790 and 1808, the number of sheep farmed there increased from 7,840 to 21,000. The Countess of Sutherland and her husband Lord Stafford forcibly resettled some ten thousand people from their lands to make way for more profitable flocks of sheep. Forty-eight villages were cleared from Assynt alone, with over 160 families evicted from their homes.

Many Highland communities were forcibly resettled on the coast and encouraged to fish instead of farm. This 'shepherding' to the coast had a precedent: three hundred years previously, James IV of Scotland issued a parliamentary decree that all 'idle persons' should be forced to work in fisheries or face banishment. Neil Gunn's *The Silver Darlings*, set in the fisheries of the Moray Firth in the first half of the nineteenth century, brings the Clearances chillingly to life: 'the landlords had driven them from these valleys and pastures, and burned their houses, and set them here against the seashore to live if they could, and if not, to die.'⁸ The Clearances, most notoriously carried out by the Dukes of Sutherland and Argyll between 1847 and 1858, compelled more than 16,500 Highlanders to leave their homes. It wasn't simply a forced exodus, but something almost amounting to a massacre: 'extermination of the population'⁹ was the term used by Sir Edward Pine Coffin, the government commissary-general.

The resettled communities were often expected to make their living without experience or equipment. Lairds bought fishing boats that they rented to the men, who had to pay back the owners from the proceeds of a successful catch. This tied the men to their new village, and to fishing as a livelihood. Landowners were known to force men to fish in the roughest weather, so intent were they on a return from their investment, but fish prices on the quayside sometimes dipped so low as to make it nigh-on impossible for fishermen to buy their freedom.

Boats tended to be crewed by family groups, much as the old farms had been run, with brothers, fathers, uncles, sons and nephews working together; catches included ling, cod, haddock and whiting. There were two types of fishing: sma' (small) lining used a light, weighted line to fish close to the shore; with great lining the men headed for deeper waters, undertaking voyages lasting many days. The catch was divided according to the 'Scottish share': two thirds went to maintain the boat and gear, with the remaining third divided between the fishermen. Along Scotland's east coast in the first half of the nineteenth century, boats averaged crews of six men: each took home one eighteenth of the total catch to use or sell.

The sea may have been a cruel mistress – boats were female too – but the water was the domain of men. Women never set foot aboard ship: a 'blood taboo' precluded it. When these communities had lived inland, menstruating women were kept away from the milk churn lest they curdle the milk. On the coast, the belief in the blood curse continued. A woman should never step over fishing nets – to do so might bring about the drowning of her husband. Even a wife sitting at home combing her hair whilst her husband fished could be held responsible for his drowning, and a red-haired woman on the shore could spell disaster for the fishermen.

'Work and wait and dree your weird' (dread your fate), went the saying.[10] But more than simply waiting, women worked hard onshore. Sma' lining required fishing lines a mile long, with 600–2,000 *snids*, short horsehair threads dangling from the main line. From each snid hung a hook, with a shelled mussel as bait. At low tide, women raked mussels from the shore and stored them in *scaups*, shallow pits dug above the high-water line. Before each fishing trip, women baited the hooks with these fleshy lures, carefully – one cut or scrape from a hook could lead to blood poisoning. The lines were then coiled into *sculls*, wicker baskets carried aboard ship. Boats took at least one scull for every man aboard. This isn't ancient history: in the mid-twentieth century a fisherman from the Fife harbour of Cellardyke remembered his mother rising at four in the morning, 'when she had a baby in the cradle, with the cradle-string tied to her foot, rocking the cradle and with her hands baiting the line'.[11]

Women also waterproofed the fishing gear, *barking* the nets by dipping them in hot resin. They often sold the catch too, carrying gutted fish in creels on their backs, walking their business from house to house. It wasn't just the creels the women carried pig-a-back. Beginning a sea voyage with wet feet was unthinkable, yet before the twentieth century many smaller fishing villages did not have piers. So women bore men to the boats on their backs, walking out to where the boats lay at anchor and wading through waist-high water to deliver the men dry to their vessels. 'Fisher laddies need fisher lassies' went the proverb. The fisher lassie's lot was far from easy.

Once these tasks were done, women weren't to sit *haund idle*. If they weren't baiting, selling, cooking, mending, cleaning or barking, they were knitting. Men needed warm, waterproof apparel to wear at sea, and spinning and working the resulting yarn had long been part of the crofter's skills. Historically, women and children would have carded and spun fleece from their own sheep, but the Industrial Revolution enabled the production of strong machine-spun worsted wool, tightly plied – a perfect, almost waterproof yarn from which to knit ganseys. The inky blue worn by the British navy (hence 'navy blue') only became the colour of their uniform in the nineteenth century, following the development of synthetic aniline dyes. This combination of wool, dye and seafaring communities brought about the creation of the gansey.

Ganseys are almost always of one colour, without vibrant patterns of contrasting shades, so can in theory be knitted from a single strand of yarn. Their patterns, no less intricate than colourwork, use different stitches to texture the wool, discernible not just to the eye but to the fingertip. Whilst fisherwomen worked their needles outdoors when the weather was fine, for half the year they knitted in the smoky darkness of their homes. Much of the gansey would have been worked with a bare minimum of light: these patterns could be knitted in almost total darkness. Until some designs were recorded by folk historians in the twentieth century, most were never written down; literacy in coastal communities, living isolated from their inland cousins, was said to be lower than for the Scottish population as a whole.

What can I knit by feel alone? I pull out a pair of small straight needles and a ball of DK yarn and begin with the Scottish flag pattern, also called the 'kilt pleat'. A popular gansey motif, its lines of purled maritime signals flutter against a background of knit stitches. Tiny triangles made in purl, plotted onto paper charts, they are held permanently flying by lines of straight stocking stitch. Five, four, three, two, one – each line decreases the purl and increases the knit to form a flag. I cast on twenty-two stitches, enough for three flags, and close my eyes.

The first row is fine: knit one, purl six, repeat. I turn my needles round to work the pattern back along the needle: purl two, knit five. Back and forth across six rows I knit the flag – though I have to cheat and peek to keep me right. As I work, I find it's easier when I don't look, when I can't count with my eyes but instead trust my fingers. I can feel the flag forming under my fingertips, the knit stitches flat and the purl raised.

Next I try the Thurso flag, named for Scotland's northcoast port and made like the Scottish flag but doubled, so that each pennant comes up twice as large and is held to the mast by its longest side. Turn the flag on its side and it becomes a chevron, which can be doubled or mixed with single lines of purl to make a zigzag. The Thurso flag forms perceptibly in my hands, but my work is slowed as I stop to check each line. Working by the light of nothing brighter than a *creusie*, the smutty handmade oil lamps common in pre-electrified cottages, women would have devised patterns by feel as much as sight, combining knit, purl and cable stitches to suit their skill and whim.

Then I come to cabling, and have to look to see my way. Cables are three-dimensional ropes of knitting usually made by working yarn on and off a stubby cable needle, they can curve to left or right, winding over and under each other like a boat's thick lines. Any cabling I've done before has been against a ground of purled stitches, but here I have to learn a new trick: in Scottish ganseys, moss stitch rules OK, its dimpled texture, formed from little nubs of stitches alternately knitted then purled, the preferred foil for a Scotch cable. My first cable lurches clumsily to the right, its tension favouring my stronger hand. I need more practice.

Knitting a gansey takes even experienced knitters over a hundred hours. An average adult size is made from rounds of at least 250 stitches, and many have more than 300 stiches per round. Whilst the size of the wearer in part determines the stitch count, so does the pattern. Thick cables worked over moss stitch produce a dense, tight fabric. You need more stitches to the inch to cover your wearer with this pattern, but the resulting fabric is thick and beautifully warming.

Traditional handmade ganseys were made to measure, to fit the men who wore them, mirroring the bend of their back and the swell of their stomach. This level of intimacy, non-sexual and practical, is almost unknown in our world of *prêt-à-porter* and off-the-peg. Before I start to knit in earnest, I need to choose and carefully measure the man who will wear my gansey. Someone who is in need of its dense warmth, who spends much of their life outside.

I do not know any working fishermen. My husband earns his living at a desk and behind a lectern, my brothers at their computers. The only person I know who works outdoors every day is my father. At seventy, he earns his keep digging, pruning and planting, bolstering his pension with little bits of cash in hand. He lives a scant few miles from where he was born, and has done so all his life. Dad knows who has recently lost a husband or a wife, who might need their hedges trimmed and their borders kept in check, and can read the clouds and birds to tell the weather. Out in all seasons, a gardener might benefit from a gansey every bit as much as a fisherman.

I go home for the weekend, and take out my tape measure as Dad stands in the sitting room with his arms outstretched. I lean forward to wrap the tape under his armpits, and as I do so I realize that this is the closest I have been to him since childhood. Ours is an undemonstrative family, more given to thumps on the back than cuddling, a love that substitutes gruffness for affection. Six feet tall – 'when I stand up straight', he says – my dad is a big man who left school at fourteen and worked in foundries and machining shops before turning his hand to gardening. The tape pulled taught, his chest measures 46 inches. I check the gansey size guide in Rae Compton's *The Complete Book of Traditional Jersey and Guernsey Knitting* (1983); it only goes as far as 44 inches.[12]

I sigh; my dad grins. I get my youngest brother to hold the tape at Dad's shoulder and I check the length at his waist: 27 inches. This at least is within the guide's scope. Then we work from shoulder to wrist: Dad measures 30 inches. The guide stops at 20. 'He's off the scale,' I wail, and Dad roars with laughter. Arms 10 inches longer than the biggest pattern, but with a short barrel chest, Dad seems to be part-gorilla. This is not really a revelation. On my wedding day, Dad turned up in a smart second-hand tweed jacket, a hand-me-down from someone tall but of normal proportions. The jacket sleeves stopped halfway down Dad's forearms.

Fortunately, the size guide notes that patterns can be easily extended in any direction by increments of 2 inches, so I add

2 to the chest, 10 to the sleeve, and keep the body an average length. Traditionally, ganseys were short at the waist and the sleeve, lessening the chance of them snagging aboard ship and dragging a man down to the deeps, but I do not want Dad to have cold wrists. Gansey gurus on Ravelry recommend fourteen 50g balls of five-ply wool for the smallest gansey and nineteen for the largest: I add another to cover the extra sleeve-length and make it twenty.

Monday morning arrives with a bundle of gansey wool: ten tightly packed balls, each weighing 100 grams. An entire kilo of wool. This wool was spun by Thomas Ramsden of Guiseley in West Yorkshire, and on the paper band, ships sail across compass-lined seas. Although I knew the jumper would be huge, the package of wool when unbound measures half a metre square. Each ball contains 224 metres of wool: over 2 kilometres of sturdy wool to knit. The old name for gansey wool is 'seaman's iron'.

As well as at least a kilometre of dense wool, ganseys also demand long needles. Today most knitters work jumpers and cardigans on circular needles, the better not to drop their stitches; traditional ganseys were worked on long double-pointed pins, as circular needles were unknown before the 1900s. My usual double-pointers measure 20 centimetres – I try to cast on the requisite 300 stitches, but fail to fit enough loops on each needle. I order a new set of extra-long points from a specialist gansey company in Cornwall, Frangipani Yarns, run by husband-and-wife team Russ and Jan. Five needles arrive in a long tube stapled shut, and I unsheathe 40 centimetres of shiny stainless steel ending in a rounded point. These needles could be weapons, their shining tips flashing a warning – don't get too close. I cut up a wine cork to make needle guards to protect myself, my husband, and the sofa.

Now I have wool, needles and my dad's measurements; I lack only a textured pattern for the gansey's body. I pick up *The*

Complete Book of Traditional Jersey and Guernsey Knitting and peer at grainy-grey pictures from Shetland to Southwold showing bearded men with broad chests displaying patterns of flags, cables and zigzagging chevrons. The patterns have names like 'seeds and bars', 'Betty Martin', 'rope and ladders' – a swathe of knitting terms particular to ganseys. At first, 'bird's eye', 'cats' teeth' and 'hailstones' seem to differ from town to east-coast town. But Compton notes that the three motifs are merely variations on the simplest stitches, the building blocks of knitting: moss stitch, purl, knit and cable make up the gansey's algorithm.

Compton notes that in Thurso, on Scotland's northern coast, the gansey is patterned on the sleeve-tops and yoke only, whereas the ganseys of the Moray Firth and Yorkshire include patterns down the sleeves as well as across the body. The rest of the gansey is knitted plain: rounds of stocking stitch, knit upon knit. This variation surprises me: the distance between Yorkshire and the north of Scotland is some 350 miles. I would expect the designs of Thurso and the Moray Firth to be similar, given that they are hundreds of miles closer than Wick and Whitby. Why is this so? I need to find out more.

Adventure wakes me early, before the late winter sun is up. I leave home as dawn arrives and, coming over the hill on the way to the station, see that the town that nestles in the next valley has disappeared, hidden under a thick fleece of mist. Past the primary school we slow to a crawl, the pelican crossing's warning lights yellow smears in the wet air. Measuring our progress against the dashboard clock, I jump out of the car before it's fully stopped, dragging my suitcase from the boot. But the train's not yet on the platform – fog slows everything down.

Once the train draws away from Cupar, I wedge myself into a corner seat, pull out my needles and jam headphones over my ears. I cast on 300 stitches across four needles, and use the fifth to knit the first wide round. The gansey is a huge piece of work, the needles covering my lap. I struggle to keep 2 metres of steel within the confines of a cramped ScotRail seat. At Markinch, a woman squeezes in beside me and I try to change the angle of my needles to keep from jabbing her as I knit. Instead I poke a hole in my tights and accidentally hook myself to the hem of my dress.

After boarding the east-coast mainline train at Edinburgh, we speed south and everything is bright blue on this late winter morning: sky, sea, the bridge at Newcastle, a hot-air balloon sailing high above the Tyne. The train swallows a hundred people at each stop, hurtling past the Angel of the North and Durham's scaffold-wrapped cathedral. Doncaster is upon us, then York station's long tunnel of metal and glass.

An oft-repeated gansey tale is that each east-coast town and village had its own distinct design, the men's jumpers acting as a knitted 'lost and found' tag, an identifiable shroud to wrap a man in should he be drowned at sea far from home. It is an eerie tale – but is it true? I am on my way to Yorkshire to find out. Many places along Yorkshire's east coast claim their own gansey patterns. One classic Staithes gansey is made of bands of 'bird's eye', its pattern composed of moss-stitch dots alternated with rows of 'ridge and furrow', emblem of the gardens kept by fishermen. Robin Hood's Bay, the old smuggling village that runs steeply to the sea, uses the patterns of the Storm family, a dynasty of Bay-dwellers since at least the sixteenth century. The Storms preferred their ganseys moss-stitched, with cables knitted close for warmth, the forearms and waist left plain.

Scarborough, Yorkshire's biggest coastal town, has its own ganseys, but their roots are harder to trace, influenced by the constant flux of fishermen and holiday-makers. The oldest style recorded includes a yoke of double moss stitch, known as 'hit and miss', step-stitched to the shoulders. Filey, a few miles south of Scarborough, used the same 'hit and miss' pattern, mirroring the pebbles on its seashore, and 'marriage lines', the double zigzags wryly said to represent the ups and downs of connubial life. One Whitby gansey combines triangular 'ships' flags' with 'rope and ladders' and diamonds, the angular shapes supposed to echo the 199 steps that link the harbour to the abbey on the clifftop.

In Scarborough, I start at the Maritime Heritage Centre, a tiny museum crammed into two rooms close to the seafront. Ganseys dangle from the wall, and a cheery volunteer sits me down in their small library. He brings books, printed slips and photocopied newspaper articles, all on ganseys. I gleefully open Gladys Thompson's *Patterns for Guernseys, Jerseys and Arans*, published in 1955.

Thompson was one of the first people to write down instructions for these jumpers as standardized knitting patterns. Prior to this, they were handed, down the female line, like mitochondrial DNA, or copied on sight. In the early 1950s, Thompson travelled throughout England, Scotland and Ireland to learn about ganseys from the women who made them, a pilgrimage that sounds at times hair-raising. While being driven across the causeway to the Holy Island of Lindisfarne by a boy of sixteen, in a car 'at least thirty years old and covered in rust and sand', she is alarmed to see water beginning to come up through the floor; the driver's advice is a robust, 'Put yer feet on the seat.' Sixty years ago, gansey knitting was so regionalized that Thompson recommends exactly where to buy the right yarn: 'The wool can be bought at Richardson's in Whitby, or Hammonds of Hull, and is special 5-ply worsted for guernseys.'[13]

Thompson lists more than fifty patterns she finds along the coast of Yorkshire and Northumberland. Flamborough yields four gansey styles; the tiny port of Filey fourteen. She finds two at Scarborough, eight in Whitby. Even tiny Staithes yields five. Heading north into Scotland, she picks up five patterns named 'Scottish fleet' in Musselburgh, including two different designs from the small harbour at Fisherrow. She found it was common everywhere for working ganseys to be patterned only around the yoke, leaving the forearms and waist plain so they could be easily reknitted. 'Sunday best' could be patterned all over and last much longer.

'I went over to Anstruther in gale of wind with frequent snowstorms,' Thompson writes. In that Fife harbour she spots a pattern she recognized from Whitby on a fisherman, who sends her to see his wife – they have a box-bed in the corner of their kitchen, 'the real Scottish kind, warm and cosy'. She chases one be-ganseyed sailor to the door of The Fisherman's Inn, working out the pattern as he walked, but notes only four different panels before he disappears where she 'was not brave enough to follow'.

In the museum, I peer closely at the photographs of fishing crews. Many, though not all, are wearing ganseys. One shows four nineteenth-century Crimlisk brothers – James, John, Francis, Thomas – all sporting jumpers with different patterns. By checking their ganseys, how would anyone be able to identify these brothers as coming from the same family, let alone the same

village? In Michael Pearson's *Traditional Knitting* (1984), patterns are attributed not to the place they came from, but to individual knitters: 'Miss Verrill', 'Mrs Wilson', 'Esther Rutter'.[14] My grandmother was Esther Rutter, but I've never before met another. I like this serendipity – our names connected through our knitting.

One important factor in the transfer and development of knitting patterns between communities was the herring trade. Herring is a slippery fish, greasy with oil and needing quick curing. As the demand for herring boomed with the expansion of Britain's urban population in the nineteenth century, the need for food that could be transported and stored in cities made the commercial fish-curers increasingly powerful in coastal economies. It was they who smoked and salted the fish for sale, who drove up the profit on the catch. They offered advance payments and subsidies to the fishermen in exchange for their haul, sometimes mortgaging them up to a whole season in advance. By the 1830s, it is believed that some four hundred fish-curers worked along Scotland's east coast. But the fish-curers didn't work alone – they needed an army of gutters and curers to process the catch.

While Scottish herring had been exported to the Continent since the fourteenth century or earlier, from 1808 the British government subsidized the herring catch for boats over 60 tonnes, and paid a bonus for herring sold abroad. Herring could be fished from British waters throughout the year: in winter and spring, the herring shoaled along Scotland's east coast. Come the summer, the north coast and Shetland reaped the catch, while in the autumn the fish swam south to waters off the east coast of England. From Lerwick to Lowestoft, as many as 30,000 boats fished for herring by the end of the nineteenth century.

Herring are drag-netted; there is no need for baited hooks. Scottish women, used to the hard work of baiting the sma' lines, were a workforce willing to earn what the fish-curers would pay them. Dubbed 'the Herring Girls', regardless of age, they travelled the length of Britain to work at the fishing ports from Shetland to East Anglia as the season demanded. Wearing heavy aprons and tying clouts around their knuckles to protect their hands, they could gut a fish in seconds. As the herring trade expanded, the gutters followed the fish along the coast, migrant workers chasing the catch. By 1907, two and a half million barrels of herring were exported annually from the UK to Europe; more than three thousand women had gutted them by hand.

Everywhere the Herring Girls travelled, their knitting went with them. Many came from the far north of Scotland, from Shetland, the Hebrides and the Caithness coast, and they brought their needles, worsted wool and knitting belts with them to the herring yards – their *weirs, wusset* and *whuskers*. These three *w*s were the tools of their trade. Photographs of the Herring Girls in Yarmouth, Scarborough and Lowestoft show them knitting on the sea front, working their pins as they walk. Whereas knitting in public had long been common in Shetland, with women proud of their skill, this behaviour was anathema in the East Anglian ports. Although the last Herring Girls came to Suffolk in the 1960s, this public knitting is still remembered and remarked on there today.

Gansey patterns were shared and spread by these women, thereby knitting the fashions of these distant communities together. They also copied patterns they saw in the ports, and legend has it that someone wearing an unusually patterned jumper as they walked along the quay would be followed by a gaggle of knitting women, all trying to copy it. From Shetland to Southwold, the Herring Girls shared and shaped and wore their ganseys.

As I follow the trail of these working women, I think back to my studies of Old English. At university, we pulled apart Anglo-Saxon kennings, trying to crack their meanings like squirrels after nuts. To the earliest English speakers, the sea was known as the *hron-ræd, segl-ræd, swan-ræd, hwæl-weg*: roads for the whale, sail and swan; the way of the whale. To the Norsemen, the sea was not something that kept communities apart, but that drew them close. To sailors, the sea is a road; only landlubbers see it as a barrier. The Herring Girls took the old road as they followed the catch – the *hæring-ræd.* Sea is an insufficient syllable.

After Scarborough, I head for Whitby, home of gansey guru Deb Gillanders. Famous as the setting for the shipwreck in *Dracula*, Whitby clusters below the ruins of a Benedictine abbey. Its alleys are heady with the scent of frying fish and chips. Shop windows shine darkly with the oily glamour of Whitby jet, the polished lignite that made the town popular with fashionable Victorians with an eye for mourning jewellery. Whitby remains a place where mainstream and macabre meet. I turn up a narrow alley flanked with shops, on the lookout for a health-food store. Ahead I see a compact red-haired woman standing in the street and enthusiastically waving fingers raised in a V. It's not usually a sign of welcome, but it turns out Deb Gillanders is having her picture snapped by a local photographer with a portfolio to build. From 15 metres away, I can see she's wearing a navy gansey. The photoshoot finished, we step inside her shop to talk.

The health-food shop is hung with ganseys. Arms outstretched above the teas and pulses, they welcome shoppers with a woolly hug – pale blue, grey, dark blue, bright red. Measuring only 5 centimetres across, the smallest is pinned proudly beside the till, knitted on lace-maker's pins by Rita Taylor. A bin bag full of Shetland fleece is on sale beside hanks of five-ply ecru worsted heaped into a wicker basket. Frangipani gansey wool is ranged in cones, their names a seaside litany: Falmouth Navy, Ocean Deep, Sea Spray.

Deb first fell in love with ganseys at a house party. In the hall-way, she found a man on his knees, fag in hand, so amused by the story he was telling that he couldn't move for laughing. He wore smart jeans and an eye-catching navy jumper gleaming with the patina of use. This was her first meeting with a gansey – and with trawlerman 'Hippy' Alf Hildred. Like Scottish tartans, ganseys can be tribal garments for those who wear them. Deb was transfixed by Alf and his gansey – but she wasn't from the tribe that made them. 'Give me a hundred quid and I'll knit you one,' said Alf. Two years passed, and still no sign of a gansey. After inviting Deb for a fitting once the gansey had been knitted as far her armpits, Alf declared the fit too loose and immediately unravelled the whole thing. 'That gansey was twenty-one months of begging and three months of capitulation,' Deb says with a grin. Finally handing over the gansey, Alf told her its pattern was called 'rope and ladders'. It reminded her of ratlines, the thin ropes that connect the rigging on ships to make a ladder for sailors. Researching ganseys, she'd seen the pattern elsewhere. 'Isn't it called "Betty Martin"?' she asked. Alf looked sideways at her, sucking on his fag. 'What do I know?' he shot back. 'I only knit the bloody things.'

As we talk, Deb pulls out gansey after gansey from a bag behind the counter. Smoothing them flat with a careful hand, she introduces me to each like an old friend. She tells me the men wore navy blue for work days and grey or cream for best. But in truth, ganseys were knitted from whatever came to hand – there are several 'salt and pepper' ones, made from the marled hard-wearing wool often used for socks.

Deb spreads Steve Locker's oatmeal-coloured gansey out across the counter. Worn by two generations of Steve Lockers, father and son, it is grubbed a yellowish grey at the neck, pale cream flecked with age and wear. Its armpits are like sunsets, turning red where deodorant kept Steve smelling sweet in the 1970s. Another gansey has huge holes ripped under the arm, the wool rubbed thin with daily use; a third has been darned at the gusset, patching old to new.

These 'mucky old jumpers' speak for themselves. They were made for a purpose; useful garments worn when working, sweating, drinking and even being buried. Deb is proud of this hands-on heritage: her word for it is the neat portmanteau 'Propagansey', and every year she puts together an exhibition of well-worn ganseys. 'Classic' is Deb's word for historic ganseys, used in place of the trickier 'vintage', and all that might imply.

We look at another gansey, donated by Doug Heselton. The donors, the wearers and the makers all combine to make the story of each 'proper gansey'. This isn't knitting history so much as genealogy. Making sure we don't forget, connecting people whose remaining touch on the world is in this wool, Deb reads ganseys like tea leaves, conjuring stories from seams and gussets. Discussing gansey myths and traditions, Deb shakes her head at the idea of women 'knitting shrouds' for their men, working patterns into their jumpers to identify a man found drowned. Nonsense, she says – the logistics of returning a body to a family would have been extremely difficult. Emotional upset aside, burials were an expensive business for families scraping by on the breadline. Deb has scoured the churchyard of nearby Old St Stephen's, whose tombstones record generations of families whose lives and deaths were shaped by the sea. On only four of the 800 graves is it recorded that the body had been returned home for burial.

The shop bell tinkles cheerfully and in comes Robin for tea and marmalade. A retired shepherd who walks with a crook, Robin settles onto a chair beside the counter and Deb rustles up his order. Robin shepherded on the moors above Goathland, and he grins like Mr Tod as he tells me about his sheep, his smile crooked above his blue woollen sweater. Robin is a Philpott, descended from generations of Yorkshire miners, jet carvers and lifeboatmen. He's a regular at Deb's, and she selects his marmalade carefully, wraps his Assam in a paper bag.

The family of ganseys look down on us from the window, comfortable as crumpets and hot tea. As we chat, Deb continues to serve customers, but suddenly runs short of change. 'Could you pop to the bank for me?' she asks, thrusting £20 notes into my hands. 'Twenty pounds of £1 coins and the rest fivers.' I'm obedient with surprise, taken aback at her trust in me, a stranger in her shop. Yet we're not really strangers: we're part of that peculiar 'family' of gansey knitters, bound together by our yarns.

Talking to Deb reminds me that knitting patterns were transmitted directly from one knitter to another, rarely written down, and that few authenticated original patterns survive. Instead, textile historians often 'reverse engineer' traditional designs, working back from archived garments or photographs to create patterns. A 'Sheringham Gansey' may simply be one design as worn by a Sheringham fisherman in the early 1900s, copied from a sepia image. As we cease transmitting skills and stories orally, the desire to 'fix' a pattern to a particular place seems to strengthen.

Does this adaptation strengthen or diminish the concept of tradition? Today's knitting historians are to textiles what Robert Burns was to folk songs: important collectors, innovators and transcribers, embedding traditions into history by writing them down. But the communities that inspire them had no one way of making ganseys. Like a folk singer who learns a tune, then adapts the words and tempo to suit her voice and temperament, I decide to be a tradition-bearer in this mould. I will combine the knitted motifs I like with traditional gansey knitting techniques to make something simultaneously old and new.

On the train home, I plan the gansey I will make for Dad. I've started with a ribbed welt, common to almost every gansey I've encountered, as its knit-purl rib hugs the wearer's waist. There is no traditional Suffolk gansey style, nothing specific to the county's major herring ports of Southwold and Lowestoft. Searching online for ganseys brings me to the Isle of Man's

Manx National Heritage catalogue, where a patched and mostly plain one catches my eye. This island holds a special place in our family lore: my dad used to build and race motorbikes and would head to the Isle of Man for its notorious Tourist Trophy road races for many years. We went to watch the races, and some of my earliest memories are of picking heather on the hills with the whine of motorbikes flying past behind me.

The Manx gansey is very plain. Stocking stitch and rib only, it boasts no cables or flags, no moss stitch, wave or cable motifs. The pattern is easy to follow, though no needle size or weight of wool is given, simply a tension from which to work. I will use this simple shape as the foundation for the gansey, but add my own particular combination of stitches to make a pattern specifically for Dad.

In Whitby, I visited the Sutcliffe Gallery, looking closely at Frank Meadow Sutcliffe's photographs of Yorkshire fishermen for inspiration. There I saw initials worked into the backs of ganseys. Rae Compton says that numbers would sometimes be included too, often telling the number of children born to a fisherman. My dad needs the initials MFR and the number three. As he doesn't fish, I'm keen to include some motifs more relevant to him. 'Ridge and furrow' sounds about right for someone who grows their own vegetables, and it's a good stitch to work around the shoulders. 'Railroad' echoes his own father's trade, mending and replacing sleepers on the railways.

On graph paper, I plot the yoke's pattern of 'ridge and furrow', interspersed with broad swathes of 'railroad' backed by moss stitch, representing gardens, railways, the Isle of Man. I add in trees and leaves and apples; for all his motor-biking passion, Dad is a Suffolk boy with a lifelong love of plants. After the broad welt, I plot his initials at the right hip and three narrows lines of purl at the left – my two brothers and me. This gansey is for my dad, and no one else.

Every spare moment is given over the gansey. In front of the television and in bed before I sleep at night, the gansey is my dark-blue familiar. It grows slowly, a moss-like companion. Heavier in my lap as it swallows yarn, it is as helpless and comforting as a baby. Whilst the Herring Girls knitted as they walked, my lack of knitting belt and sheath forces me to be stationary. For the sheer time they take, ganseys have always been a labour of love as much as necessity. This one is no different.

As February draws to a close, I find that I have not yet finished the gansey's broad chest band, with the yoke and arms and neck still to make. This gansey is more than one month's work, demanding more wool, more time, more of myself. It will follow me as I explore knitting's history in the ten months left of the year, a promise to fulfil in time for my dad's birthday as this year becomes the next. Ganseys are not just a part of Scottish and northern English culture; they also play an important role in the fishing cultures of England's southernmost counties. Later in the year, when the weather is fine, I'll head to the far south-west to learn more about the jumpers of these fishing fleets. For now, I concentrate my attention on the growing navy mass upon my lap.

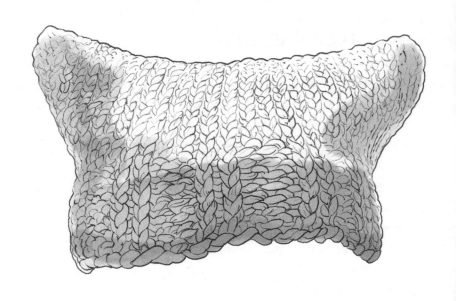

3

Revolutionary Knitting

March should herald spring, but here in Fife, daffodils shake their heads at cold and stormy weather. Inside, I keep vigil with the gansey, working round after round after round of stocking stitch. I slip my knitting one stitch clockwise with each round, moving the increasingly heavy work to avoid a ladder forming where the stitches rest upon the needles. Its familiar woollen loops slip through my fingers like beads on a rosary.

Another knitting project calls. The gansey has become too heavy to carry comfortably and it is time to start a new knit, something smaller and more portable. Laying the gansey aside is a relief: its 46-inch circumference has begun to bore me with its endless circling repetitions. I'm ready to feast my hands and eyes on something new, something less hard on the eyes and hands than tightly wound and greasy dark-blue yarn that must be knitted by the window, so light-absorbing are its stitches.

Most knitters have several simultaneous works in progress – wips, in knitting's abbreviating tongue. A baby's jumper lies half finished, stalled by a mistake at the neck. The second of a pair of socks, abandoned after the flush of success in completing the first – I've got to make another? My relationship with all but the simplest of patterns follows a predictable cycle. Excitement at the beginning – keen to cast on, to create – that fades to frustration (this pattern is difficult), or boredom (so far still to go), and sometimes both. I fall out of love, lay it aside, make something else. Then a deadline looms – birth, birthday, Christmas – and I'm pressured into picking up my pins again.

Planning a new project is giddying: you can start with yarn, a beautiful ball or skein too gorgeous to resist. Or maybe a person – their upcoming visit or birthday swims into focus. In an idle moment online, a particularly lovely design catches your eye. Excitement rises in you like spring sap. You shell out for a pattern, carefree in response to beauty and vulnerable to a need you didn't know you had.

Then it's off to the stash, the knitter's glorious hoard of yarn. Some take up whole rooms, others are little more than a few balled-up odds and ends at the bottom of a knitting bag. On the hunt for a suitable bundle of fibre, forgotten friends emerge: skeins in candy colours, undyed shades soft against your fingers, dip-dyed sock wool in neat balls. Quite often, what you're after simply isn't there, so it is with pleasure – tinged with a frisson of guilt – that you acknowledge the need to buy more.

Knitting festivals give yarn fanatics the chance to indulge their addiction. One of Britain's biggest is Edinburgh Yarn Festival, taking place each March in Scotland's capital. As the skies cloud with the promise of spring showers, I head to the city's Corn Exchange. This will be my first yarn festival; until now, I have relied on local yarn shops and the internet to source my wool. I am also here for inspiration, to decide what to knit next.

The festival begins before I arrive at the Exchange. Waiting for the bus by Waverley, I hear two women talking. I glance across – one wears an intricate Fair Isle jumper, the other a swirling lacy shawl. I diagnose both as serious knitters. Once on the bus, I head to the back seats, where three women sit wrapped in winter coats. On the lapel of one I spy a beaded badge in the shape of a sheep; the next warms her hands in beautiful colourwork mittens; a third spills a striped scarf down her chest. As the bus rattles through the city, the badged one plots the bus's course on the map with her finger, cocking her head under the low ceiling to follow the route. Reading out road names, her voice sounds like my aunties'. I can't resist the urge to ask them where they are from. Pilgrims with 400 miles already behind them, they come from Suffolk, my home county.

We compare woolly credentials. Sheila can weave with a stick, and offers to show me on the spot. Val not only knitted her scarf but dyed and spun the wool herself. Jane likes to bead her knitting, handing over the badge for my benediction. They are members of Framlingham's Guild of Spinners, Weavers and Dyers, and know my mum, who spins with a nearby group. The woolly sisterhood is a network reaching across the country.

Arriving at the festival, we go our separate ways: they bought tickets in advance, whereas I'm chancing my luck, turning up and hoping to squeeze in. Behind me in the long queue, a midwife from Ulverston talks her companion through her day. Up on the early train and back on the late, she has left her husband and children a tea they can reheat. As we stand in line, she works a circular needle, simultaneously making two socks in yarn that turns from blue to purple. She's not the only knitter plying their pins whilst we wait: any queue disappears the quicker when you knit.

Once inside and branded with a wristband like a teenager at a gig, I squeeze myself into a corner to plan my visit. The Scottish Highlands, west Wales, Northumberland, Cornwall, Yorkshire – here in Edinburgh, the UK is mapped in yarn. Women pass me, talking about how much they will allow themselves to spend. Numbers in the hundreds are bandied about between exclamations about bank accounts. I must manage my addiction with a small dose: £50 is my limit. Quite a sum for me; small change for others.

The festival fills many rooms with yarn and knitters. My first challenge is where to start: over a hundred beautifully branded stalls vie for my attention. Because I began this year with Shetland yarn, I decide to commence with Shetland. These windswept islands at the UK's topmost corner, their population smaller than that of a mainland market town, have sent four stalls to the festival. I head to Shetland Handspun first: a tiny booth decorated with a paper banner and patterns in Ziploc bags, printed on folded A4 paper.

Shetland Handspun is the brainchild of Elizabeth Johnston. A Shetlander who learned to knit so young she cannot remember not knowing how to work her wires, Elizabeth not only knits and designs but also spins and dyes the wool she sells. Until recently her own flock supplied the raw wool, but now she buys her fleece locally. Her older sister, Margaret, is with her. 'Here I get to boss her about,' says Elizabeth, her eyes twinkling. As children, they were taught to earn extra pocket money for themselves through knitting – 'A kind of slavery, really,' jokes Elizabeth with a grin, and she confesses to a long-held dislike of making the classic islands' patterned yokes. 'I hate knitting them, and hate wearing them,' she says with spirit.

I watch the sisters conjure sunset-orange fleece into golden strands, and for the first time I become acutely aware of this yarn's story. At this festival, I am surrounded by as many farmers and spinners as I am knitwear designers; knitters are here to buy direct from the source – from a company, a person, or, in some cases, even an individual sheep. Both raw fleece and exquisite yarn exchange hands for serious sums of money; once bitten by the woolly bug, a knitter's passion can be difficult to control.

Making my way through the festival, I squeezed past long queues and knots of enthusiastic shoppers to meet weavers from the isle of Mull; farmers from the Cotswolds; crofters from tiny Iona with a trunk full of yarns dyed to match the island's stones and sky and sea. These skeins are things of beauty, rich in personality, and most come from very small farms, often family-run concerns that have struggled not only to make money, but even to cover the costs of feeding, keeping and shearing sheep. Producing speciality yarn from rare-breed sheep is one way that small-scale producers can carve out a niche.

Like most knitters, I began knitting not with luxury wool like this, but with mass-produced acrylic yarn, tough enough to stand trips through the family wash. Whilst my mum did spin at home, her yarns were for weaving, not passed on to me for clumsy craft experiments. My knitting mentor, Suzanne, gloried in working with second-hand yarns picked up for a song and a gossip in charity shops: soft angora mixed with acrylic was knitted up into a pale-blue winter jumper for her daughter's birthday; postbox-red yarn turned into washable mittens and a hat for Christmas. This was affordable, practical knitting with a purpose. Much of the yarn available in non-specialist shops is not woollen but acrylic, made from oil and highly flammable, but also hard-wearing and comparatively inexpensive. Whereas woollen clothes biodegrade relatively quickly, acrylic garments may degrade but do not rot. Like the plastic trays we buy food in, they may be with us for centuries – not as heirlooms, but as landfill.

In the same way that the 'slow food' and organic movements have reshaped our diets, concern about provenance and the ethics of production of fibres is changing the way many knitters think about and buy their yarn. Wool with a story, with a traceable provenance, has become a necessity for many. Some vegans will not knit with woollen yarn, uncomfortable with the treatment of sheep in large-scale modern farming. Yarns made from other fibres are subject to similar ethical rigour. Silk yarn can be practically and morally problematic: if silk-moth larvae are left to chew their way out of their cocoons, the length of the threads is shortened, making them more difficult to spin. This means that often the worms are boiled to death inside their own cocoons. The Natural Fibre Company, based in Cornwall, now spins yarn with 'cruelty-free' ahimsa silk, which uses naturally discarded cocoons. By choosing to knit with sustainable yarn from ethical sources, yarn shopping can become a political act. In a capitalist market, purchasing can be prison turned to power.

After a morning of intoxicating wool fumes and ardent conversation, my bags and I find a quiet corner close to the knitting bookstall, and I wriggle myself into a space on the floor. As I give my purchases a second inspection, I notice that the woman sitting next to me is doing the same. Marsha has come all the way from Arizona for the Edinburgh Yarn Festival – pure-breed wool in such a localized abundance is a novelty, and Marsha has made her first pilgrimage over the pond on the hunt for yarn.

We go through our goodies: I have dark four-ply Wensleydale from the Cotswolds, samples of organic Welsh wool from Garthenor, two bright-coloured cakes of Ionan yarn. Marsha's prize find is the smooth, psychedelic Cuthbert's Sock yarn from Whistlebare in Northumberland: a skein of orange, silver and blue twists that slinks over her hand like a river at sunset.

Marsha rummages through her bags and pulls out her knitting notebook. Handing me this small paper-bound book, she challenges me to decode a mystery. On the first page is a list of numbers, banded in ascending groups of five. Against each group is stuck a strand of yarn, their names an exotic litany: Lilac Mist, Sea Foam, Marlin, Flamingo. On the following pages are the days of the year, running from January to September. Each day has a number between forty-seven and a hundred. I can't make sense of it – until Marsha reminds me that Americans chart the temperature in Fahrenheit. The numbers show each day's mean temperature for nine months of 1988, taken from the almanac from San Francisco International Airport. For every day that Marsha carried her unborn daughter, she recorded that day's temperature: it is the story of her baby's gestation in degrees, from 8 to 38 Celsius.

Turn the clock forward twenty-nine years and Marsha is using the charts to knit her daughter a coming-of-age present to tell the story of the year she came to be: a scarf in shades of purple, blue, green, pink, yellow and red. Marsha plans to end the scarf with a flourish of silver to mark the day her daughter was born. At first glance, Marsha has simply made her daughter a colourful striped scarf. Yet to them, it is an umbilical metaphor, the link between mother and daughter, the tie between two bodies, rendered in yarn.

Around us passes a handmade fashion parade. I spot a stunning lichen-green cardigan wrought with cables and knots so intricate I couldn't sketch it, much less knit it. Fine lace shawls drape shoulders in mustard, umber, maroon; Fair Isle yokes dazzle from jumpers in shades from rose to slate, fawn to scarlet, cream to darkest brown. My blue-grey jersey dress, which I knitted years ago as a man's oversized jumper, is a simple, muted addition – but I'm glad I've worn it, adding my own voice to the symphony of homemade knitwear.

But there is one garment I see over and over again: a pink hat with jaunty little ears. This is statement knitwear, an indicator of political intent: the Pussyhat. Designed by Kat Coyle from her California yarn shop, The Little Knittery, the Pussyhat started life in November 2016 when two regular customers, Krista Suh and Jayna Zweiman, wanted to create a simple unifying and identifying garment for the planned Women's March in Washington, DC. The pattern was given away for free online, with yarn shops across the world distributing it to their customers. On 21 January 2017, over a million women took to the streets to protest against the anti-women sentiments expressed by America's forty-fifth president. The National Mall in Washington was awash with protestors sporting Pussyhats in shades from strawberry to fuchsia, magenta to rosé. Watching from thousands of miles away, my social media feed became a sea of pink and placards. Powerful and political, women had knitted themselves into the public gaze.

'Craftivism',[1] a portmanteau of 'craft' and 'activism', is a new term for a long-standing creative form of protest. It takes traditional domestic skills such as needlework and knitting and uses them as a platform for political engagement: think of the banners of trades union workers and the tricolour rosettes and ribbons of the suffragettes. Knitting and protest too have a long history. Best-known of our knitting sisters-in-arms are the women of the French Revolution, *les tricoteuses* – 'the knitters'. Representations of the *tricoteuses* in British culture owe much to the popularity of Charles Dickens, who dramatically – and creatively – reimagined these *citoyennes* in the shape of Madame Defarge in *A Tale of Two Cities* (1859).[2]

Driven by the murder of her own kin to see members of the Evrémonde family meet their end at the guillotine, Thérèse Defarge is the novel's malevolent constant, plying her needles whenever she appears. We are first introduced to her as she sits behind the counter of her wine-shop, glancing around 'in a casual manner', taking up her knitting 'with great apparent calmness and repose of spirit, and [becoming] absorbed in it'.[3] When her customers are engaged in conference with her husband, 'Madame Defarge knitted with nimble fingers and steady eyebrows, and saw nothing.' Like an automaton, she is 'the one woman who had stood conspicuous, knitting, still knitted on with the steadfastness of Fate'.[4] Dickens's reference to Fate echoes the Moirai and the Norns, of Greek and Norse mythology, spinning, measuring and cutting the thread of life, and the reader senses that the power over life and death, omnipresent in Paris's newly invented guillotine, may be within Madame Defarge's grasp.

Although she appears at first as a shadowy cipher, we learn that she is actively engaged in the work of the Revolution. Madame Defarge knits with purpose: in a chapter entitled 'Knitting', her craft is revealed to be of great practical import. Her needles are busy constructing the Revolutionaries' register of those deemed fit for death. At another meeting in the wine-shop, Monsieur Defarge is asked if keeping a register is safe, and he passionately defends his wife: 'If madame my wife undertook to keep the register in her memory alone, she would not lose a word of it – not a syllable of it. Knitted, in her own stitches and her own symbols, it will always be as plain to her as the sun. Confide in Madame Defarge. It would be easier for the weakest poltroon that lives, to erase himself from existence, than to erase one letter of his name or crimes from the knitted register of Madame Defarge.'[5]

This vengeful cipher records Madame Defarge's observations about those destined for the guillotine. In the chapter 'Still Knitting', Thérèse is at her sentry-post in the wine-shop, 'knitting away assiduously' on a stifling hot day. When an unfamiliar client enters, she drops her knitting and her regulars melt away as he orders water and a cognac. He compliments her on the brandy, and she resumes her knitting. He is a spy, working for the Ancien Régime, and comments, 'You knit with great skill, madame' – 'A pretty pattern too!' He asks her why she knits thus, and she replies, sphinxlike, 'Pastime.' 'Not for use?' he asks, and she responds: 'That depends. I may find a use for it one day.' His final remark on the Revolution glides off her like so much bourgeois pomade: 'Ah, the unfortunate, miserable people! So oppressed, too – as you say.' Thérèse Defarge and her stitches get the last word: '"As *you* say," madame retorted, correcting him, and deftly knitting an extra something into his name that boded him no good.'[6]

Madame Defarge is not a lone knitter in *A Tale of Two Cities*, holed up in the wine-shop with her pins. Dickens paints a vivid picture of the district of Saint Antoine, where, sitting 'on door-steps and window-ledges' and on 'the corners of vile streets and courts', groups of women meet each evening. 'All the women knitted. They knitted worthless things; but, the mechanical work was a mechanical substitute for eating and drinking; the hands moved for the jaws and the digestive apparatus: if the bony fingers had been still, the stomachs would have been more famine-pinched.'[7] Knitting keeps the desperate just one step further from the grave.

As night falls and the church bells compete with the beat of the military drums, the women knit, like their gansey-making sisters, by feel alone. This is more than a literal gloom; it prefigures the spectre of the guillotine. 'So much was closing in about the women who sat knitting, knitting, that they their very selves were closing in around a structure yet unbuilt, where they were to sit knitting, knitting, counting dropping heads.'[8]

As with Margaret Thwaite endlessly plying her needles in The Retreat in York, the function of knitting to provide distance from mental or physical discomfort is well documented. In March 1912, Virginia Woolf, then Virginia Stephen, wrote to her future husband, Leonard, 'Knitting is the saving of life.'[9] That year she had experienced one of many severe episodes of mental illness, necessitating a stay in the private asylum Burley House, and this letter hints that knitting helped provide a steadying hand for a whirling head.

Being both process- and product-focused, knitting can reinforce capacity and confidence in the knitter, building skills and self-belief with each completed item.[10] But more than this: it appears that knitting helps to lessen the after-effects of traumatic experience. In April 2004, a group of researchers from Cambridge University's MRC Cognition and Brain Sciences Unit examined the function of performing repetitive tasks to reduce people's likelihood of flashbacks after experiencing trauma (in this study, video footage of car crashes). They concluded that those who engaged in activities such as knitting suffered far fewer flashbacks than those who did not.[11] Even for those who have not witnessed something disturbing, knitting has been shown to improve both physical and mental wellbeing. In 2007, a study by a team at Harvard Medical School showed that knitting reduced participants' heart rates by on average eleven beats per minute, lowered blood pressure and lessened muscle tension – the 'relaxation response', which 'can be elicited by a number of meditative techniques, such as diaphragmatic breathing, yoga, progressive muscle relaxation, jogging – even knitting'.[12] Even knitting, indeed.

Virginia was not the sole knitter in the Stephen family: in 1912 she wrote to Leonard that her brother Adrian 'has taken to it too'.[13] In that year, her sister Vanessa painted a portrait of Virginia, showing her slumped in an armchair, knitting with reddish-pink yarn. Her face is an impressionistic, almost featureless blank, eyes disappearing into daubs, and all but the nose is smearily unclear. There is a passivity, mirrored in her knitting and her posture, at once creative and dejected. It avoids the viewer's gaze. In Vanessa's portrait, Virginia embodies the 'paradoxical aesthetic of creativity'[14] – the idea that passivity is an essential part of the creative process. Dame Edith Sitwell's voice crackles with something like envy when she remarks in a letter following Virginia Woolf's death, 'I enjoyed talking to [Virginia], but thought nothing of her writing. I considered her "a beautiful little knitter".'[15]

The Stephens were not the only knitters of the Bloomsbury Group. Lytton Strachey also plied his pins, writing to John Maynard Keynes in September 1914 that he was knitting a navy-blue scarf 'for the neck of one of our sailor lads. I don't know which, but I have my visions.'[16] This was far from a one-off creative endeavour for a lover; throughout the First World War, Strachey spent many evenings 'knitting mufflers for our soldier and sailor lads', sighing with the resignation of a slow knitter, 'but I expect that by the time I've finished with them the war will be over, and they'll be given to Henry [Norton] and Duncan [Grant].'[17] In a photograph taken by Lady Ottoline Morrell in June 1926, Strachey sits in a deckchair beside Dora Carrington, Stephen Tomlin and Walter Sprott, straw hat perched above his round glasses and thick beard and round glasses. He is holding a piece of knitting, working the needles with long, slender fingers. Strachey delighted in challenging Edwardian norms of behaviour, particularly those concerned with sex and gender: one can discern a distinct thrill in his imagining the sailors he might warm through his knitting.

Woolf wrote knitters into her novels, most memorably Mrs Ramsay in *To the Lighthouse* (1927). Matriarch and lodestar, she is introduced as she discusses the weather with her husband, their son James on the drawing room rug before them. Mrs Ramsay expects it to be fine, a proclamation made as she knits, 'making some little twist of the reddish-brown stocking she was knitting.' She is making a stocking for the lighthouse-keeper's little boy, a child 'threatened with a tuberculous hip'.[18]

Mrs Ramsay is widely believed to be based on Julia Stephen, Virginia and Vanessa's mother, who died when Virginia was thirteen and whose death precipitated the first of many mental collapses. Virginia Woolf's biographer Hermione Lee draws on Virginia's remembrance of her mother 'knitting on the hall step while we play cricket'[19] at their summer home in St Ives; and the parallels between Mrs Ramsay and the late Mrs Stephen run to the smallest domestic detail. 'Flashing her needles, confident, upright, she created drawing-room and kitchen, set them all aglow.'[20] Mrs Ramsay and her knitting are no marginalized domestic nonentities, but vital, creative and essential. They send out coded messages of warmth, welcome, security and safety to her family, and become a metaphorical beacon to mirror the lighthouse without. But this reassuring reflection is not without cost: 'So boasting of her capacity to surround and protect, there was scarcely a shell of herself left for her to know herself by; all was so lavished and spent.'[21]

To the Lighthouse can be read as Woolf's reworking of Homer's *Odyssey*, with Mrs Ramsay as faithful Penelope, working the stocking in place of weaving her shroud.[22] Knitting is also an important mechanism for protecting Mrs Ramsay's self and sanity as a mother. As she sits alone at the end of the evening, 'she continued to knit, and sat upright, it was thus that she felt herself; and this self having shed its attachments was free for the strangest adventures.' Her nimble fingers and her mind work in tandem: 'Not as oneself did one find rest ever, in her experience (she accomplished here something dexterous with her needles), but as a wedge of darkness.' She sits watching the lighthouse's beaming pulse, identifying with the longest stroke: 'She looked up over her knitting and met the third stroke and it seemed to her like her own eyes meeting her own eyes, searching as she alone could search into her mind and her heart, purifying out of existence that lie, any lie.'[23]

Woolf's knitting women are parts of Woolf herself, observing and creating simultaneously. Present and passive, yet actively creative, each knitter 'performs' her craft in public – and her character is often one of social cohesion or creativity. The critic Sayaka Okumura notes that there are more women who knit than write in Woolf's fiction, and that they seem to be more emblematic of her identity as a writer than those who put pen to paper.[24] In the Bloomsbury world, knitting not only connected people – Mrs Ramsay knitting for the lighthouse-keeper's boy, Lytton Strachey making gifts for imagined lovers – it also allowed Woolf the space to connect with her creative self. There are many ways of being revolutionary, but all require creativity.

Heading to London after Edinburgh Yarn Festival, my visit to the capital coincides with a march protesting against a possible visit to the UK by the US president, Donald Trump, echoing the Women's Marches in Washington, Baltimore and New York. One will take place outside the Houses of Parliament and I decide to join it, to publicly register my disgust at a presidency that allows misogyny, violence, xenophobia and racism to take a comfortable seat in the White House. But first I need a Pussyhat.

Pussyhats must be made, not bought, so I head to Islington to pick up bright pink yarn from Loop, arriving at the shop minutes before closing and leaving with a squishy bundle of Debbie Bliss's Roma yarn in 'Hot Pink'. Settling myself in a nearby pub to wait for a friend to finish work, I cast on using 5 mm needles – the only pair I have to hand – disregarding from necessity the recommended needle size of 12 mm. Even for this simple pattern, little more than a strip of stocking stitch with a garter rib, the going is tough, the tension too tight to be comfortable. Yet on I knit; I want to stand and be counted in this hat, and there's no time left to source new needles. Knitting is often a matter of using what's to hand rather than careful shopping or design.

I'm soon joined by my friend, who is intrigued by my knitting. 'Can I have a go?' she asks, and before long is wielding pins with aplomb. She'd learned to knit at school but hadn't touched it since. Now a civil servant, she is forbidden from protesting outside Parliament, but in contributing to the hat she makes a small stand of her own. We work our way through a bottle of wine and, despite our best efforts, by the time we say goodnight the hat is still not done.

As I prepare for this protest I consider what sort of protestor I am comfortable with being. My mind turns back to Madame Defarge: is she just a gross caricature of Dickens's invention, or does she epitomize the real women of the French Revolution? Certainly, women were prominent in eighteenth-century Paris: in 1797 they made up 53.8 per cent of the city's population, numbering at least 40,000.[25] Many women came to Paris to work as servants; it was more common for men to remain in the countryside to farm,[26] and during the French Revolutionary Wars of 1792–1802 the army also absorbed many younger men into its ranks.

Not only were they present, they were politically engaged. From the beginning of the Revolution, women became vital agents in their country's battle for change. On 5 October 1789, several thousand men and women had marched from Paris to the royal palace at Versailles to call for measures to relieve the starvation faced by the French people; their call of 'Bread, bread' has echoed down the ages, as has Marie-Antoinette's apocryphal response: 'Let them eat cake.' Whereas the Storming of the Bastille on 14 July had failed to bring down the monarchy, after the march, six women were admitted to the palace to petition Louis XVI directly, an action that saw the palace's grain stores opened and their contents distributed. The following day, a further group of women gained entry to the palace and a skirmish ensued; Louis and his much-reviled wife then agreed to return to the city and face the public's judgement.

Many of those who marched on Versailles were working women, though witness statements from the time mention men disguised in women's clothing as well as several wealthy and prominent figures, both male and female. Testimonies of the events include that of Madame Madeleine Glain, a charwoman; nurse Jeanne Martin; and linen-worker Anne Maguerite Andelle.[27]

Women were visible in Paris's public places, including the gardens of the Palais-Royal, its walks lined with perfume, jewellery and dress shops. They were prominent at the Palais des Tuileries, where they gathered to observe the Convention Nationale, the first French republican government, which sat as a single-chamber assembly of 749 deputies from 20 September 1792 to 26 October 1795. They were visible too at the Palais de Justice, where the Revolutionary Tribunal passed death sentences on some 2,600 people, and at the Place de la Révolution, where the guillotine stood in macabre glory. This act of witness was an important one, as these revolutionary bodies deliberated in the public eye.

Among these women numbered many dressmakers. Whilst some had served long apprenticeships and made clothes for the aristocracy, many more were untrained and lived hand-to-mouth by their needle.[28] They might be employed on a casual basis by merchants, or they might be drafted in by couturiers for specific commissions. Women could sew almost anywhere, and would work while attending the debates. In addition, rampant unemployment often drove female workers without work to the Revolution's places of public assembly.

Did these women also knit? The historian Dominique Godineau believes they did, both in the galleries and in women's clubs.[29] However, she notes that 'knitting' did become synonymous with any form of needlework; as they listened to the debates women also sewed, and tore up linen to dress the wounds of soldiers.[30]

Why, then, were these women known as *tricoteuses*? The word itself, meaning 'knitter' or 'one who earns a living by knitting', first appears in French during the seventeenth century, but it is not until the 1790s that it is recorded as having political resonance.[31] A picture from 1793, *Les Tricoteuses Jacobines*, now in the Musée Carnavalet in Paris, is one of a series of gouaches by Jean-Baptiste Lesueur depicting scenes from the Revolution; it shows three women, two of them sitting knitting tubes of roughly stocking size with double-pointed needles from a ball of yarn each in the pockets of their aprons. Below the picture is the caption, 'There were many who were given 40 *sols* a day to go to the tribune of the Jacobins to applaud the revolutionary motions.'[32] This detail reveals as much about the political persuasion of the artist, printer or intended audience as it does about the knitters themselves. Just as it was believed that some of the women who attended the march on Versailles were paid to be there, counterrevolutionary accounts were quick to imply that the women's presence was economically rather than politically motivated. An image can be unreliable.

Les Tricoteuses Jacobines, ou de Robespierre.
Elles étoient un grand nombre, à qui l'on donnoit
40 sols par jour pour aller dans la tribune des Jacobins
applaudir les motions Révolutionnaires.
An 2.

The derogatory use of *tricoteuse* was popularized by counter-revolutionaries after the fall of Robespierre in July 1794.[33] As historian Paul Friedland notes, several vivid 'memoirs' of the Revolution have perhaps coloured the collective memory of these times;[34] for example, the autobiography of the actor Fleury (Abraham-Joseph Bénard, 1750–1822), published posthumously in 1836, includes the following description of Revolutionary women: these radical females, 'shrews, had the work of surrounding the scaffolds, exciting people, and letting loose shrill cries during the spectacles. If they were old, they were called *tricoteuses*; if they were young, they had the name *furies of the guillotine*. As for me, when I saw them assemble for the first time, the women and the men ... it seemed to me that I was watching ... uncoil a horrible legion of the damned, screaming, yelling, throwing their tangled hair into the wind, turning, ever turning.'[35] In time, *tricoteuse* became shorthand for any Revolutionary woman, used to designate, and denigrate, female militants.

Dickens's acknowledged source of inspiration for *A Tale of Two Cities* was Thomas Carlyle's *History of the French Revolution* (1837), a book Dickens claimed to have read 'five hundred times'.[36] Writing some thirty years after the Revolution, Carlyle described in detail the 'Knitting-women' who attended the Convention Nationale and the Revolutionary Tribunal. Carlyle's *tricoteuses* filled the galleries: 'Citoyennes who bring their seam with them, or their knitting-needles; and shriek or knit as the case needs; famed *Tricoteuses*, Patriot Knitters'.[37] While male Jacobins respond to debates and trials 'with angry roar', the Patriot Knitters expressed their disapproval 'with angry shriek'. They are evidence of the changes to Jacobin society, where 'High-rouged dames went once in jewels and spangles; now, instead of jewels, you may take the knitting-needles and leave the rouge.'[38]

Whereas Carlyle's knitting-women shriek and roar, Dickens silences Madame Defarge, depicting her as emotionally cold and disengaged, her knitting a visible public transgression of a normally private activity. Public and private clash in the body of the *tricoteuse* as she becomes a revolutionary icon: how could a woman, intent on the intimate, domestic task of knitting, be so callous as to knit during the bloodthirsty Revolution? Dickens nails this fear with Madame Defarge, a sinister, needle-bearing automaton. Godineau pierces the marrow of the horror, contrasting the image of women knitting at home, an image suffused with warmth and tenderness, with that of the *tricoteuse*, engendering feelings of violence and morbidity.[39] Politically engaged women as either screaming harridans or frigid automata: these are tropes that continue to echo in our own time.

There is another symbol of the French Revolution almost as powerful as that of the *tricoteuse* – the Phrygian cap. Inspired by the *pileus*, a wool or leather cap worn by emancipated Roman slaves, in the eighteenth century the Phrygian cap became an icon of both freedom and revolution. Over time, the headwear of the Phrygians and other inhabitants of Anatolia and the *pileus* became conflated into the *bonnet rouge*, 'the red cap of liberty'. The Phrygian cap is first documented as a piece of Revolutionary headwear in France in 1790. Along with the term *sans-culottes* (those who did not sport the fitted knee breeches fashionable among the wealthy), *bonnets rouges* became sartorial shorthand for the Revolutionaries. There was a precedent in France for the association between *bonnets rouges* and revolution: in 1675, during the Revolt of the *papier timbré* (stamped paper upon which all legally binding information had to be recorded, and subject to a specific tax), Lower Bretons donned red caps to protest against this taxation. The Phrygian cap has since been widely appropriated as a potent symbol: it appears on the seal of the US Senate, and has been stamped on numerous American coins over the last two centuries.

Were these crimson precursors of the Pussyhat knitted? It is difficult to know; as with many historic fabrics and garments, few have survived, and the authenticity of those that have is debated. The Museum of Fine Arts in Boston has a nineteenth-century red woollen cap of French origin in its collection, complete with tricolour cockade, but it has been cut and sewn from woven woollen fabric rather than knitted. Historical evidence for a connection between the caps and the *tricoteuses* appears to be more convenient contrivance than verifiable fact. In the gouache *Les Tricoteuses Jacobines*, the women are knitting what look like stockings rather than caps. Still, the allure of an easy-to-make symbol of revolution continues: power placed in the hands of the maker adds an element of autonomy to the – protest which vanishes when the symbol is mass produced and exchanged for money.

What Dickens has Madame Defarge make is not caps or stockings, but an encrypted record of the revolution: a knitted roll of justice. Knitted code is a form of steganography, where information can be hidden in plain sight, so that people do not suspect that they are there.[40] And because Madame Defarge's register is knitted, as her husband says, 'in her own stitches and her own symbols',[41] she has devised a cipher and encrypted it with her knitting.

Popular knitting mythology avers that knitting code has been part of the tactics of warfare since at least the late nineteenth century, but physical evidence for this is thin. One widely repeated story concerns the militant knitter Molly Rinker of Philadelphia, who during the US Revolutionary War spied on British troops billeted in her home. Rinker apparently wrote down the troops' conversations and wrapped this incendiary paper in a ball of yarn to disguise it. She then went to the woods to sit and knit before dropping her ball of yarn there. A Revolutionary soldier would then pick up the yarn, thereby finding out British military secrets.[42] The knitting itself held no secret messages, but the unsuspicious domesticity of the activity provided a handy cover.

Another popular knitting hero is the Frenchwoman Madame Levengle, alleged to have knitted whilst watching German troop movements from her window during the First World War. Using her feet, she tapped a message on the floorboards for her children to copy down in the room below.[43] Again, knitting provided a means to disguise espionage, not a means for encryption.

Phyllis Latour Doyle, a female operative with Britain's Special Operations Executive (SOE) during the Second World War, is sometimes cited as an encrypting knitter. Having joined the RAF as a flight mechanic, Latour Doyle was parachuted into the Calvados region of Normandy with the code name Paulette, tasked with sending intelligence back to Britain in code. In 2014, the *Daily Telegraph* published an article about Latour Doyle, who, at the age of ninety-three, was being awarded the *légion d'honneur* for her part in wartime espionage. She said that she sent 135 coded messages and used her knitting to conceal them.[44] However, Latour Doyle's own testimony reveals that it was not her knitting that was coded, but the silk, she used. As her codes were on a piece of silk, when she had used that code she would prick the respective piece of silk with a pin before wrapping it round a knitting needle to hide it.[45]

The Great War provides the only substantiated stories about knitting in code, chiefly from the British Secret Intelligence Service, MI6. In 2009, the BBC produced a series of programmes to celebrate the service's centenary. One described how, in 1914, MI6 worked with members of the Belgian Resistance, who, detesting the occupation of their country by Imperial Germany, sought out older women living in houses with windows that had views of railway yards. As they knitted, they would knit one for a troop train or purl one for an artillery vehicle.[46] In the Second World War, the US Office of Censorship banned the sending of knitting patterns abroad, in case the instructions contained encoded military information.[47]

Perhaps the most interesting element about knitted code is our perennial fascination with it. The possibilities of hiding coded messages in knitting have long captivated the public imagination; perhaps because the idea of knitters as secret agents seems deliciously preposterous – at least to non-knitters. Knitters, adept at reading the codes of their patterns, know better. Developing and adapting their own garments has honed their skills in analytic geometry, abstract algebra and topology. Knitting is an exercise in exploring and interpreting the world.

Before the protest back in London, I make a pilgrimage to see the Woolsack, the huge wool-stuffed seat in the House of Lords, which stands as an emblem of Britain's historic wealth and power. Entering Parliament is like taking a flight. Belt and shoes off, bag stripped of laptop and phone, pockets emptied. At the bottom of my bag, the unfinished Pussyhat hangs guiltily from my bamboo needles. Through the scanner we go – I think of the half-done hat and hold my breath – and we're free to continue inside. I get to the Great Hall and am met by a smiling security-woman, who walks me through gates, yards and buildings. It's a busy day, she tells me – three lobbies and a demonstration, the Brexit bill in the House of Lords, a visit from US congressmen and women. I keep quiet about the yarn and needles in my bag.

After exploring the halls and corridors of power, I put the finishing touches to my hat on the Embankment, twenty minutes before the march begins. I hastily finish the hat, using a straightened paperclip as a makeshift needle to work in ends of yarn, lest my inglorious concoction unravels. Jamming the hat onto my head as I cross the road to join the protest, I realize it's far too small and barely stays on. The ears are wonky, and as I was slightly short on wool, there's a slight hole at the top. It's not the most beautiful hat I've ever made, but sometimes looks are not the point. The Pussyhat is a twenty-first-century reimagining of the *bonnet rouge*, today's Phrygian cap. It is me saying, 'I am here, see me, count me in.' From buying sustainable yarn to taking to the streets in a Pussyhat, the *tricoteuses* live on.

4

Highland Kilts and Stockings

Back home in Fife, April dawns, and a run of sunny days warms us into spring. As the days lengthen past the equinox, I feel the pull of the mountains, the draw to be out in the hills that have been wind-battered, snow-drenched and frost-frozen since before the old year ended. Throwing a rucksack and a pair of boots into the back of the car, I point it north and speed towards the Highlands with the lengthening shadows. The Cairngorms, regal under mantles of recalcitrant snow, look soft as ermine in the sunshine. Below them, the last of the day's light skims off the lochs, where a scum of ice still grips their edges.

I am bound for the Highland Folk Museum, on the trail of Scotland's woollen past. Founded in a church on the island of Iona in 1935, the museum now spans more than a square mile in Newtonmore, in the central Cairngorms. Dr Isabel Grant, the HFM's prescient and dynamic creator, saw that the traditional Highland way of life was in danger of disappearing in the maelstrom of the twentieth century, and made it her mission to preserve of it what she could. By knocking on doors, rifling through rubbish and bidding at auctions, she built a physical record of rural Highland life in what became the UK's first mainland open-air museum, after her initial collection was removed from the vicissitudes of Iona's weather. Today, the museum also houses an enormous archive of domestic material from across the north of Scotland – hundreds of thousands of items that tell snippets of stories of lives that might otherwise be unremembered, all cared for at Am Fasgadh, 'The Shelter', a purpose-built collections store.

Walking through Am Fasgadh, I see box after box of coloured woven textiles, from an elaborate wedding tartan made into an *earasaid* (a long plaid worn belted or loose by Highland women), to simpler blankets and plaids. Although woven fabric featuring stripes and checks dating to the third-century CE has been found in Scotland, when the so-called 'Falkirk Plaid' was discovered with a Roman coin hoard near Stirling,[1] no evidence of tartan as we would recognize it today dates from before the sixteenth century,[2] and there is no one word for tartan in Gaelic.[3] The closest is *breacan an fhèilidh*, a name first used for the belted plaid. *Breacan* on its own means 'pattern', though it can also be used as shorthand for 'tartan'. Its root, *breac*, means 'spotted' or 'speckled'. A plaid can refer to any textile woven from two or more coloured threads, its origins in the Gaelic *plaide*, meaning 'coarse cloth' or 'flannel', whereas tartan's history is uncertain and disputed. One possible etymology is that the word comes from *tarsuinn*, Gaelic for to 'cross transversely', reflecting the crossing nature of the weave;[4] another is the French *tiretaine*, the name for cloth made from half wool, half linen or cotton.

The clan 'setts', those distinct checked patterns on which today's tartans are based, were not formalized or even widely used until the nineteenth century. Checked fabric was certainly worn – with red shades being popular (and possibly signifying status), as were blues and purples.[5] This fabric was worn hanging below knee-length at the wearer's back, where it was doubled, so that the top layer could be pulled up and wrapped around the shoulders; in front it was kilted at or above the knee for ease of movement. The short kilt, or *philabeg* (*fèileadh beag*), a modern, knee-length version of the *breacan*, was folded into pleats rather than worn double at the back.

The *philabeg* first appears in written English in the eighteenth century, in the prohibitive Dress Act of 1746, which aimed to bring the Highlands into the British fold and reduce the power of the clans. Following similar earlier Acts, this unpopular decree, enforced from 1 August 1746, stated that: 'no Man or Boy [...] shall, on any pretence whatsoever, wear or put on the Clothes commonly called Highland Clothes (that is to say) the Plaid, Philabeg, or little Kilt, Trowse, Shoulder Belts, or any part whatsoever of what peculiarly belongs to the Highland Garb.'[6] Punishment was six months' imprisonment without bail for a first offence; thereafter, it was transportation.[7] Woven checked trowse or trews, *triubhas* in Gaelic, were worn by Highlanders on horseback and in inclement weather under the kilt. Tailored to be close-fitting,[8] trews were made from the same colourful cloth as the *breacan*. The ban did not apply to women,[9] but for men, the kilt became the preserve of the British military – officers and soldiers were exempt from the Act. Made from a coarse weave of combed wool, this 'hard' tartan continued to be worn by soldiers in the Highland regiments until Queen Victoria abolished it in 1872. Drenched by rain and whipped against the backs of the knees by fierce winds, hard tartan cut soft skin like a knife; after seeing the ragged knees and calves of the 93rd Regiment, the Guard of Honour at Ballater, 'the Queen was graciously pleased to direct that soft instead of hard tartan be in future supplied to Highland regiments'.[10]

Surrounded by farming implements and row upon row of wooden Highland dressers, Am Fasgadh's curator turns on the lights in the textile store. They illuminate a table full of knitwear – socks, shawls, even a knitted doormat – but most numerous are pairs of brightly coloured stockings. Named for the 'stocks' that held felons by the ankle, stockings were the legwear of choice across Europe from the sixteenth to nineteenth centuries, both as everyday undergarments and striking fashion pieces. They superseded hose, woven strappings covering the leg, garments that by the 1580s were thought 'too base'[11] for the fashion-conscious Londoner, but live on in our word 'hosiery'. Close-fitting and smoothly knit, stockings came to be worn by men and women from all strata of society, the finest and most expensive being knitted from silk. Spanish silk stockings, in particular, were renowned for their quality – and were prohibitively expensive for all but the very wealthy. In *The Anatomie of Abuses* (1583), his critique of perceived cultural excesses (including the availability of many different types of hats), Phillip Stubbes sharply notes, 'The time might well have been when one might have clothed all his body well, from top to toe, for less than a pair of these [silk] nether stockes will cost.'[12] Stockings also provided the terms to describe knitting, so closely were the two connected: 'stocking stitch' is named for rounds of continuous knit stitches that make up that garment's form, with the rounded garter that grips the top of the leg standing shorthand for a round of knit followed by one of purl.

In Am Fasgadh's collection, the most common type of stockings are diamond-patterned military stockings. Also known as regimental hose, these were developed to be worn with the short kilt after the Dress Act. Most have been knitted with bold diamond patterns overlaid with contrasting diagonal lines; by the 1890s this style of textile, whether knitted or woven, had become known as 'Argyle', as it was based on the Argyll sett of the Campbell clan from Scotland's west.[13] Most of the museum's military stockings have been knitted in the pink, red and white of the 92nd Regiment of Foot, better known as the Gordon Highlanders. Several pairs have initials knitted into their tops, traces of owners long since departed, and a few have a banded pattern that works its way in two-tone stripes around the stocking leg. From the raising of the regiment in 1794 until the late 1840s, regimental leg coverings were made of white and scarlet cloth known as *cathdath*, cut on the cross and sewn together, held in place by rosettes and garters made of red ribbon. After 1847, knitted stockings in the same colourful pattern took the place of *cathdath* hose; by 1856, the design switched from red and white to what is known as 'Rob Roy' tartan: overlapping blocks of red and black. This continued until 1952, when the pattern reverted to the red and white dice – without feet and designed to be worn over grey stockings.[14]

Whilst much of Scotland's historic woollen production centred on weaving, commercial hand-knitting could be found in pockets across the country. In 1680, hand-knitting was an extremely ill-paid occupation on the Scottish mainland, though it formed the basis of an international market: 'The women of this country are mostly employed in the spinning and working of stockings [...] which the Aberdeen merchants carry over the sea; it is this which bringeth money to the commons; other ways of getting it they have not.'[15] In 1749, James Rae writes in *A Compleat History of the Rebellion* that in Aberdeen, 'The manufacture here is chiefly of stockings, all round the adjacent country, and every morning women bring in loads to sell about the town to merchants who have them scoured for exportation to London, Hamburg and Holland.'[16] Women were the chief knitters and their industriousness was remarked upon by the minister of Glenmuick, on Deeside, who wrote in the *New Statistical Account of Scotland* in 1845: 'While I accuse men of indolence, I should do great injustice to the women if I did not exempt them from the charge, by whose industry and diligence their families are, in a great measure, supported.'[17]

Much of the wool to be knitted came from the Borders. In 1685, Bailie Alexander Skene of Newtyle wrote that 'Aberdeen merchants brought the wool from the south of Scotland and sold it out in "smalls" to the country people, who spun it and [...] knitted it into stockings'[18] – there was 'a very large number of old women' in the rural counties of Inverness and Ross-shire occupied in spinning the yarn needed by the knitters. However, it appears that the Lowland fleeces may have been less fine, resulting in lower-quality stockings; the Highland historian Isabel Grant believed it was 'of the fine scanty wool of the original Highland sheep that the very fine stockings were made'.[19]

Before leaving the archives, I unearth a piece of paper headed with the words 'Gairloch Knitting Pattern', reissued in 1982 by the Gairloch and District Heritage Society. It is for stockings similar to those I saw in the museum's stores, worked in two shades of undyed yarn with criss-crossing paler lines over a darker ground, wrapping the legs of the wearer in distinctive bands. But these stockings are also decorated with a stag's head, the symbol of the Mackenzie clan. Legend tells that in 1265, King Alexander III was charged by a stag in the forest of Mar; his life was only saved by the skill of Colin Fitzgerald, progenitor of the Mackenzies, who shot the stag with an arrow. In return, 'the grateful monarch granted to Colin a stag's head puissant as his armorial bearing'.[20] This elaborate pattern, known as *caberfèidh* or 'stag's horns', was designed to be shown off on the turn-over tops of men's stockings worn with the kilt, and in 1912, the Gairloch and District Heritage Society noted that 'these knee-length stockings are still worn by game-keepers and sportsmen'.[21] Discovering the pattern lights inspiration's touch-paper for my next knitting challenge: I will recreate a pair of Gairloch stockings.

Gairloch takes its name from the Gaelic *gearr loch*, 'short loch', around which its small townships huddle. Almost unique in Scotland, the Gairloch estate, covering some 56,900 acres by 1996,[22] has been owned by the same family since 1494. In six centuries of Gairloch Mackenzies, one in particular stands out: the eleventh laird and fourth baronet, Sir Hector Mackenzie (1757–1826). Widely regarded as a popular, generous and humane landowner,[23] he inherited the estate at the age of twelve.

Unusually, Sir Hector did not employ a factor; instead, he communicated directly with his tenants regarding rents and the management of their land. Sir Hector and his descendants did not evict the tenants on their land and – in sharp contrast to much of Highland Scotland – Gairloch's population increased from around 2,500 in 1755 to an all-time high of 5,449 by 1861. Although there was some voluntary migration as the nineteenth century wore on, mostly to Canada, it was only in the twentieth century that the parish's population dropped below 4,000, and by 2011 it numbered 2,300, roughly the same as when Sir Hector was born there some 250 years before.[24]

Sir Hector's son, Sir Francis Mackenzie (1799–1843), continued to run the estate according to his father's ethos, without a factor and with an emphasis on supporting crofters. Outliving his father by only seventeen years, Sir Francis left the estate to his eleven-year-old son, Kenneth, who was thought to be too young to manage such a huge domain – at that time encompassing some 170,000 acres. For the ten years until he came of age, the estate was run by his uncle Dr John Mackenzie (1803–86)

and by his mother, Lady Mary Mackenzie (1812–1901). Both had a powerful, positive and long-lasting influence on the lives of the people of Gairloch. Dr John continued the even-handed work of Sir Hector and Sir Francis, firmly believing that 'the population of the Highlands can be supported by soil, without being obliged to emigrate';[25] together with Lady Mackenzie, he implemented a new system of crofting that they hoped would be entirely self-sustaining. The land was surveyed in minute detail by George Campbell Smith, and in 1854 the Mackenzies created six hundred planned crofts, each with around four acres of land. This differed markedly from the runrig system of annual allocation; the Mackenzies gave each tenant a plot of land close to that which they already farmed, and also created several new townships and a few larger farmsteads, including one near their home, Flowerdale. The crofters built their own thatched drystone houses, using the roof timbers of their former turf dwellings, and the land that had not been allocated to the new crofts was given over to common grazing.

For all its progressive land management under the Mackenzies, Gairloch was still affected by the Potato Blight of 1846 that ravaged Ireland and the Highlands. The impact on livelihoods was, however, lessened because Lady Mackenzie had set up a new local business to give the women of Gairloch a way of increasing their household income. In 1837, she had 'employed a lady from Skye who was staying at Kerrysdale to instruct twelve young women in knitting nice stockings with dice and other fancy patterns'.[26] Six years later, as one of the estate's trustees, Lady Mackenzie 'started the manufacture of Gairloch stockings in earnest, having spinners, dyers, and knitters, all taught and superintended' during the ten years she lived at Flowerdale. 'Now dozens of pairs are brought by the women to the hotels and steamers, and large quantities go to Inverness, Edinburgh, and London; £100 worth has been sold in one shop.'[27]

By 1847, Lady Mackenzie had over '100 women employed spinning wool who work up about thirty-five stones [222 kilos] per week which is then knitted into stockings or woven into coast cloth'.[28] Gairloch designs were represented at the Exhibition of Modern British Crafts and the Great Exhibition held at the Crystal Palace in Hyde Park in 1851. In 1886, J. H. Dixon wrote in *A Guide to Gairloch and Loch Maree* that Gairloch 'is justly celebrated for its hose', noting that stockings were being knitted 'in an immense variety of pattern and colour, some being in imitation of old forms of tartan'.[29] In 1890, Lady Mackenzie began a competition for knitting stockings, and throughout her life held exhibitions of local knitwear. Together with Lady Fowler, who organized a spinning and hand-weaving industry at Loch Broom, 50 miles north-east of Gairloch, Lady Mackenzie had a small depot for completed knitwear at Strathpeffer near Inverness.[30] Some estimates give the annual value of knitted exports from Wester Ross at £500 in 1900, and in 1895, Gairloch knitters were winning prizes at the Highland and Agricultural Society Show.[31] By the end of the nineteenth century, several schemes like Lady Mackenzie's had been developed.

Harris Tweed became the best known of these. First produced on the orders of Catherine Murray, Countess of Dunmore, in 1846, *An Clò Mòr*, 'the Big Cloth', is the only fabric in the world whose manufacture is governed by an Act of Parliament, which forbids any person from 'selling, exposing or offering for sale or having in his possession for the purposes of sale – any material which is represented as Harris Tweed but is not Harris Tweed'.[32] Having inherited the Dunmore lands on Harris from her husband, Lady Dunmore asked her tenant farmers to weave the Murray tartan on their looms in blue, green and red. The islanders had woven textiles for their own use since time immemorial, but this was the era of the Potato Famine, and Dunmore's tenants were facing starvation; new economies were sorely needed across

Scotland. Impressed with the results, Lady Dunmore then promoted the islanders' tweed to her wealthy friends. Yarn left over from weaving was put to use and knitted up into *geansaidh bobain*, jumpers made from Harris Tweed yarn.

Smaller schemes for supporting local crafts formed part of the Scottish Home Industries Association. Set up by the Countess of Rosebery in 1889, the SHIA was the result of 'a strong upper-class interest in fostering household industries' and aimed to provide a market for these handmade goods, as well as 'to improve the quality of the productions by instruction and the circulation of information, to promote the sale of products and to ensure the payment of a fair price to the workers'.[33] It was hardly a grass-roots Highland movement: this upper-class institution based its Board of Management and first depot in London. In 1896, it was formally registered with capital of £10,000 and had expanded to include depots in London, Harris, Lewis, Golspie and Edinburgh, as well as employing 'a travelling inspector to control the quality of the tweed'.[34]

The SHIA was divided into four branches (Northern, Eastern, Central and Western counties), whose emphasis was on tweed, needlework, linens and art embroidery respectively. Sales were low at first – totalling £2,303 1*s*. 9*d*. in 1894 – but as the organization developed, they began to rise. Two problems were apparent from the start: local merchants, who were responsible for supplying the depot with wares, were not willing to place large orders, as it left them financially vulnerable; and the producers themselves could only make a limited number of products as they invariably had little working capital. They had to sell what they made when they made it, instead of driving up prices by denying the markets.

Another 'problem', as it was seen at the time by those at the top of the SHIA, was the workers' attitude to their own craft. In England, craftspeople had specialized in and depended upon one particular skill for their livelihood since at least mediaeval times. Across Scotland's north, it was common for people to have developed a more diverse set of abilities, necessary for communal township and later crofting life: they would combine farming, spinning, weaving, fishing and myriad other tasks as the seasons demanded. Spinning, knitting and sewing all had to be fitted in around the demands of the croft and creel; the workers were not accustomed to working solely on one project to fulfil an order. This was a strength when it came to working the land, but went against mainstream market principles

The interrelation between craft, farming and fishing remains particular to the crofting way of life, and Gairloch stockings continued to be produced in Wester Ross into the twentieth century, partly owing to the area's continuing success with small-scale crofts. In 1910, the chairman of the Parish Council of Gairloch made a report to the House of Commons on livelihoods in the parish, noting that the population of Gairloch, numbering about 4,200, 'is chiefly dependent on fishing and agriculture. There is no industrial occupation [. . .] but there is a certain amount of home industry in spinning, knitting, and tweed manufacture.'[35]

Before I can begin to knit my pair of Gairloch stockings, I must find the right yarn for the job. Four-ply yarn is the most common modern weight for making socks, and I am keen to use wool from as close a breed to the old Highland type as I can. Isabel Grant's description of the 'fine scanty wool' gives me my first clue. Prior to the 'improved' Cheviot and Blackface breeds, the Highland sheep were small, with fine, double-layered fleece, similar to Soay and other Northern European short-tail breeds. As most breeds recognized today were developed and codified in the nineteenth century, we now cannot know exactly what these sheep were like, but parish records and the statistical accounts indicate they were not of a uniform type. In Caithness and Sutherland to the north, they were known as the 'Kerry' – black-faced, narrow-framed and slow to grow. Those from Orkney, the north-west and the northern Hebrides were most like the Shetland – descriptions indicate they were short-tailed and of various colours, and frequently piebald – whereas on Arran and in the west the sheep were tan-faced, with no mention of a short tail.[36] Where can I find the descendants of these sheep today?

It's a cloudy morning as I climb aboard the tiny twin-engine plane that will take me to Britain's western edge, to the Outer Hebridean islands of North and South Uist and Berneray. Seated by the emergency exit, a flicker of fear goes through my chest as the plane hangs between propellers rotating so fast they blur to nothing. We vibrate along the runway and throw ourselves into the sky with a leonine roar. A little under an hour later, we land in the Outer Hebrides, where I pick up a tiny car from a family-run hire company at Benbecula airport.

The Western Isles stretch for 130 miles between Barra Head and the Butt of Lewis, caught between mainland Scotland and the Atlantic. Knitting has long been part of life on the Outer Hebrides, though not on a commercial scale as in Gairloch. Early-twentieth-century photographs and films of the Hebrides by the ethnographer Werner Kissling show women shearing, spinning and dyeing wool and working metal knitting needles, marled yarn crooked over their fingers. The author and broadcaster Finlay J. Macdonald, who grew up on Harris in the 1920s, remembers his great-aunt Rachel knitting socks while she brewed her tea. After filling a pan with spring water and heating it over the peat fire, she threw in half a handful of tea and 'the brew was made to boil vigorously while she knitted a measured knuckle of sock which she had calculated long ago took her ten minutes'. But time moved more quickly than Great-Aunt Rachel: 'The fact she got arthritic and slower as she got older didn't alter anything. As far as she was concerned, an inch and a half of sock was still ten minutes, and that was the duration for which tea boiled.'[37]

As I arrived at the Kildonan Museum on South Uist, I see a large black cauldron filled with lichen and wool standing sentinel by the door. The pot is one of many given to the South Uist townships by their previous owner, Lady Gordon Cathcart, who married the son of the widely hated Colonel John Gordon of Cluny. In a portrait from 1876, now in Aberdeen Art Gallery and Museum, Lady Cathcart is shown with a ball of pale yarn and two double-pointed needles in her hand. One she holds like a pen, and neither has any cast-on stitches. It is a pose of knitterly idleness – or ignorance. Lady Gordon Cathcart became notorious for forcing her tenants to migrate to Canada and is believed to have visited the lands she owned in the Hebrides only once. In 1908, she took a group of crofters, known as the Vatersay Raiders, to court, for having the temerity to croft on a then-empty island.

Round three-legged iron cauldrons such as this one were used for dyeing wool. Crotal, the general term for lichen used in dyeing, would be scraped from the rocks using an old spoon and brought back to the croft in a pail. Shorn and separated fleece would be laid in the cauldron on top of a layer of shells or stones, to keep the fiercest, scorching heat off the wool. Then a layer of crotal would be followed by another of fleece, and the pot filled with water. Heated over a fire to a simmer that lasted all day, it would then cool overnight before the wool was spun into yarn.

Today, much of the yarn spun on Uist remains undyed. Although Finlay J. Macdonald, writing his memoirs in the 1980s, saw knitting as a relic of a past generation,[38] today Hebridean knitting is experiencing something of a boom. Uist Wool, launched in 2016 after several years of research, fundraising and training, is a community-benefit society that spins undyed yarns from breeds including Hebridean, Scottish Bowmont and Cheviot sheep. A small but dedicated team produce high-quality yarn from the Hebrides, ensuring that the crofters who supply the fleece receive a fair price for their yarn, and also educate and inspire people to make things from Uist Wool. The yarns have evocative Gaelic names, encouraging knitters to look more closely at their provenance, colour and texture.

Arriving at the company's mill at Grimsay on North Uist, my hire car struggles to keep moving as the causeway I'm crossing threatens to disappear under water. It is a *reothart*, or spring tide, the time of the month when there is the greatest difference between the waters at high and low tides. Uist Wool have a yarn named 'Reothart', which goes from deepest chocolatey black to palest cream, a gradient carefully spun. Its sister skein is 'Conntraigh', all soft greys and creams – named for the neap tide, when there is little variance between low and high water.

I leave with a skein of Canach (Cottongrass) in oat-coloured 'Corca', perfect for the paler parts of the Gairloch stockings. A silky four-ply with soft slubs like seed pearls, it is spun from the fleece of the Scottish Bowmont, a cross-breed of Shetland and Saxon Merino developed in the 1990s by the Macaulay Land Use Research Institute (now the James Hutton Institute). Alas this breed is not hardy enough to be farmed on the Hebrides, so in a modern echo of the seventeenth-century south-to-north movement of wool for spinning, the raw fleece is flown from Aberdeenshire to be spun on Uist. Paired with a skein of dark 'Dorcha', it will form the contrasting bands that wind around the calves.

After a morning at the Grimsay mill, I head to Berneray, the tiny island, only a mile long, in the Sound of Harris. Driving across the causeway, the rain has lifted and I see a scattering of low islets in the sound. I have come to visit Meg Rodger, artist and crofter, on her Sunhill croft. Meg owns and manages The Birlinn Yarn Company, named for the specially adapted rowing boats, or *birlinns*, used by the Vikings to navigate the rock-strewn Hebridean waters. It's a well-chosen name: it is thought that the hardy Hebridean sheep that Meg farms, which belong to the Northern European short-tailed family, may have been introduced to the Hebrides by the Vikings. Meg's sheep are still seafaring: they are brought to and fro between her croft on Berneray and offshore islands in the Sound of Harris for grazing. What's more, Meg's husband, Andrew, once crewed the birlinn *Aileach* from Glasgow to the Faroes; in a moment of Hebridean happenstance, I realize I have seen the very boat he sailed. By the Kildonan Museum stands the *Aileach's* curved hull, resting here following her ocean voyage in 1992.

Viking-era ships similar to the *Aileach* are believed to have been powered by woollen sails, spun and woven from the double-layered fleece of the ancestor of many of today's Northern European short-tailed breeds, the *villsau* (literally 'wild sheep'). Made from one-ply yarn spun clockwise in the warp and usually widdershins in the weft, the sails could be *einskept*, woven from one thread passing over and under another; *tuskept*, with two threads under and over a single warp; or *prinskept*, with two weft and two warp threads.[39] The Norse Gulatingslovi, laws dating from around 1,000 CE, decreed that sails must be stored in churches, such was their value and importance: 'The man on whom responsibility falls and who lives near the sea, shall store the sail in the church. If the church burns this man is responsible for the sail.'[40]

In 1990, part of one such lanolin-rich *villsau* sail was discovered in the roof of a twelfth-century church in Trondenes, northern Norway, its original function still identifiable by the sail's eyelet holes. The following year, the Coastal Museum on the island of Hitra, west of Trondheim, decided to recreate such a sail; Amy Lightfoot, head of the Tømmervik Textile Trust on Hitra, was the person skilled enough to make it. Though no one in Norway had made woollen sails for over two hundred years, people still knew how to make *wadmal*, a thick cloth used as both currency and clothing by communities across northern Europe from the Viking era until the end of the eighteenth century. Lightfoot used these techniques to reproduce a woollen sail.

It was no small task. The sail needed to measure 85 square metres; such a large piece of cloth required the fleece of 2,000 comparatively rare *villsau* and *spælsau* sheep. Sorting the fibres took four people six months; spinning them into some 165,000 metres of yarn and then weaving them into a sail took more than two years. The sail needed to be strong enough to bear the brunt of Arctic gales, the tensioned pull of wind against rigging. Too heavy and it cannot be raised by hand; too light, and it cannot withstand the weather. It must flex enough to fill with air, but not bend so much, or be so flat, that it cannot propel the boat. The spinners' and the weavers' skills are paramount to ensure sailing success, twisting threads to just the right degree and weaving the resulting yarn into a cloth dense, flexible and strong.[41] As they worked, Lightfoot and her team realized the importance of Viking women in producing these sails; the ships were truly a communal resource and responsibility. The resulting sail was able to propel a replica Viking ship around 10 per cent faster in an upwind direction than a modern sail.[42]

At Sunhill croft, with its backdrop of the stormy-skyed Sound of Harris, my hands luxuriate in a basket of woolly colour. Meg sells yarns in many hues, some the colour of their natural fleece and some over-dyed. The result is a rich rainbow to reflect the Hebridean landscape. I leave with a ball of 'Cearc Bhreac' ('Speckled Hen'), perfect for the foot of the stockings, which will be pounded by determined feet. A marled four-ply yarn, it twists together strands of peaty-brown Hebridean and storm-grey Cheviot wool. Marled yarn was most often used for making socks and stockings, its barber-pole stripes of pale and dark wool disguising stains from sweaty feet. This yarn was often cheaper too, good for using up wool that varied in shade. Although I cannot get my hands on yarn from the old Highland breeds, this yarn represents Scotland's ovine history: dark Hebridean bound to long and lofty Cheviot.

*

Back on the mainland, I head for Gairloch, sleet and snow buffeting the car as I wind my way along increasingly narrow roads. Wester Ross, with Gairloch at its western edge, gets its weather fresh from the Atlantic. Under heavy clouds, I wend my way along the narrow road, darting into passing places to let a handful of cars pass. Sleet drums on the roof as I arrive at Gairloch Museum and I pick my way carefully up the museum's circular iron staircase to find two large boxes full of stockings. Knitted in red and blue, purple and cream, teal and brown, each bicolour pair is unique, made for specific legs and feet. Others are Argyle-patterned, diced green and black and banded with the red and white of the Mackenzie tartan. I also find prototypes of my Gairloch stockings: knitted from undyed yarn, their alternate bands of dark and light snake across imagined shins.

Leaving the museum, I head south to Torridon, arriving at my rented cottage in the grey half-light that precedes a snowstorm. The long, low bulk of Stalker's Cottage hunkers down on the shores of Loch Torridon, and inside its chairs are cushioned with heavy tartan, the doorways topped with antlers. Large Victorian paintings of stags and cattle loom from the walls, set against a backdrop of their homeland hills. Stags have become an immediately recognizable symbol of the Highlands. After the large sheep flocks were introduced, the price of British wool dropped as imports from its colonies flooded the market. Sheep were no longer as profitable as had been hoped, and were replaced with herds of deer. The Mackenzies also turned their rougher moor and hill land over to deer forest, totalling 38,000 acres by 1842. Deer are still farmed here; the car's headlights caught their eyes as I juddered down the lane to the cottage. Next door is a small, macabre deer museum, hung with skulls and skeletons.

Before the cottage is a high wire fence, penning the deer into the parts of the estate where young trees have not been planted.

Beyond them rise the scree-filled flanks of Seana Mheallan, Beinn na h-Eaglaise and Meall Dearg, dusted with snow across their upper reaches. Last summer's bracken has died back to leave a reddish smear on the mountains' lower slopes, and between us stretches the old loch's salted, marshy edge, bisected by the rivers Torridon and Abhainn Thrail. It is the perfect place for a week of knitting.

By the flickering, smoky warmth of the cottage fire, rain rattling on the windows, I lay out the skeins of 'Corca', 'Dorcha' and 'Cearc Bhreac', and wind them into balls round the legs of the tweed-covered chairs. As the wet weather worsens outside and the wind rises to a howl, I make a start on the first stocking, beginning with the decorative top. Casting on seventy-eight stitches across five 3.25 mm needles and working a broad k3, p3 rib, I then knit the *caberfèidh*'s proud horns and upright nose in 'Dorcha', stark against the pale 'Corca'. Once the top band is completed, I turn the socks inside out and continue knitting with the wrong side outermost as the tops of these socks will be worn turned down, the stag's heads visible just below the knee. I then work and shape the bands of dark and light grey, tapering the calf towards the ankle. Some of the stockings at Gairloch Heritage Museum were only half-finished, and showed that some knitters worked the leg as a flat piece, knitting and purling back and forth on two pins, before forming a tube at the ankle and working the heel, instep and toes in the round on double-pointed pins. Others have been knitted in the round; this too is my preference, as sewing seams is not a part of garment-making that I particularly enjoy.

Gairloch stockings were intended for men to wear with kilts. Although my husband, Tom, is not a Scot and therefore has never donned his adopted country's traditional dress, I make these long socks for him. As an ardent hillwalker, he can test them against the tug of gorse and heather, the sump of bog and burn. Back home from my week of knitting, I present him with the stockings. He pulls them on under his trousers, and laces up the thick leather boots he keeps clean and waxed for the next hill walk. Much longer than his usual walking socks, they fit tight around his calves.

Legs clad warmly in wool, we head for the Cairngorms. Compared to Torridon's dark, glowering slopes, their steep, forbidding corries picked out in winter's snow, the Cairngorms look inviting, shadowed by the morning sun before the day breaks fully over them. Over breakfast in a cafe, we crack the map's new fold to plot the route; across the Ordnance Survey's familiar squares the Spey snakes along beside the railway line. We will follow their parallel course on foot.

Curlews have risen long before us. Oystercatchers peep, lapwings ring like telephones: the world belongs to these gods of the morning, and we creep into their chorus like postulants. A raptor, striped in a merlin's buff and black, tumbles out of the ruins of Ruthven Barracks at Kingussie. Jinking sideways, then gliding down to view its world from a fencepost, it pays us no heed. We sit with our backs against the stone walls of the barracks, the sun full on our faces, and my husband rolls down his long socks, too effective at conserving heat on this rare hot April day.

We walk to Glenfeshie, a narrow valley running north to south through the western Cairngorms. As afternoon wears on, the sky clouds over and the heat fades from the day; after our picnic lunch, the stockings are rolled back up, their warmth now welcome. We press on in the fading light, covering 20 miles before returning to Kingussie. Rewarding ourselves with a pair of pints, my husband covertly slips off his boots and socks under the bar table. His feet are hot but dry – and unblistered. Fortunately for our fellow drinkers, they smell only of wool, a sweetish lanolin scent. These stockings have passed their Highland test.

5

A Not-So-Itsy-Bitsy Bikini

Back at home, May dawns sunny-bright as grape hyacinths thrust their deep blue heads through the garden's undergrowth. They are several shades more purple than the inky indigo of the gansey, which patiently waits for my attention. After knitting lightweight stockings and a quick-to-finish hat, returning to the increasingly hefty gansey requires physical effort. Its rounds of stocking stitch will now cover Dad from waist to armpit, but even half-finished it is already densely heavy, its bulk too much to carry with me as I travel south for the next chapter of this knitting quest. In these warming days, sturdy lambs peppering the fields, I turn my attention to the Border region, historically disputed lands that bind England to Scotland. The area has a history rich in stories – and tales of wool production in particular.

The Borders' woollen industries started almost a thousand years ago, with the founding of abbeys at Kelso, Melrose, Jedburgh and Dryburgh. Indeed, Scotland's oldest extant agricultural records, dating from 1150, detail specialized commercial sheep farming at Kelso.[1] While the monks spent their hours in prayer, contemplation and reading, lay brothers set up sheep farms nearby at places including Eildon and Gattonside, on lands gifted to the abbeys by King David I of Scotland.

The Border abbeys farmed sheep in their thousands. Kelso's grazing lands extended from Whiteadder Water near Berwick, on the coast, to Fulhope Burn in western Northumberland. By the fourteenth century, records attest that Melrose's flocks alone numbered 17,000. The monks sheared, sorted and graded the wool, but did not make their money from manufacturing yarn or cloth; rather, they exported their fleece from the nearby port of Berwick to Italy and the Low Countries, whose extensive textile industries were eager to spin and weave British wool.

Much of this wool came from the now-extinct Scottish Dunface, a breed also known as the Scottish Shortwool. A short-tailed hardy sheep with, as the name suggests, a dark brown face above a pale fleece, the Dunface reigned supreme in the Border counties until the sixteenth century. In 1503, James IV introduced some five thousand Blackface sheep into Ettrickdale. With a small body, its eponymous black face and black legs, this hardy sheep eventually replaced the Dunface – but its wool was not of the finest or softest quality.

The development of the Cheviot breed, however, in part led to the creation of a large-scale wool spinning and weaving industry in the Borders. Named for the hills that run between Sauchope Forest in the west and Wooler at the eastern edge of Northumberland, today's hardy Cheviots boast a white face and legs, and wool that is dense, strong, lustrous and 'lofty' – with a good degree of springy bounce. Identified as a breed by the founder of the British Wool Society, Sir John Sinclair, in 1791, the Cheviot was the first sheep to have its own Flock Book, dating back to 1893. Edward Harrison, chairman of one of Scotland's best-known woollen companies, Johnstons of Elgin, from 1920 until 1966, saw national identity writ large in the Cheviot: 'the wool would seem almost to have taken on the character of the true native Scot, in that, under a slightly rough exterior, it is sound and honest at heart.'[2] It is an ironic comparison; after 500 Cheviot gimmer ewes were introduced to Caithness by Sinclair in the eighteenth century, their subsequent success helped to precipitate events that saw the area's human population cleared from the land.

Another important Border breed is the Border Leicester, known colloquially as the 'Great Improver'. Bred by crossing Robert Bakewell's New (or Dishley) Leicester with the Cheviot, they combine the heavy Longwool fleece and meaty carriage of the Leicester with the resilience of the hill sheep. Bakewell was one of the pioneers of selective breeding, developing a type of genetic crossing known as 'in-and-in', or line-breeding, where sheep are bred with their close relatives. On Bakewell's death, part of his Leicester flock was brought to Glendale in

Northumberland by the brothers George and Matthew Culley. The Culleys crossed the Leicesters with their local Teeswater breed, and two strands developed: the 'Blue Cap' and the 'Red Legs'. By 1850, the hardier Red Legs had become known as Border Leicesters, the Blue Caps going on to form the basis for the rare Black Wensleydale breed. The Border Leicester's fleece is ideally suited to knitting's capacity to hug the body's curves as its fibres are natural elastic and warmly insulating. With the development of this long-fibred fleece, knitting's time had come in the Borders.

In spring's watery sunshine I arrive in Hawick, a mid-sized market town in the Teviot valley. The Border towns, set by fast-flowing rivers and surrounded by sheep farms, were perfectly placed for working wool on an industrial scale: Galashiels's Weavers' Corporation was established as early as 1666,[3] with the town's earliest fulling mills dating from the late Middle Ages (1250–1500CE). But whilst the knitting industry flourished further north in Scotland from the sixteenth century, it wasn't until two centuries later that commercial knitting boomed in the Borders. Straddling the River Teviot and on the main rail and road routes linking Edinburgh and Carlisle, Hawick was ideally positioned to power mills, transport wool and finished knitwear, and to share its fibre expertise with the world.

From the late eighteenth until the mid-twentieth century, Hawick flourished as Britain's main producer of machine-knit woollen undergarments. Pringle, Dior, Chanel – all have produced knitwear in the town, and some still do. Instead of being knitted by hand on sets of double-pointed needles, Hawick's knitwear was produced on knitting machines. Designed by Nottinghamshire clergyman William Lee in around 1589, early frame-knitting machines looked much like a weaver's loom: large wooden frames almost 2 metres high, with a simple seat at one end. Opposite the seat stood an iron 'carcase' with toothy rows of needles laid in a plate. The knitter swung the heavy yarn carriage across the teeth, turning spun fibres into fabric as they pushed down the presser bar. Knitting was ahead of its time: the invention of the knitting machine preceded the mechanized spinning wheel, the 'spinning jenny', by some two hundred years, meaning that yarn could be industrially knitted before it could be mechanically spun.

By the end of the seventeenth century, as much as 90 per cent of England's stockings were being made in the East Midlands, as Leicester, Derby and Nottingham developed huge frame-knitting industries. Different towns specialized in knitting different fabrics: Derby had its silk mills, Leicester its woollen and worsted. Hand-frame knitting required not only keen eyesight and good coordination but also brute strength to manipulate the swing carrier, so it was often men who worked the frames. With their skilful manipulation of the machines and sharp eye for detail, hand-frame knitters were regarded not as manual labourers but as artisans, paid not by the hour but by each finished piece. Hand-frame knitters were essentially self-employed, having the freedom to set their own hours and to employ members of their family in associated tasks such as winding yarn and seaming. For almost two hundred years, from around 1600 until the end of the eighteenth century, a hand-frame-knitting family could feed and clothe themselves from the proceeds of their labour.

After the Union of the Crowns in 1603, Scotland strove to emulate the success of England's stocking knitters. Acts were passed in Edinburgh controlling the export of raw wool, granting privileges to new companies, and encouraging an inflow of skilled labour: all measures designed to promote Scotland's manufacturing capability. Yet the country's woollen economy was slow to grow – whilst skilled hand-knitters in the Highlands and Islands continued to turn out exquisite stockings, these items were costly compared to machine-knit stockings made in England. In the late eighteenth century, the *London Tradesman* noted that, 'Knit-Stockings are much preferable in Durableness and Strength to those made in the Loom; but the time employed in knitting stockings of any fineness raises their price too much for common wear.' Scotland's knitwear industry had to become competitive: to do so, it needed its own knitting machines.

This was no easy task. Knitting machines were heavy, cumbersome and awkward to transport on the unmetalled roads. Before the Union of the Parliaments in 1707, it was illegal to transport technical machinery between Scotland and England without paying hefty customs duties. Nevertheless, in the spring of 1682, two narrow-bed foot-powered knitting frames were smuggled from London to Scotland by packhorse. They were destined for Haddington, in East Lothian, where the New Mills Cloth Manufactory had been founded in 1681.

By 1684, Lothian's New Mills frames were rattling out not only silk stockings but also warmer worsted woollens. Fashionable colours for stockings ranged from red, buff and gold to green, blue and black, all with wide ribbed tops. Whilst commercial hand-knitters continued to produce very fine garments, frame knitting had the edge of speed – and therefore profit. The difference in speed between frame- and hand-knitting was marked: where an expert hand-knitter could make a hundred loops in a minute, the frame churned out a thousand.

By 1812, some five hundred of Scotland's 1,450 frames were in Hawick, then a town of around two thousand people.[4] This concentration of frames was in large part due to the energies of alderman John Hardie, who first brought knitting frames to Hawick in 1771. Soon several small 'stocking shops', specializing in woollen stockings and half-hose, had sprung up, and before long Hawick's hosiers had organized their own unions to protect their lucrative trade. By the 1840s, the Borders were home to about two thousand of Scotland's 2,065 frames, churning out over a million pairs of stockings every year.

Today, only one narrow-bed foot-powered frame remains in Hawick, in the museum at the Borders Textile Towerhouse. Hand-made by Glasgow's Gavin Lennox in 1798, the frame proudly bears its maker's name and date, etched gracefully into its top bar. Looking at this exquisite machine, beautiful but mysterious in stasis, I realize that I need to see one in action to understand its workings. The museum's sole survivor is for display only, but staff suggest I visit the Framework Knitters Museum in Ruddington near Nottingham, over 200 miles away, where their historic frames are still in use.

After an early start and a long morning on a series of trains, I arrive at the Framework Knitters Museum, a neat brick cloister at the heart of Ruddington village. In a small machine room on the ground floor, the youngest member of the Worshipful Company of Framework Knitters coaxes one the country's oldest knitting frames into clattering life. Holly Batley, currently the only frame-work knitting apprentice in the world, perches her small frame on the machine's rough eighteenth-century seat. In front of her are rows of bearded needles, their hooked barbs lying in neat leaded pairs. Each framework knitter would need to melt and cast lead to make their own needles; theirs was a trade requiring skill in metalworking as well as manipulating yarn.

Eight individual movements are needed for a single row of stitches, and take a week or more to learn. First, Holly hangs weights like solid cowbells from the machine to set the tension. Within the broad wooden carriage hang the needle plates, which hold the sinkers, metal pieces that push the yarn into loops. Every alternate sinker is pushed down by levers called 'jacks'; the other sinkers are attached to a bar and alternate with the jacks to create successive loops of yarn. Pushing the yarn loop to the edge of the needle, where it is caught in the 'beard', the sinkers then retreat and down comes the presser bar to close the beard and push off the latest row of loops. Completing all eight movements as a smooth and seamless motion was known as 'meeting the presser'.

This eighteenth-century machine is a narrow-bed frame, the twin of the one I saw in Hawick, and requires Holly to lay yarn across the needles by hand. Only one stocking at a time could be made on the narrow-bed frame, and the fabric can be widened or narrowed as desired by removing or adding individual needles. But this 'full fashioning' takes time and skill, and by the early nineteenth century wide-bed frames, capable of knitting many strips of fabric simultaneously, were being developed. With their automated yarn carriers, they could churn out knitted fabric much more quickly than the narrow-bed frames. The small stocking-shops started to disappear as factories crammed row upon row of wide-bed frames into large rooms – but, unlike weaving looms, which were beginning to be steam-powered, knitting frames, whatever their size, continued to be hand-powered until the later part of the nineteenth century.

With the development of the wide-bed knitting frames, knitters of fully fashioned stockings were going out of business. In 1810, reports into the framework knitting industry in the East Midlands show that 'poverty and wretchedness' was endemic amongst the stockingers. 'Poor as a stockinger'[5] had become a common phrase, so meagre was the living possible from the frames. Although stockingers could work at home, their houses were often 'ill drained, damp and unhealthy'; the work was so poorly paid that the income barely covered the cost of house and frame rent.

Yet families struggled to leave the trade. A seven-year apprenticeship was relatively costly, and a trained framework knitter was unlikely to bear the expense of retraining in a different profession. They also had to pay off the cost of renting a machine from the master hosier, something that could take years. So the frame became 'sanctuary and cell' for generation after generation, tied to a trade whose value dropped year on year.

By 1811, the framework knitters had had enough of pitiful pay and hungry bellies. Rioting and destruction of frames had been a problem since at least 1788, when the Protection of Stocking Frames Act was passed to prevent workers from smashing the wide-bed frames in the factories that threatened their livelihoods. Punishment was transportation, forcing the perpetrators to spend up to fourteen years in the colonies. But workers were at the point of starvation; to protect themselves and their families, they had to take action.

Ned Ludd, also referred to as 'King Ludd', was a semi-mythological figure in the mould of Robin Hood, whose name allowed dissatisfied workers to take revenge anonymously: the Luddite movement saw the destruction not only of Nottinghamshire's knitting frames but also of modern machinery across England's industrial heartlands. In 1812, Parliament revised the Protection of Stocking Frames Act to make frame-breaking punishable by death. As I passed a pub called The Frame Breakers on my way to the museum, I saw stencilled in sharp black on the white-painted brick wall one of the eponymous workers, his mell raised over a knitting frame.

Back in the Borders, I pick up the trail again, on the hunt for more modern knitting machines. By 1891, 95 per cent of the UK's knitted goods were factory-made,[6] and commercial knitting companies had abandoned hand-powered frames in favour of William Cotton's patented steam-powered machines, the industry's standard until after the Second World War. Capable of producing 10,000 loops a minute, they worked at ten times the speed of the hand frames, producing five million pairs of stockings a year, along with undershirts and drawers. The urban Border landscape changed from one centred on small-scale stocking shops to towns thronged with large-scale mill complexes. It wasn't just knitting, either; come the mid nineteenth century, over half of Scotland's industrial spinning was being done in the Borders, as was almost half of its weaving.

At the peak of the Borders fabric boom, Adam L. Cochrane and Brothers built the majestic four-storey Netherdale Mill in Galashiels. Completed in 1873, by 1881 the building was one of twenty mills in the town, where a century earlier there had been merely four. In 1922, Netherdale went from being a commercial mill to a training facility for the Scottish Woollen Technical College, which in 2005 became Heriot-Watt University's School of Textiles and Design.

Walking between the former mill buildings, I thrill at the knowledge that fabric is still being designed and made here. Heriot-Watt is one of only a handful of universities worldwide offering degrees in knitting, and students come from thousands of miles away to study at the industry's historic centre, to learn how to operate knitting machines both ancient and modern.

I am shown around the workroom of hand-cranked knitting machines by Emily, a slender imp from Oklahoma, who crossed the Atlantic to study knitwear design. She is dressed head-to-toe in stylish black, her eyes shaded behind dragonfly dark glasses. As a master's student, Emily has designed and made her own 'Shetland Dandy' ganseys. Combining the rugged masculinity of the fishermen with the foppish sensibility of the dandy, Emily's ganseys are wide-necked, cinch-waisted, short-sleeved. In cherry red and navy, they stand out on their tailor's mannequins, rare garments combining two very different pasts into one knitted present.

Emily talks me through her creations, scattering our conversation with two new-to-me words: 'Dubied' and 'Shima'. The first sounds like 'doo-byay', French in its omission of the second glottal *d*. Embarrassed by my ignorance, I ask Emily what they mean. 'They're the machines I used to make these,' she tells me with a smile. I thought the garments had been hand-knitted on Emily's skilful needles, but in fact they were made using the smaller, hand-operated machines in place of fully automated computer-aided ones. 'Shall we take a look at them?' she says, and ushers me into the workshops.

Row upon row of coloured yarn cones greet us by the door. I am momentarily speechless at the quantity and variety of colour and texture, and reach for my camera to capture this rainbow. Emily walks quickly past them with the indifference of an intimate, pulling me through the stacks. Arrayed before us is a stationary army. Pale green, dull metal, thirty skeletal Dubied machines look back at us, arms raised in salute. On their heavy metal frames lie long beds of needles, with hundreds of hooks raised to take the threads. In the next room, a cluster of more modern Shima machines stand idle, their neat white frames waiting for instruction. Japanese company Shima Seiki is a byword for innovation: in 1964 the inventor Masahiro Shima developed the first fully automated glove-knitting machine, and in 1996, the Shima Seiki SWG was the first commercial computerized whole-garment knitting machine, able to produce totally seamless outerwear.[7] The industrial hand-flat Dubieds, named for their Swiss founder, Edouard Dubied, have two smooth metal beds set back to back, and can hold fourteen needles for every inch of fabric. No longer manufactured, they were originally used to fashion sample garments, as a single operative could experiment with knit, slip and tuck stitches on each machine. They are now are used to teach and inspire new generations of students here in Galashiels.

Emily quickly threads up a machine, dipping into the stash of spare donated yarn for our experiment. I have chosen contrasting dark and light green threads, and Emily loops the two colours swiftly through the raised hooks of the machine. As anyone conversant with a sewing machine will know, it is essential that every

loop and hook greets the thread in a precise order. One omission
and the whole thing unravels, tangles, twists. I'm glad of her
steady expertise.

Once the yarn is threaded and hooked, Emily carefully weights
the end of the frame below the machine to create the tension. Tear-
drop weights, smooth by design and scratched by use, dangle below
the main frame. Emily passes the carriage across the hooks and in
seconds a neat line of stitches has formed. Looking at me with a
smile, she says, 'Your turn.' I take the rubber handle and slide the
steel carriage over the prepared hooks. With a swift swish and the
click of release, my first line of machine knitting is complete.

I am entranced. I push the carriage again, enjoy its swish and
click, back and forth, forth and back, laughing at the ease of it.
Before long a strip of green stocking stitch emerges beneath the
carriage. Emily takes it to the end of the room, where a clutch of
small machines like butter churns wait by the wall. Turning one
machine's handles, she links the two ends of knitting together
with the rotation of a wheel. 'What's this machine called?' I ask.
'A linker,' comes the matter-of-fact reply.

I ask Emily what drew her here. Having studied fine art and
made shoes for Nike, she left her home, thousands of miles away,
to come to this Border town to improve her knitting, wanting to
understand the machines that high-end fashion brands still use to
make their luxury goods. In 2012, Chanel bought Hawick's Barrie
Mill, established in 1903 by Walter Barrie and Robert Kersel.
Barrie has long been a byword for class, for fine design and cat-
walk output. To work there is Emily's dream – and to do so she
needs to know knitting machines back to front.

'What are you going to knit from the Borders? Maybe some Y-
fronts?' Emily jokes, but I am seriously tempted. Barrie, Pringle,
and Lyle & Scott – Hawick's knitwear giants today – all began life
as underwear manufacturers. William Lyle and Walter Scott started
producing woollen stockings on hand frames in 1874; by 1914, their

company, Lyle & Scott, had grown to be one of the largest firms in Hawick, with net sales of over £59,000 a year, offering not just stockings but undergarments in every imaginable style.

The growth of the leisured middle class in the nineteenth century saw an increased demand for what *Field* magazine termed garments 'allowing participation in any sport where bodily freedom is essential', and the race was on to offer new underwear for modern lives. As well as hose and drawers, companies offered 'Interchangeable Part Combinations' – neck-to-ankle woollies worn throughout the winter during the Victorian and Edwardian periods. Another of Hawick's successful hosiery firms, Peter Scott Knitwear, prided themselves on their combinations. In 1914, a delighted customer wrote saying that his Peter Scott woollens had seen him through the previous nine winters, and he anticipated at least six or seven more, as they were yet to need any darning. It was the yarn that did it: Peter Scott incorporated an extra thread into the yarn used 'for all parts liable to strain'.

In 1925, this 'liable to strain' element came into its own, as in that year short trunks made of cotton went on sale for the first time, thanks to Joseph Golomb, founder of the boxing brand Everlast. 'Boxers' might be perfect for the ring, but in the euphemism of the time, they lacked sufficient 'masculine support' for everyday wear. The jock strap had been designed specifically for the cycle messengers known as 'jockeys'. But it wasn't until 19 January 1935, in Chicago, that men were able to buy Y-fronts – or, as they were first marketed, Arthur Kniebler's Jockey briefs. Proudly displayed in the shop's window, over six hundred pairs were sold on the first day, with more than 30,000 sold in the following three months. Kniebler's briefs were made of cotton, not wool, but were machine-knitted much the same.

Back in Hawick, Lyle & Scott were keeping an eager eye on this new development. The immediate popularity of jockey briefs was either a threat or an opportunity to a company specializing in knitwear, with competitors in Hawick champing at the bit for their market share. Lyle & Scott embraced the Y, and in 1938 secured exclusive manufacturing rights to produce Y-front jockeys in the UK, France and the Netherlands. From then onwards, any Y-front worn in these countries would come from their cut-and-sew factories. Knitting of underwear continues to this day, though not in Hawick, and usually combines spandex or Lycra with cotton: close-fitting Y-fronts require the stretch and strength of knitted fabric, not the crisp structure of the woven textiles used for looser-fitting boxers.

It wasn't just Y-fronts. From 1967, Lyle & Scott teamed up with professional golfers to bring out bold and colourful knitted golfwear bearing the company's Flying Eagle logo, known as 'the Birdie'. They clad the winning team for the Ryder Cup in 1981, for the Hennessey Cup in 1982, and in 1986, Greg Norman, sponsored by Lyle & Scott, won not only the Open at Turnberry but also six other international tournaments. The company continues to turn heads and open wallets today, as do their rivals – and Hawick neighbours – Pringle.

In 1890, knitwear company Robert Pringle, precursor of today's Pringle of Scotland, began to advertise 'hose for golf and cycle', shorts for rowing, and 'cycle drawers'. Pringle is also credited with the invention of the twinset, the pairing of a knitted jumper and cardigan by the Austrian designer Otto Weisz. Coco Chanel had pioneered the wearing of close-fitting jumpers and cardigans, but had sold them as separate items; Weisz was the first to combine them and sell them as a set. Weisz worked for Pringle from 1934, recruiting his designers from the Glasgow School of Art, and his knitwear rose above the quotidian into the realm of art. Legend has it that the word 'twinset' was coined on Hawick high street in the mid-1930s. Weisz had originally dubbed the garments a 'double-set' but, seeing a pair of identically dressed twins, hit upon 'twinset' as the name for his new design.

This story comes to me from Gordon Macdonald, a retired knitwear mechanic who worked at Lyle & Scott. Born and bred in Hawick, Gordon began his working life as a teenage apprentice at George Woodcock and Sons, knitwear engineers. In the 1960s, the Hawick mills each took on thirty or more apprentices three times a year, when the high school spat out its termly cohort of teenagers. Gordon worked with knitwear engineers from Germany to Japan to make Hawick's knitting machines the envy of the world.

Many of Gordon's peers still live in the town and I meet one of them, Irene Scott, a grand woman with heavily ringed hands, her hair stylishly tinted. Now retired, she trained at Pringle, and, like most apprentices to the trade, attended Henderson Technical College. Although mending became Irene's speciality, apprentices were shown the full process, from yarn to shop-ready garment, during their first year of training. Clothes began life 'on the greasy side', made up from yarn greased with synthetic oil to help it cleave together. After machines knitted the main panels, the panels were taken to the body linker, who hooked the garment's constituent parts together on a smaller machine, the joins then finished by the seamer. The finished piece would then be subject to close inspection for defects, and mended by hand if required. If you worked on the greasy side, it was imperative to wear an apron, as the oil stank and stained your clothes.

Once approved, the (almost) finished garments were placed in a Hoffman press for a final steam, before the tabbers added labels, using intricate tabbing machines. After a final examination with menders on hand, the clothes would be folded and bagged, then hung with swing tickets if required. Whilst a sample could be made from start to finish in a day, and there was a separate team to do just this, big firms such as Pringle could produce a thousand or more garments at any one time, with a start-to-finish time for each line of a matter of weeks.

Most people worked in eight-hour shifts across twenty-four hours, but as a trained mender, Irene was able to work from home once she had children, to her own schedule. Every day, a box was dropped off at her house from the factory, containing bundles of garments in lots of eight. She was paid one old penny for mending the chunkier knits with a bigger gauge; for finer garments this increased by a ha'penny. Even with a lamp directly over her work, Irene missed the big double strip-lights of the factory when it came to the finer-gauge repairs. The box would be collected the following morning, and the next batch dropped off. Many a time, Irene would be sitting up into the small hours to finish a batch for the morning – if the weather was fine or the house needed attention, this work could be put aside until everyone else was in bed.

Irene was thereby able to work after her marriage, something rarely permitted to earlier generations. Interviewed in the *Scots Magazine* in 1971, Mrs Jessie Graham remembered that during the four years of her apprenticeship in the 1910s and 1920s, she 'never knew anyone that worked on', noting that it was 'in the war that married women started working again.'[8] As Irene did, thirty years later, Jessie had to learn every process involved in making up garments. Early starts and long working days were the norm, 'though we used to jook over to the canteen to buy a piece and a cup of tea'.[9] For this long week, the first-year apprentices got 9s. 11d., rising to 29s. 11d. in the fourth year. After that, the flat rate was £2. The youngest apprentices stopped their work at four o'clock, not to go home but to sweep and tidy the remnants that littered the floors. In the 1920s, knitting apprenticeships were different for the boys and men, who were trained to use the knitting machines. Jessie's husband, Jock, started on 5s for a fifty-five-hour week, rising through a four-year apprenticeship to 30s when he 'got a frame' of his own to work. And 'getting a frame' was the ambition of every apprentice, for these machines that knit the yarn – at that time for hosiery and underwear, nowadays for high-quality cashmere sweaters and cardigans – were the mainstay of the factories. Often, it meant a long wait for the eager apprentice, because there was no retirement age: Jock Brown spoke of one old man who still worked his machine at the age of eighty.

In 1924, the Browns were able to marry on Jock's salary of less than £3 a week. But they married in the shadow of the Great Depression, which heralded short time in the mills and hard times in the town. Three months after his wedding, Jock Brown was 'on the burroo' – forced to borrow money to make ends meet. The Browns did not stay in Hawick to go hungry: one by one the mills went short of work, and they, like many Borders people, moved to Canada for a better life.

Rather than knocking up a pair of knitted knickers, I decide to make another of Hawick's famous exports: swimwear. Announcing this intention raises eyebrows and elicits worried shudders among my family. Wool's inevitable sag and droop plays on the mind. But knitted swimwear, with its charm-like ability to stretch, liberated women from the head-to-toe swimming suits made from heavy flannel, serge or 'stout brown holland' in which they had previously floundered. Until the very end of the nineteenth century, even swimming 'costumes', which included the daring innovation of pantaloons, covered women from wrist to neck and ankle.

One-piece costumes have their roots in knitted 'combinations'. Worn as both underwear and sportswear, they started to become popular for swimming thanks in large part to the Australian swimmer Annette Kellerman, who in 1907 was arrested on Revere Beach, Boston, MA, for the 'indecency' of her fitted one-piece swimming costume.[10] Kellerman was a prize-winning diver and swimmer whose 'unitard' allowed her great freedom of movement; she not only popularized her sport among women, but also spoke out about women's need to dress safely and appropriately in the water.

In 1919, two young American swimmers, Charlotte Boyle and Ethelda Bleibtrey, were arrested for swimming in fitted woollen one-pieces; the outcry following their imprisonment saw the adoption of short swimming costumes by American women, particularly once the Portland knitwear designer Carl Jantzen began mass-producing fitted knitted swimwear in the 1920s.[11] Today's form-fitting swimsuits are still, in the main, knitted: like jersey briefs, a warp-knitted fabric can follow the body's curves seamlessly,[12] ensuring both greater comfort and speed in the water. In 2010, the use of knitted swimsuits in Olympic competitions was banned by the sport's governing body, FINA, who noted that Speedo's 'Fastskin' suits, modelled on the texture of shark's skin and knitted from nylon/elastane thread, gave swimmers an unfair advantage in the pool. Twenty-six knitted stitches made up 3 centimetres of fabric, creating a ridged texture that sucked water closer to the swimmer's body, thereby reducing drag by as much as 4 per cent.[13] FINA called for swimwear to be made from textiles – i.e. woven, not knitted fabrics – in place of the advantage-giving Fastskin.

I search for a pattern from a time when knitting swimwear was an ordinary, everyday domestic activity. Hand-knitted swimwear creeps into pattern books from the late nineteenth century onwards, reaching a peak post-war, when bikinis became fashionable and fabrics were rationed. The bikini, launched in Paris in July 1946 by designer Louis Réard and model Micheline Bernardini,[14] was designed to cause a storm: named for the Pacific nuclear test site Bikini Atoll, it daringly revealed not only a woman's figure in relief, but also her stomach, chest and thighs. By the 1960s, bikinis had become ubiquitous on beaches from Cannes to California, and in 1964 the Austro-American designer Rudi Gernreich unveiled the risqué 'monokini', a pair of high-waisted briefs secured round the neck with two narrow ties – with the wearer's breasts left bare. Needless to say, it was not a commercial success, and I have no desire to replicate it.

The oldest knitwear patterns in my collection date from the 1940s and include a couple of Bestway designs. Costing a mere 3*d.*, they were simply printed in black and white on folded pieces of A4 paper. On their covers, small-waisted women with hair rolling to their shoulders model jumpers entitled 'Streamlined', 'Sweet and Lovely', 'Trimly Tailored', 'Smart and Slick'. The design names reflect the aspirations of the time; it was desirable to be 'Gay', 'Dashing', 'Trim' and 'Charming'. During and after the war, 'keeping up appearances' was deemed to be of paramount importance to the country's morale. From 1941 until 1949, rationing was in place for clothes, as it had been for bacon, butter and sugar since 1940. A colour-coded points system was introduced, fluctuating with available supplies. An adult's full-length lined coat could set you back sixteen stamps; a pair of stockings needed two, pyjamas eight. This did not mean that clothes were free – they still had to be bought, but only to the value of one's allotted coupons.[15] Yarn was rationed too, and many contemporary patterns detail how many clothing coupons were required to knit them.

Written with the privations of rationing still in mind, my copy of *Practical Knitting Illustrated* (1949) provides 'A recipe for happy families [. . .] garments to suit every mood and occasion of every member of the household'.[16] It includes, 'new for this season', 'swimwear for male and female – to be had in many beautiful colours and in all sizes'. Beneath a black-and-white snap of a slim fair woman sitting on a wooden groyne, legs repeated in shadow beside her and one hand awkwardly raised in staged salute, is the caption 'Come and take your place in the sun!' It promises to be 'an easy to make beach suit for summer days'.

Make a beach suit while the sun shines! This suit is a three-piece outfit. A brassière top and shorts for the swim; a gored skirt that goes with a swing, easy to slip on when you take your place in the sun.

For May, this month of warming temperatures and unexpected showers, I will knit a bikini – an 'itsy bitsy, teenie weenie, yellow polka-dot'[17] one – from twists of golden yarn, flecked with cream and buttercup yellow in place of polka dots. With my mother-in-law's warning question, 'But won't a knitted swimsuit itch?' ringing in my ears, I buy six skeins of Alpaca Tweed Silk, the softest washable yarn I can find. A blend of alpaca fleece, silk, Merino and bamboo, this yarn is spun at the nearby Border Mill at Duns – perfect for a Borders bikini.

Today, most people do not hand-make their own clothes, so have little need to precisely measure the shaping of their bodies. Even those of us who might turn out a hat or jumper, skirt or shirt would rarely attempt underwear or a swimming costume. Concerned about our health or weight, we might check our waist, eager to be below those government recommendations, and women usually know their bra size. Beyond that we usually have no cause to scrutinize. When women brave the high street, they only need to know if they're closer to a size ten or twelve, aware of which shops offer hope or despair in their sizing. We hold an image of our 'size' in our heads, but the relationship between us and the amount of space taken up by our bodies can be shaped as much by memory and imagination as the scales or measuring tape.

Knitting this bikini requires me to get to know my own body better. It will have to hug my curves, precisely fit the intricacies of myself. The knitting of something that touches the genitals and breasts seems such an intimate act that I cannot imagine making a swimming costume for even the closest friend. That implied proximity of touch makes me uncomfortable: the maker's hands touch this yarn, which in turn will touch the most intimate parts of the wearer. It is too invasive. My soft stomach, dimpled at my belly button, is pale beneath the tape measure. Never before have I known the distance between my crotch and navel (13 inches, or 33 centimetres – the pattern's in imperial so I must measure accordingly). I measure from where the bikini's edge will cling to my skin, and add 2 inches to the pattern.

After balling up my yellow yarn, I begin knitting the bandeau top, starting in the middle of the back. Casting on 12 stitches, I knit 8 centimetres of 'fancy rib' – also known as 'fisherman's rib' – alternating purl one, knit one below, purl one, with rows of knit one, purl one, knit one below. I then increase my stitches to match the swell of my bust before decreasing again, finishing with another 8 centimetres of straight ribbing. To secure the bandeau, I thread thick elastic through the top and bottom of the fabric, and add another length to ruche it in the middle and anchor it behind my neck in a broad bow.

The pattern's constant repetition of stitches shows up inconsistencies in my knitting. Hurtling through the stitches, I notice that when I think I knit 'k2tog' – knit two stitches together into one slick loop – I make instead its purly inversion, 'p2tog'. An unconscious reversal picked up long ago, this mistake leaves a noticeable surface stitch. Unless you ask for help, once you've mastered the basics, rarely does someone look closely at your knitting. For the novice knitter, this provides the privacy necessary for trial and error, for practising the making of stitches until you are confident enough to show off what you've made. But this can also mean mistakes go unnoticed for days, weeks, months, years and even – as in my case – decades.

Whilst I am a returnee to knitting, several adult friends have taken up the craft for the first time in recent years. Knowing of my interest in all things woolly, one of them, a coder with a degree in architecture, shows me her first garment. It is a baby's jumper worked in dark wool, its intricate pattern of slipped stitches creating a leaf motif across its tiny arms and tummy. I can hardly believe it is her first knitted piece: the stitches are tiny, perfect, and, although I scrutinize it from wrist to neck, I cannot find a single fault. Exclaiming over her proficiency, her response is casual. 'It was easy,' she shrugs, 'I just followed the pattern.'

Alice's mind is ordered, mathematical, precise. A neat, taut woman, she spends her weekends climbing, hiking and challenging herself with triathlons. After seven years studying architecture, she trained as an investment banker before learning to write computer code. Her approach to life is one of consciously applied effort, of exact and structured thought. Likewise, her knitting is precise and perfect, beautiful in its accuracy, controlled.

My knitting is rarely, if ever, without fault. In summer's warmth, yarn sticks to my sweaty fingers and my knitting loses its meditative quality, instead becoming a race for the finish line. Like the bandeau top, the bikini bottoms begin with fancy rib, but this time I work in the round, from the waist downwards; once the rib is complete, I swap to stocking stitch. These bottoms are high-waisted and encase the full scope of my behind; not for the first time, I wish there was less to cover. I plough on, dividing the stitches onto two needles to create the gusset, and finishing each short leg with another round of fancy rib.

I finish the bikini just in time to test it under the summer sun with a group of old university friends. Living scattered across the country from London to Fife, we gather in Northumberland for a once-a-year jamboree. After a walk to Embleton Bay, a sandy crescent north of Dunstanburgh Castle, I strip down to my two-piece before running into the sea. I don't stop until my feet can't touch the ground.

Like a wetsuit, the bikini doesn't feel wet instantly, but instead grows progressively damper as the water soaks the fabric. As I kick my feet and windmill my arms, I feel the bikini heavy against my skin, but it doesn't move: the pattern's elastic and negative ease, designed to encase me closely, is doing its job. I swim a few strokes, accompanied by one brave friend familiar with Hampstead Ladies' Pond. It's so cold my hands and feet go numb: I can stand only a minute before coming out. Walking back to land, I keep a hand on both the bottoms and the bandeau top in case of slip or sag, but both are tightly anchored to my body and keep their place. I emerge to shouts and claps, passers-by offering their approbation. I wriggle out of my knitwear in the sand, wrap myself in a towel, and crack open a celebratory lemonade. I have made and swum in my own handmade bikini.

6

Carding, Combing and Cricket

Summer draws on and as my knowledge and experience of knitting increases, I realize I have skipped an important step: spinning, knitting's necessary precursor. Despite her reluctance as a knitter, my mother is a competent spinner, so I learned to spin before I could knit, though long ago dropped the tricky skill of manipulating a spindle or wheel for the comparative ease of knitting. Now, as I look back over the completed gloves and Pussyhat, stockings and bikini, I realize that to truly understand wool and yarn, I must return to spinning.

Truly unspun wool cannot be coaxed into knitted garments – not ones that would bear up well, anyway. At most, woollen fibres can be felted to form fabric, encouraged to stick together through the application of heat and pressure. To be knitted or woven, fibres must be formed into a long continuous string, drawn out and twisted together. The tighter the twist, the stronger the resulting thread.

All fibres, whether plant- or animal-based, must be spun into yarn before being knitted. Most must be processed before spinning: those from the stems of plants (jute, flax and hemp) need *retting* – soaking in water to break them down. Animal fibres, whether sheep's wool or the hair from goats, oxen, alpacas and so on, also require preparation before spinning, with one notable exception: silk. Silk fibres are produced in the digestive tract of *Bombyx mori*, the domestic silk moth, which feeds on mulberry leaves, or *Anthereae* species, the tussah moths, which feed partly on oak. The fibres are gummed with sericin and spun as the silkworm shapes its cocoon around itself, the fibres issuing from spinnerets on either side of its head as it waves it in a figure-of-eight motion.[1] The cocoons are then boiled or steamed to soften them so that the silken threads can be extracted. Whilst spiders also spin, their threads are so fine that they cannot currently be commercially collected.

'Wool' is really a collective term for clusters of individual fibres. Each strand has a central cortex, usually hollow and made from millions of long cells linked and folded together. When stretched, these fibres unfold but, like paper turned into origami, they remember their fold lines: when no longer under tension, they return to their original position. This gives wool its unique springy elasticity. Encasing the cortex, like tiles on a roof, are textured overlapping cells that provide the fibre's sticky grip, making it ideal for the spinner's coaxing hand. Around these tiled irregular cells wraps a semi-permeable membrane, which repels most water yet allows some absorption through its minute pores, thereby generating wool's well-known warmth.[2]

In the pocket of my waterproof coat, that little jumble of wool from my January walk at Heald Brow lies curled, and now I take it out again, smoothing it with my fingertips. Each fibre, like an individual hair, looks extremely fine to the naked eye, its thickness measurable only in microns, millionths of a metre. Yet this is a coarse type of wool. Being Herdwick, its fibres are somewhere between 36 and 40 microns. By contrast, Spanish Merino, famed worldwide for its fineness, can measure a scant 11 microns, the same thickness as mulberry silk.[3] Most knitting yarn is spun from wool of between 17 and 35 microns. Before the more-than-pinpoint accuracy of the micron, wool was measured according to the Bradford or Quality Count. Devised by the wool merchants of Bradford, the count denoted how many 560-yard single-ply hanks could be worsted-spun from a single pound of combed fleece. A pound of Merino could yield sixty skeins or more; hefty Herdwick only forty.

To spin requires me to return to my roots, to go back home, where there's a spinning wheel to be used. My mum honed her skill with wool on the textile course at Harrogate College in the 1970s, when she lived above a chip shop and stayed at home to spin in the evenings, too terrified to go out lest she met the Yorkshire Ripper on his rounds. As a child, I remember her huge loom stabled in the shed, a monster in bright wood; in her bedroom was her spinning wheel, and beside it a pair of spiked, heavy carders. It is time to go home and relearn what my mother taught me over twenty years ago.

Nestled between Norfolk, Essex, Cambridgeshire and the North Sea, Suffolk is a county without a city. East Anglia lacks the powerful rivers and mineral deposits of more northern and western counties, and so the industrial revolution wrought little change to its landscape – the small mills scattered across its arable fields were mostly wind-powered and used for grinding corn. With few hills and little native stone to quarry, Suffolk keeps itself modestly low against the sky, a meagre skim of land squeezed between fen and sea. Above the fields rise the spires of the county's great stone churches, knapped in flint. What today are small villages – Lavenham, Long Melford, Kersey – boast vast mediaeval churches, now out of proportion with their tiny congregations.

During the early mediaeval period, East Anglia was densely populated, relative to much of England. The coastal ports of Ipswich, Colchester, now-drowned Dunwich, Yarmouth and Lynn sat at the mouths of East Anglia's broad rivers, meaning that wool from across England could be brought here and sold directly to the major cloth markets of the Baltic and the Low Countries.[4] Sheep farming was popular and profitable by the end of the thirteenth century, in the reign of Edward I, export duties on wool were the primary source of revenue for the English Crown. By 1300, England was home to around ten million sheep, which produced 40,000 sacks of wool, each weighing 364 pounds, every year.[5]

At first, wool could only be sold in 'staple' towns (from the Old French *estaple*, meaning 'market')[6] on the Continent, primarily in Flanders – Antwerp, Bruges and Mechelen, which relied on English wool to make exquisite cloth. This soon changed: by 1353, Edward III had overseen the creation of staple towns in England, four of them in East Anglia (Lynn, Yarmouth, Ipswich and Norwich). Each had its own member-elected 'Mayor of the Staple', who held immense local influence with his knowledge of the 'law merchant'.[7]

Whilst the trade in raw fleece boomed, England's cloth trade remained a small and exclusively domestic concern, producing a limited quality of textiles and virtually none for export. It was only in the 1300s that cloth production began to thrive – again, thanks in large part to East Anglia's proximity to the Continent. Although Flemish emigration to England had been taking place since at least the Norman Conquest, it was the great St Lucia's Day flood of 1287, wreaking havoc upon Flanders' coastal regions, that caused a sizeable influx of skilled wool workers into East Anglia. During the Hundred Years' War (1337–1453), Huguenot spinners and weavers, capable of producing cloth of unrivalled quality, sought sanctuary in England's eastern counties. Part of their skill was down to their 'extreme fastidiousness' when sorting wool; in fact, the mixing of different types of wool was strictly prohibited in Flemish guilds.[8] Fuelled by these influxes of spinners and weavers, East Anglia became important, powerful and wealthy through its production of woollen cloth.

*

I arrive home in Suffolk to find the sitting room in thrall to spinning. Mum's Ashford, a classic upright wooden wheel, stands amid bags of fleece. Each is stickered with its breed: Wensleydale, Suffolk, Jacob, Herdwick. The table is heaped with bristling carders and bald bobbins, their naked bodies waiting to be wrapped in yarn.

Mum hands over a little pink booklet marvellously entitled *The Insatiable Spinner*. It is the yarn fanatic's hippy handbook for home-spinning, detailing everything from buying fleece to dyeing yarn. Although mostly aimed at those spinning sheep's fleece, there is a detailed section on the possibilities of spinning dog, cat, camel and even musk-ox hair. Someone I know once spun the hair of her favourite but sadly deceased dog into yarn and then had it woven into fabric and made into pillows – an animal lover's version of a Victorian hair locket.

There are more than sixty breeds and hybrids of sheep in Britain, divided into four broad classifications: Mountain and Hill; Shortwool and Down; Lustre and Longwool; and Medium. As one might guess, Mountain and Hill sheep are bred for those areas where the weather conditions are colder, wetter and windier. Their fleece is coarser, better at turning water. Shortwool and Down are their lowland cousins, with denser, springier fleece – perfect for milder, drier lowland climates. Lustre and Longwool fleece has an inviting sheen, derived from its larger, light-reflecting scales. Medium scoops up everyone else.

Of key concern to the spinner is the 'staple', a fleece's natural lock length. Whereas microns measure the width of the wool's individual fibres, the staple, measured from root to tip of a clump of fibres, can be anywhere from a scant 3 centimetres for a short-haired breed like Merino, up to more than 30 centimetres for Longwools such as Masham, Teeswater and Wensleydale. In breed names, we find Britain in miniature: Welsh Mountain, Manx Loaghtan, Derbyshire Gritstone, Norfolk Horn. Britain's polyglot history of exchange with the Continent is here too: British Texel, British Friesland, British Bleu du Maine.

My childhood friend Elly, whose mum taught me how to knit and with whom I collected sheep's wool from around the farm as a child, comes to lend a hand. We both know well the beguiling challenge of wool. Growing up side by side, as adults we both retain a love of fibre craft: Elly crochets; while I knit. Can we create something beautiful from this wool, daggy with muck and flecked with straw? The physicality of the challenge still compels.

Mum has a bought a fresh raw fleece for us to turn to yarn. The first sheared coat of a yearling Suffolk, it is pale cream, with a waved, soft staple, 7–8 centimetres long. Downland sheep like this were developed across England's arable counties, with breeds specific to Dorset, Hampshire, Shropshire, Oxfordshire, Suffolk and the South Downs region of East Sussex. The Suffolk's origins are an accidental mix of breeding Southdown rams with Norfolk Horn ewes;[9] first identified as a classified breed in 1810, it is ideally suited to thrive on East Anglia's sandy soil. Suffolk is good, inexpensive fleece for knitting, wool with a moderate staple whose fibres resist felting.

Laying an old sheet down in the yard, we roll the fleece out, its soft underbelly to the ground. We start at the literal bottom, the tail end, clagged with dung, and pull out the worst. Next we skirt the fleece's edge, pulling away mats of felted wool, and Mum points out the kemps, wiry unworkable hairs often produced by a sheep under stress. Out come too-short tufts of unspinnable wool, the staple clumsily cut by the shearer. In the sunshine's warmth, we spend two hours on our knees, cleaning and sorting the fleece into the best, the worst, and the middling. The finest will be spun, the filthiest composted.

Back inside, we gently open up the best fleece along its staple, laying it out in lines across a sheet. With sun streaming through the window, we prepare a feathery pile of creamy fleece, teasing out fibres smooth enough to not need carding. They are not straight, but beautifully waved, like human hair uncoiled from a braid. This 'crimp' is another indicator of a fleece's fineness: our eyes scan the fleece for these waving fibres to add them to our pile.

Next, we card the remaining wool, using rough paddles spiked with short, fine nails. The first recorded use of carders in processing wool comes from thirteenth-century France;[10] the name for these broad brushes apparently stems from their similarity to the spiked poll of the teasel – *carde* being French for 'teasel-head'.[11]

We will spin 'in the grease', the natural fat in the unwashed wool helping its fibres bind together. As the fibres grow, the sheep's fleece exudes greasy *suint*, ovine sweat that combines fat with potash salts, also known as 'yolk'.[12] Lanolin, fatty matter in the grease, has a pleasant smell, but too much yolk on a fleece can gather in globules and requires degreasing before hand-spinning.[13] This Suffolk fleece is just greasy enough, and a comforting sheepy odour envelopes us as our hands become smooth with lanolin.

Yarn spun in industrial mills must be scoured, lest its excess grease and dirt clog up machines. In 1749, London's monthly *Universal Magazine of Knowledge and Pleasure* advised that: 'To use your wool to the best advantage, you must scour the fleeces in a liquor, a little more than lukewarm, composed of three parts fair water, and one of urine.'[14] After drying in the shade (to prevent the sun's heat making the fibres 'harsh and untractable'), the wool was then 'willowed': laid across wooden hurdles and beaten with slender sticks to remove further debris. Today, as in 1749, the wool is then mixed with oil, up to one quarter of its weight – traditionally using tallow, lard, butter or even goose grease – so that it can be turned into an even yarn. Our unscoured wool can be simply spun as it is.

Mum takes out a drop spindle and, holding the fleece in her other hand, expertly spins the wooden body of the spindle in front of her, twisting the fleece into a long, smooth strand. Elly and I try to copy her, but our threads break, our spindle juddering to a halt. For novice hands, using this simple rod with its circular block of wood is harder than it looks.

Drop spindles have been used to spin yarn since Neolithic times. At their most basic, they are little more than a weighted stick, a slender shaft of wood that pierces a stone or chunk of wood, around which is tied a wisp of fleece. The spinner uses the downward pull of gravity, combined with a twisting flick of her wrist, to meld the fleece together to form thread. Whorls, the stones used at the base of the spindle, have been found in archaeological digs across the world. It is said that watching the spindle twirl gave humanity pause for thought, eventually leading to the development of other rotational technologies using gravity. The most famous of these is, of course, the wheel.

The spinning wheel is believed to have been invented in modern-day China or India over a thousand years ago, but did not reach Europe until the late Middle Ages. Using a spindle and a distaff, a pronged stick to hold the teased or carded wool, women spun threads of such fineness that a pound of wool could yield half a mile of hand-spun thread. Distaffs were so ubiquitous as household objects and their use as primarily a woman's occupation that the maternal branch of a family was known as 'the distaff side'.[15]

Mum sits at her wheel, beautiful in its wooden smoothness, and reminds us how to thread the bobbin, adjust the brake, and use our hands to create one smooth strand of yarn. At first, she pushes the spinning wheel slowly with her palm, giving our hands time to relearn how to think. Like patting your head and rubbing your tummy, spinning wool needs both hands to do different things. One holds the yarn to create the required twist against the turn of the wheel; the other feeds in just enough.

Whereas Mum's yarn is even and smooth, mine swells and shrinks like an earthworm. The thread is full of neps and slubs, its twist uneven. Mum's is fine enough to ply into a two-threader strand finer than my single thread; she twists strands together on a bobbin as she turns her wheel counter-clockwise. Plying is an art of balance: the S-spun (clockwise) twists of the individual strands strengthen by Z-plying (anticlockwise) them into a twisting whole. Tension is a force added; the meeting point of the fibre's natural energy, its gene-deep curl and flex, with the intention of the spinner. To spin successfully, your threads must meet at this critical juncture, dictated by material and weight. After an hour at the wheel, first spinning then plying, Mum hands over a bobbin of creamy two-plied perfection. I then wind the yarn into a hank, looping it round and round the niddy-noddy, three conjoined wooden bars that keep the fibres tensioned. Tying off the hank with two slips of string to keep its shape, I then take it to the sink to be washed. Rather than shell out for expensive wool wash, I use a little soap, followed by an acidic rinse with vinegar, balancing the wool's natural pH.

As Elly and I run the yarn under the bathroom tap, a memory of standing at another sink with our sleeves rolled up comes to mind. Over twenty years ago, we stood side by side, much as we are now, as I washed wisps of fleece gathered from farm fences. Elly eagerly asked when it would be her turn to wash the wool, but, being bigger and older, I commanded the sink, relishing the crunch of warm, wet fleece against my fingers. With a child's easy callousness, I denied her a turn. The exact words of our argument have been lost to time, but I know that, in thirty years of friendship, this debacle constituted our one great falling-out. Today we laugh at the memory, and wash the fleece together.

Hearing about my experiments in spinning, a generous friend says she has a special gift for me. 'This is Britain's real Golden Fleece,' she tells me, pressing a bag of Cotswold wool into my hands. Inside is light turned to fibre. The rich golds and soft creams, pale and glorious, make the fleece's long waving locks glow and sparkle in the sunshine. Rumpelstiltskin's task reversed, this wool seems have been made from gold. These lustrous locks come from Rob Harvey Long's award-winning 'Pickwick' flock of Cotswold sheep based near Cirencester, and their siren call draws me west.

Whilst East Anglia's affluence was built on the strength of its weaving, and its ability to trade readily with the Continent, it was the sale of raw fleece that made the Cotswolds wealthy. Stretching over 800 square miles between Birmingham, Bristol and Oxford, these limestone uplands have long been a keystone of Britain's woollen trade, its 'cheef tresour in this land growing'.[16] The word 'Cotswold' seems to stem from the sheep folds or 'cots'[17] that were once a common feature of these rolling wooded hills, and the ovine influence lingers on in other Cotswold place names, among them Sherborne (the shearing stream), Shipton (the sheep hill), and Sheepscombe (sheep valley).[18]

Today, 'Cotswold' refers not just to the region, but also to a specific, classified Longwool sheep breed, with a heavy fleece. Though the breed was not formalized until several centuries later, direct antecedents of the modern Cotswold are thought to be fine-woolled sheep farmed by Cistercian monks. Abbey sheep walks, the tracts of pasture land used to graze sheep, spanned large areas of what were in the Middle Ages comparatively remote areas: the Abbot of Evesham grazed his sheep at Stow-on-the-Wold, whilst Northleach was home to the flocks of the Abbot of Gloucester,[19] and Westminster Abbey kept flocks at Bourton-on-the-Water, Moreton-in-Marsh and Todenham.[20] Cistercians excelled at developing commercial sheep farming, producing high-quality fleeces and expertly sorting them; an inventory of wool producers made by the Florentine merchant Bardi at the end of the thirteenth century lists more Cistercian houses than any other religious order – about 85 per cent of their suppliers.[21] Along with the families of Frescobaldi and Pergolotti, the Bardi family founded the *Arte della Lana*, the Florentine Wool Guild, which controlled the production of the most highly priced cloth in western Europe. Richard Martin of Cotswold Woollen Weavers notes that Cotswold fleece was also highly prized by Flemish weavers as early as the twelfth century.[22]

After half a day of driving due west from Suffolk, I arrive in the Cotswolds as the warm light of evening strikes Northleach's pale stone buildings. In the middle of the pub-fringed market square stands a wrought-iron sign declaring 'Granted Annual Market Charter 1227'. The words encircle a church and a huge white short-fleeced sheep, standing proudly atop a woolsack, for Northleach was the home of a large sheep market, as well as a three-day fair in the last days of June that followed the yearly shearing. The wool from the abbey at Gloucester and the church at nearby Winchcombe was sold at Northleach, and Cirencester Abbey's sheep were walked here to be shorn. By the end of the 1300s, the wool dealers of Chipping Camden, Burford, Cirencester and Stow-on-the-Wold descended on Northleach to attend its wool market. The Cotswolds' proximity to London ensured a steady supply of quality fleece to the capital throughout the mediaeval period; those transporting wool from Cistercian lands were granted free passage, exempt from the tolls that others paid for road use.[23]

Many of Northleach's oldest buildings were built from the proceeds of the wool trade. The 'Cotswold Lion',[24] so called for its curling 'mane' of wool, had immense buying power: in the thirteenth century, fleeces from England's western counties commanded 14 marks for a 364-pound sack of wool, compared to a measly 4 marks for short-stapled East Anglian fleece.[25] This money helped England to buy back its king: in 1192, Richard the Lionheart was captured near Vienna and subsequently imprisoned, first by Leopold V, Duke of Austria, and then by the Holy Roman Emperor, Henry VI. Eager for money to fund his conquest of Sicily, Henry spent over a year negotiating the terms of Richard's release, finally agreeing to free him for the huge sum of 150,000 silver marks. This represented three times the annual income of the English Crown, the coins weighed 30 tonnes, and would be worth some £2 billion in today's money. The king's ransom was paid in part from the proceeds of the entire annual wool crop of England's Cistercian monks;[26] upon his return, Richard was crowned king for a second time, in an attempt to demonstrate his devotion to those who had paid for his release, and his commitment to English causes.

Grandest of Northleach's mediaeval edifices is the Church of St Peter & St. Paul. As I walk from the market cross to the churchyard, the sun's warm evening rays catch the church's west

end and, shining through its window, they illuminate the entire length of the building, exploding the east window into jewels. The church glows, its golden fireball heart bursting into sudden life as a faithful few head through its door for evensong. I follow them inside, where the nave and aisles stretch for 30 metres, with the tower and the chancel soaring above. The pale stone floor is pockmarked with flat brass plaques – not the tiny, bitter-sweet ovals that attach names and dates to benches, trees and buildings, but life-sized human figures wrought in brass, now smoothed by centuries of feet.

In the floor of the arcade near the pulpit, I find a full-length brass figure of a man. His pointed shoes stand one on a polled sheep with long curling fleece and the other upon a bulky sack of wool. This marks the tomb of John Fortey, a wool merchant who in 1458 left the church £300 'to complete the new work already by me begun'[27] – that is, to add this nave and aisles to the pre-existing chancel and tower. He also wished to be buried 'in the middle aisle of St Peter',[28] but concerned churchwardens in the 1960s removed his plaque to this quieter space.

Around him are six circular medallions wreathed in ivy leaves, each displaying the initials J.F. around a central cross – Fortey's merchant's mark. Each merchant had their stamp, often an angular composition of their initials, a cross, and sometimes the 'Sign of Four', the enigmatic reversed four believed to hold ancient mystic power. Once the fleeces had been shorn and graded, they were packed into 'tods', sacks weighing 28 pounds (a tod was an ancient measure of weight particular to the wool trade, its Germanic roots shared with Swedish *tott*, 'a mass of wool', and Dutch *todde*, meaning 'burden'). The tods were then packed into 'sarples', coarse canvas packing cloths capable of holding 80 tods of wool, and delivered to 'the king's beam' at London's Leadenhall market to be weighed. It was the woolman's task to take the sarples to Leadenhall, each with the merchant's mark.

Whilst the 'Cotswold Lion' once filled the Crown's coffers with gold, their wool no longer forms the lion's share of the local economy. The fleece of today's improved breeds, particularly those with their roots in the close-gene breeding of Robert Bakewell, is usually far heavier than that of their mediaeval ancestors. Eight hundred years ago, words such as 'long' and 'fine' described fleeces that weighed as little as 1.5 pounds:[29] today, a Cotswold fleece, however fine, can weigh up to 20 pounds, or 9 kilos. Like our bodies, grown taller and broader on better diets, Britain's sheep have bulked out too. By the 1960s, only one large breeding flock of Cotswold sheep remained. In 2017, the breed was still at risk – just shy of 1,500 Cotswold ewes now make up Britain's entire flock.

Looking at my hoard of exquisite Cotswold wool, I see that the fleece's staple is long, sometimes measuring more than 10 inches, with five or six crimps to the inch. Before I spin them, these golden locks must not be carded, but combed. Whereas my downland Suffolk yarn is woollen-spun, its shorter fibres trapping lots of air as they cross each other, lustrous Longwool fibres, such as the Cotswold fleece, show their true colours best when their fibres have been aligned and separated using long-toothed combs.

In the Middle Ages, wool combing on a commercial scale was journeymen's work, tough and physically demanding. Each comb weighed around 7 pounds and measured 7 inches wide, with sharp teeth of tempered steel of increasing length set into a piece of horn and attached to a wooden handle. Before use, they were warmed on charcoal stoves to better slide through the woollen fibres. The first comb would be set on a narrow wooden bench known as a jenny (hence the term 'spinning jenny'), then woollen fibres were thrown over it before being brushed or 'jigged' with a second comb, expertly swung. After sufficient combing, the resulting 'sliver' of yarn could be drawn off and passed through a 'diz', a narrow horn ring used to uniformly smooth the fibres. Finally it would be wound into a 'top', the term still used for a unit of combed wool today. Combing methods did, however, vary across the country, as the *Book of Trades* of 1815 testifies: 'The business of the wool-comber is different in different counties; some, as the wool-combers in Hertfordshire, prepare it only for worsted yarn &c; others, as those in and near Norwich, prepare it for weaving into camblets and other light stuffs.'[30] Women also combed wool at home for domestic use, but using two smaller, lighter combs that could be easily held, one in each hand.

I have never combed a fleece – to learn, I must head further west again. Driving towards the still-pink sky, I bed down for the night at a pub close to the Welsh border, before arriving the following morning at a stone-walled, slate-roofed farmhouse. A woman with a bob of ash-blonde hair ushers me inside. She'll be with me soon, she says – first, though, she has to move a calf into a trailer. This is the expert spinner Dunja Roberts, who, with her husband, Brian, farms sheep and cattle in the Black Mountains. The couple first met in Bettws-y-Crwyn, an English village whose Welsh name means 'the chapel of the fleeces', but moved here so they could 'eat two puddings with one spoon', as Brian says – live in and farm the same place together.

Dunja shows me how to handle Longwool fibres, combing them twice to line up all their ends, ready to be worsted spun. She lays out bags of carefully labelled fleece and yarn on her kitchen table and, pushing fleecy fibres into my hand, talks me through lustre, crispness, twist. The breed, the staple length, the spin, the dye. She reads yarn like a map, both head and hand clever. Touch-dumb, I hold them in my palm like coins I can't yet spend.

As the spinning wheel flickers round, I watch Dunja turn an ounce and a half of raw fleece into smooth, dense yarn, with the slight sheen that sets worsted yarn apart from woollen-spun. Dunja knows the properties of her fleece in the raw, and lets the wool's own specific qualities guide her spinning. 'Spin to the crimp,' she advises, pushing long-stapled fibres against my fingertips. Lincoln Longwool carries around three crimps to the inch; three crimps become three twists in a spinner's hands.

I open the bag of Cotswold fleece and tease out its locks. Laying staples of the yarn beside me, I count carefully: five or six crimps to an inch. Laying the drifts of prepared fleece beside the spinning wheel, I tie a small piece of leader yarn to the bobbin, and slowly depress the treadle. As the wheel whirrs to life, the leader starts to twist and, as it turns, I lay the golden strands beside it. Like an Archimedes' screw, the leader snatches in the airy fibres, and I draw, pinch and release them, trying to keep the greedy thread fed with a consistent diet of Cotswold yarn. Dunja's mantra, 'spin to the crimp', is my guide, though often the wheel's speed and my inexpert touch leaves my yarn more tightly spun than is ideal.

After washing and winding my Cotswold yarn into a ball, I line it up beside the Suffolk spun by my mother and Dunja's hand-spun yarn, made from her own Clun Forest sheep. A now-rare breed with its roots in nearby Shropshire, Clun Forests are hardy and alert, adept at mothering and producing both good flesh and fleece. Joseph Plymley, in his *General View of the Agriculture of Shropshire*, written for the Board of Agriculture in 1803, describes them as 'all of a small sort, weighing from eight to twelve pounds a quarter, when fat'. But it is their self-preserving character that draws the most attention: 'although the fences in these vallies are mostly quick, and well made, these little animals force their way through or over them in severe weather, in defiance of all endeavours to prevent them.'[31] Cluns produce a Down-like wool that keeps its shape, with a springy staple and lots of wavy crimp.

'Homespun' has stood as shorthand for homely, simple, unso-phisticated or rustic since at least 1590, and my inexpert yarn has a roughness entirely unsophisticated about it. Even Dunja's beau-tifully uniform hand-spun wool has a quality of texture not found in commercial yarn, though I see this as its strength and charm, imparting the individual flavour of her farm and flock.

After a day of sheep and spinning, I head for home, clutch-ing two skeins of Dunja's yarn, the rich smell of sheep grease upon my hands. Dunja also passes on a few Welsh sheep farm-ing terms, a clutch of words to help me when I return to Wales later in the year: *defaid*, for sheep looked after by the *ffermwr*, the *gwlân* turned to yarn by *nyddu*. A linguistic *cwtch* for adventures yet to come.

Leaving the Black Mountains behind me as I head north and east again, I pass green fields flecked with white: not sheep grazing, but cricketers on their pitches, casting long shadows as day turns to evening. Cricket and wool-working in Britain are surprisingly intertwined. Some historians aver that cricket has its roots in a game first played by the shepherds of the Low Countries in the late Middle Ages:[32] the name may be derived from the Flemish *krik ketsen*, 'to hunt with a crutch'.[33] They also believe that the now-straight cricket bat was developed from the curved shepherd's crook, turned upside down and used like a lacrosse stick to push a ball of matted wool across swards levelled by the sheep's nibbling teeth.[34] Like many theories, this one is difficult to prove, but it is certain that by the sixteenth century, a team game called *creckett* was popular among schoolboys in Surrey: 'one of the Queenes Majesties Coroners of the County of Surrey [...] saith that hee being a schollar in the Free schoole of Guldeford, hee and several of his fellowes did runne and play there at Creckett and other plaies'.[35]

Like football's scarves and golf's diamond-patterned socks and jumpers, cricket is a sport with its own identifying knitwear. But it was only during the latter years of the nineteenth century that head-to-toe 'whites' became standard cricketing attire. Before this, players would simply strip down to their shirts and breeches for a game – shirts were usually white linen, though breeches could be colourful and some sides wore checked, striped or dotted waistcoats.

The popularity of 'traditional' cricket whites owes much to W. G. Grace (1848–1915), England's famous cricketer who swung a bat at international level well into his fifties. Grace was a sporting superstar, with a presence and personality to match: with an enormous beard and over six feet tall, he swaggered onto pitches in white cloth trousers, wide-necked white shirts and the red and yellow cap of the Marylebone Cricket Club. His views on cricket fashion were typically forthright: 'I have very seldom met with a cricketer of eminence [...] who did not impress upon his tailor the momentous importance of comfortably fitting clothes.'[36]

In 1888, Grace wrote that 'it was no unusual sight ten or twenty years ago to find an eleven or county twenty-two dressed in all the colours of the rainbow', but that now white is preferred; he describes this new aesthetic as 'both better and cooler'.[37] He also advised that, 'for the sake of health and comfort', cricketers should wear flannel or wool next to their skin. The connection between wool and health had already been extolled by Gustav Jaeger in 1880 in his *Die Normalkleidung als Gesundheitsschutz* (*Standardized Apparel for Health Protection*), which inspired the creation of the Jaeger clothing brand in Britain four years later. Grace's preference for a knitted sweater, rather than the blazer which was then popular, was because it 'fits closer to the body, is much pleasanter, and in the field on a very cold day it helps to keep you warm, which is necessary for smartness and comfort'. Even on the warmest day, Grace exhorts his acolytes, 'Always carry it in your bag, for a hot and fine morning may be followed by a cold or wet afternoon', and goes on to recommend thick woollen socks for cricketers spending long days on their feet: 'and always have an extra pair or two in the bag when travelling about. They are better made plain, not ribbed, and in natural colours they are more comfortable and do not mark the feet.'[38]

Cricket's white sleeveless slipovers, affectionately dubbed by some 'the woolly pullies', has a firm place in popular culture. Like an Aran sweater, most are knitted in white wool and heavily cabled. Although modern Twenty20 games and international test matches feature players in synthetic shirts and fleeces of every hue, cricket jumpers and sleeveless pullovers are still sported on the county grounds of England. At their neck and waist are bands of strong colour, determined by county: red and navy for Essex, blue and yellow for Yorkshire, dark blue for Middlesex.

I decide to make a sleeveless cricket pullover to fit my friend's small boy, Jack. His father's family makes their living growing turf for cricket pitches, and I am drawn to the pleasing circularity of purpose, person and identity inherent in making him a cricket jumper. I begin to knit with my hand-spun yarn, using the biggest needles I own to cast on stitches for the rib. More like the handle of a wooden spoon, each 15mm needle feels huge and heavy in my hand, and my wrists soon ache with holding them. The resulting fabric is so dense that even a few centimetres of it resembles tweed more than knitted jersey. I realize that it will be too heavy and inflexible for the cricket jumper I intend to knit; instead, I will craft one from Dunja's hand-spun DK yarn.

Cricket has been a part of my life for as long as sheep and knitting. At school, my best friend Emma had an older cousin, 'Cousy', who knew his way round a cricket bat, and, as tiny scholars in Mrs Payne's reception class, we would run onto the sports field and try to attach ourselves to Cousy's cricket whites. I'm not sure we endeared ourselves with these antics, but Cousy went on to play cricket for Essex and England as a left-handed batsman and medium-fast bowler. We clearly had an eye for talent.

As teenagers, Emma and I again decided to inveigle ourselves into the world of men and sports. We were the first girls to join a local Scout group, shunning the Girl Guides, and signed up for our school's cricket club. We weren't allowed near competitive matches, but would turn up at practices, bouncing balls off the catch nets and swinging bats around in netted cages behind the netball courts, eyeing up the boys we liked as they made heroic catches in the outfield. This curious form of flirting drew no rewards, but those warm teenage Suffolk summers are caught in an amber glow of memory.

Twenty years later, I am off to watch Yorkshire battle Essex on a sunny summer weekend. Hearing of my interest in knitting and cricket, my husband's uncle Steve has volunteered to take us to a match. A card-carrying member of Scarborough Cricket Club for more than thirty years, Steve, like his father and uncle before him, watches every match from the North Stand's old wooden benches, just as he did on his first visit.

As the scent of the sea rises on the humid air, Steve meets us by the gates to the Scarborough club. The waist-high turnstiles

are manned by three unsmiling chaps in caps, who hand out thin cardboard tickets. Unusually, Scarborough's gatekeepers keep no change. 'Exact money only,' they bark, pointing us towards another queue where we can exchange our notes for pound coins. They only let you through when precisely £16 is placed in their tins.

Before the match begins, Steve walks us proudly round the ground, pointing out the day's main players. Not those who wield bat and ball, but the stage hands and directors who really run it. Out on the sward, a stout, unsmiling groundsman inspects the crease with a critical eye, parading up and down on his turf like a sentry. The outcome of the match is in his meaty hands.

We then go to inspect the tea room, the name stencilled on its slate roof in bold white capitals; the toilets ('They were condemned last year, so it's Portaloos today'); the impressive brick pavilion, with a wide white veranda and first-floor balcony. 'That's where the players eat their lunch,' he says, pointing to a white door on the building's seaward side. For Steve, this place is the holiest of holies, each trip a pilgrimage to the past as much as a good day out in the present.

Steve is part of a family that not only watches cricket but plays it – and knits for its players. Hearing of my quest, Steve's cousin Audrey posts me her pattern for a cricket sweater. Carefully protected between the pages of a *Camping and Caravanning* magazine, this *Wendy* knitting pattern has two smart men dressed in white on its cover, one in a sweater, the other in a sleeveless slipover. Knitted in *Wendy* 'Ascot' yarn in Jersey Cream, with Blue Bayou and Magenta stripes at neck and waist, this pattern has already kept two generations of Cowtons warm on the pitch.

The first cricket woolly I see at Scarborough is not a jumper but something much bigger. Below us in the North Stand, people have arrayed themselves in folding chairs, eye-level to each ball. An older couple have come prepared: draped over the back of her chair is an enormous crocheted blanket. Like a 'woolly pully', it is mostly creamy-white, with a yellow, navy and sky-blue edging round the squares. I compliment the maker on her work; she wishes me a good first day at Scarborough. A few metres away, I spot some crocheted cushion covers in the same style, Yorkshire's sunny colours inspiring comfort.

Cricket jumpers themselves are few and far between. The four or five I do see are stretched across the stomachs of men who seem more familiar with raising pint glasses to their lips than hurling balls or swinging bats. Groups of old men sit under flat caps, trousers halfway up their chests, working their way through cups of tea and the *Test Match Special* quiz. Closest to us, a keenly attentive old boy cranes his neck towards the crease and between overs meditatively chews the arm of his spectacles.

Cricket is the perfect accompaniment to knitting. Keeping one eye on the 'action', I cast on a wide welt of stitches in Dunja's DK yarn to begin this cricket slipover. Once the knit-purl rib is done, I work in a pale blue strip of West Yorkshire Spinners' Illustrious DK yarn to mirror Yorkshire's blue, before cabling broad columns of stitches to make twelve twisting pillars that snake their way from navel to neck.

A cricket pullover must have cables, just like an Aran jumper, though there is scant connection between the cricket field and Galway Bay's windswept islands, off the west coast of Ireland. Although 'Aran knitting' is recognized worldwide, its pedigree is much contested. The historian Richard Rutt notes that though the 1934 film *Man of Aran* did much to bring the lives of the islanders of Inishmore, Inisheer and Inishmaan to the world's attention, it shows the fishermen wearing the dark ganseys and knitted caps common to Britain's fishing communities[39] – no impractical white cabled jumpers are worn. It was not until the Prussian author and clothier Heinz Kiewe saw the film that the white sweater began to be associated with the Aran islands, as Kiewe instigated the 'revival' of a 'Biblical white'[40] knitted jumper, developing a theory of influence and connection between ancient Gaelic art and Aran knitwear. Kiewe went as far as to contend that illustrations in the Book of Kells showed monks wearing white knitted garments, though this claim has been largely refuted: it is not possible to ascertain the method of construction shown in the manuscript. But though there seems to be no legitimate connection between the Aran Islands, eighth-century monks and knitwear, the legend continues to inspire thriving tourist and knitwear industries to this day.

Regardless of its debated provenance, the appeal of the cabled cream sweater endures. To the eye, if not the hand, cables' texture is created through the existence of shadow, the absence of light behind raised stitches. As the long shadows of early evening lengthen – the footprint of the built world surrounding the Scarborough pitch – the rise-and-fall geometry of my twisting stitches creates new worlds of light and shade in cables. What we do with all our making is to explore multiple dimensions, to describe space through its interplay with light.

Down on the pitch, Yorkshire's wickets tumble, but up in the North Stand I am pleased with my knitting's progress, working towards the neck's essential 'V'. Before I can begin to shape it, the late-afternoon sky has clouded over and play is halted. If allowed the luxury of four full days of a county match, I might finish the jumper – but I can only spare a day. The rest I complete back home to the familiar roll and pitch of *Test Match Special*, shaping the neck and shoulders to the comfortable rumble of Blowers and Aggers, Boycott and Tuffers.

This sleeveless pullover is not dissimilar in construction from the body of my dad's gansey as it too is knitted in the round, with cables that march regularly from waist to shoulder. As the cricket season gets up to speed in the summer's long days, I post the woolly pully south to Essex, where it can keep Jack warm as he toddles round the turf farm, exploring miles of proto-cricket pitches.

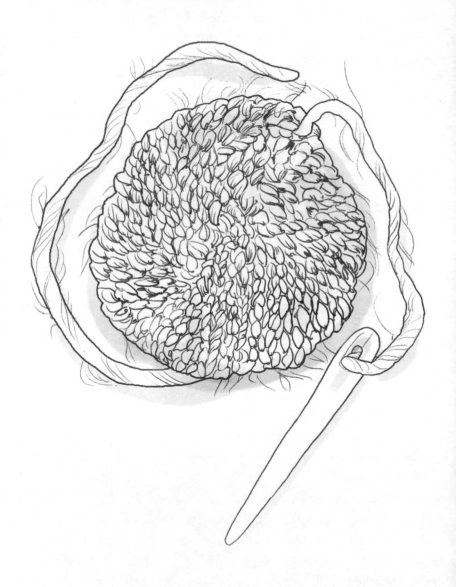

7

Vikings, Socks and
the Great Yorkshire Llama

After the heat of midsummer, rain arrives and the weather cools. July storms leave the world dripping with water. My challenge for this mixed-weather month is to recreate Britain's oldest surviving needle-made piece of clothing.

I say 'needle-made' because tracing Britain's earliest truly knitted item is something of a wild goose chase. The Victoria and Albert Museum holds some of the world's oldest needle-made garments – including two-toed Egyptian socks dating from between the fourth and sixth centuries. Split like Japanese *tabi*, they were made to be worn with sandals in the Egyptian desert, the ends bifurcated so the toes could grasp a leather thong. At first glance, they seem to have been knitted, but on close inspection their stitches do not form the smooth outward-facing loops of knitting. These socks have been 'nålebound', their thread looped using a single needle.

English generally borrows the Danish *nålebinding* – pronounced 'noll-binding' – to refer to the technique variously described as 'needle-binding', 'knotless netting' and 'needle-knitting'. Whereas two needles are necessary for knitting, nålebinding uses one large-eyed needle to pull lengths of yarn into interlocking loops. Many of Europe's oldest foot coverings, like their Coptic cousins, have been made using this looping method, usually worked from the toe up towards the leg. Only one pre-modern nålebound item has been discovered in Britain; natural fibres rarely survive the ravages of light, oxygen and time; this item dates from around the tenth century and was discovered in York.

How did this particular item come to last a millennium? People have lived and worked in York for almost two thousand years. Founded by the Romans in 75 CE as Eboracum, it became a large Roman military outpost of some five thousand men. Resettled and expanded by the Vikings, by 874 it had become the de facto capital of the Danelaw and was renamed Jórvík, a Viking corruption of the Saxon *Eoforwic* – 'settlement of Eofor', or possibly 'place of the wild pigs'. At the time of the Great Survey of 1086, recorded in the *Domesday Book*, York was a huge city, second in size only to London. At York's heart, then as now, lies Coppergate, bounded to the east by the River Foss and to the west by the River Ouse.

In the tenth century, under the rule of Norse king Eric Blood-axe, Coppergate's residents turned the wooden cups that gave this road its name – Coppergate means 'street of the cup-makers'. Dexterous Vikings also worked leather, fibres and metal, and carved bone here; waste from these trades rapidly accumulated, raising the level of the street by a centimetre or so each year. The damp soil, fed by the rivers, created a low-oxygen environment, which preserved, under the debris of centuries, not only metal, leather and wood, but also fragile textiles.

In the 1970s, 211 Viking-era items were unearthed from beneath the city's modern street to make way for a new shopping centre. Wool, plant fibres and even silk were all found here, and many of the fibres had been woven or twisted into cords. Most of the wool was quite coarse, its fibres thick and hairy, and full of wiry kemps. Unusually, much of the wool had not been shorn, but instead plucked from a dead animal's pelt. Known as 'fell wool', this fleece is short and hard to spin, as it rarely contains a full year's growth. Fell wool was not worth trading – York's archaeologists concluded that this wool would have been locally sourced, and therefore readily available, or brought over from Scandinavia as part of a finished garment.

Only one garment was made from continuous loops of yarn: the 'Coppergate Sock'. An almost complete needle-worked foot covering, it was discovered in the yard of a tenth-century wattle building. Like a little slipper, it has a gently pointed toe and swells to mirror the curve of its first wearer's toes and sole. Twenty-six centimetres long, it shows signs of darning at the base of the heel. Pale reddish-brown, stained by the peaty soil that preserved it, it stops below the ankle, bordered by a thin band of dyed red yarn. Today it is displayed at the Jorvik Viking Centre, carefully stuffed, as though its Norse owner had left their foot inside. On first glance, it looks more like a root vegetable than a piece of clothing.

The Anglo-Saxon words *socc*, *calc* and *méo* offer us a glimpse of the types of foot-coverings worn by the Norse a millennium ago. *Méo* can be glossed as 'sole-shoe', 'sock' or 'sandal'; *calc* as 'shoe', 'little shoe' or 'sandal'; and *socc* as 'sock', 'light shoe' or 'slipper'. Whether the Coppergate 'sock' was designed to be worn with shoes or as a slipper we cannot know, but what we can tell from this tenth-century remnant is that it was well-worn and useful enough to be worth mending.

Although Roman-era socks and foot bindings have been found across Britain, none of them had been knitted. A scant half-mile from Coppergate, across the Ouse at Micklegate Bar, workmen digging foundations for York's railway line and station in 1838 unearthed a Roman stocking. It was 'sprang-worked', constructed from two-ply yarn webbed together on a frame, from toe to knee. 'Sprangwork' is a little like the children's game cat's cradle crossed with weaving: loops of yarn are twisted around the fingers and then slipped onto warp rods to hold each row in place. With their winding columns of threads, sprang-worked stockings look more like fishnet tights than today's close-knit coverings.

A hundred miles to the north, on the boggy moors of Northumberland, stand the remains of Vindolanda, a Roman fort on the northern edge of that Empire. Since archaeological excavations first began in the 1930s, Vindolanda has revealed an unrivalled hoard of preserved textiles and footwear. Over six thousand shoes and many items of clothing and jewellery have so far been found, and they include a complete child-sized sock, sewn together from two pieces of woven cloth. Unravelling at the ankle, this muddy brown shape with its square toe was made two centuries into the Common Era. More remarkable still is a set of wooden tablets found close by; inked in the second and third centuries, their letters have been preserved in the anoxic moorland soil.

One of these minute scraps of wood, preserved in the watery ditch that surrounded the camp, gives us an insight into what Britain's Roman inhabitants wore. The wild, damp wind that batters the hillside on the July day when I visited was no different two millennia ago; one soldier far from home has been sent 'pairs of socks [*udones*] from Sattua, two pairs of sandals and two pairs of underpants'.[1] Sattua has yet to be discovered on a map; 'Sattuo' appears elsewhere at Vindolanda on a leather patch, likely a maker's brand or seller's name. Evidence of Roman legionaries pairing socks with sandals has been corroborated by finds from a dig at Leeming in North Yorkshire, where a rusted sandal nail shows traces of fibres clinging to its shaft. There is no evidence of *udones* being made at either Leeming or Vindolanda.

I want to make a replica Coppergate-style sock, using woolworking techniques that predate knitting and inform Britain's needlework heritage. First I need a suitable needle. Whilst it seems possible to nålebind with anything from an embroidery needle to a repurposed hairclip, the Norse used broad, flat, wide-eyed needles made of wood or bone. Mediaeval nålebound textiles have been found in Denmark, Finland, Sweden, Switzerland, Poland and Russia, and nålebinding is still practised in Scandinavia. I own no such needle, and immediately try to buy one. My husband, Tom, glancing at my hunched form peering at the computer screen, suggests that I make one. Or, he offers, I could make one for you? The desire to make things is contagious, and a smooth, whittled needle is proudly delivered to me two days later. Made from a branch lopped from a birch tree in our garden, it is as long as my forefinger, silk-smooth to the touch and creamy coloured. It has a broad wide eye, as requested: nålebinding needles need to carry thick and lofty yarn.

My next quest is to find the right sort of yarn, as similar as possible to that used by the Vikings. The archaeologist Penelope Walton Rogers, who worked closely on the Coppergate fibres and fabrics during the excavation, avers that the sock's yarn is made from two S-spun strands plied clockwise, with thirty-six rows of loops for every 10 centimetres of sock. Lightly spun yarn is essential: the lengths of yarn in nålebinding are joined by spit-splicing – twisting torn spittle-dampened ends of yarn together – which becomes impossible with tightly spun worsted yarn.

Searching for Viking yarn becomes a quest for Viking sheep. The sock dates from around the tenth century, its yarn almost certainly from a Nordic flock. The sheep closest to those kept by the Norse are not found in Britain now. Whilst sheep descended from the Viking *villsau* (*Ovis brachyura borealis*) do exist in Shetland and the Hebrides, almost all have been interbred with other types of sheep in the thousand years that have passed since their ancestors first arrived. There is only one place whose geographic and historical isolation is so complete that its sheep are as close as possible to those ancient Viking's flocks: Iceland.

On a seawashed outcrop on the Mid-Atlantic Ridge, Iceland has an ovine – and human – population that is little changed genetically from their Viking-era forebears. Unlike in mainland Europe, by and large the Icelanders did not intermix with other cultures until the twentieth century, and Icelandic sheep – another Northern European short-tailed breed – have been untroubled by outside influences for over a thousand years. White, black or *moorit* – a reddish-brown shade, *mórauthr* in Old Icelandic – their fleece can be one colour or speckled. It is also dual-layered: *tog* is the coarse, water-repellent outer later, *thel* the softer, shorter hairs close to the skin.

A Viking sock needs Viking yarn. Tom comes to the rescue again: he's working in Iceland in a week or two, taking a group of students to explore Sólheimajökull glacier. Four balls of Léttlopi, the lightly spun Lopi yarn from Ístex, Iceland's only commercial wool producer, find their way home in his luggage. The colour of well-milked coffee, their shade is 'Ax', Icelandic for 'barley'.

Viking yarn and needle in hand, I'm ready to consult a pattern for instructions. Here I am wrong-footed. Whereas knitting's abbreviated code – k2, p2, k2tog – is familiar to me, nålebinding patterns look like alien calls echoing from space. UU/OOO, UOU/OUOO, UUOOUU/OOUUOO – U standing for under, O for over, the slash for a turn or change in needle direction. Devised by Danish textile historian Egon Hansen in 1987, this shorthand is one of many systems used to notate nålebinding. The stitch used for the Coppergate Sock, named as Coppergate or York stitch by American craft expert Larry Schmitt, is written as UU/OOO in Hansen's notation. But in the 1950s, Margarethe Hald, textile curator of the National Museum of Denmark, called it 'Stitch Type IIa' and illustrated it with hand-drawn diagrams; 'II' refers to the number of loops from the same row through which each new stitch runs.

Eager to understand more, I consult YouTube, essential tool of the twenty-first-century crafter. Disembodied voices and deft hands talk me through the stitches. Oslo, Darby, York or Coppergate: many of the stitches are named after the location of archaeological digs where early nålebound garments have been found. I discover that the Coppergate is not really a beginner's stitch, because it determinedly twists around itself. I find myself dangling the yarn towards the floor to untwist it, encouraging gravity to work out the coils my hands have added.

Needle in my right hand and yarn in my left, I measure out two arm-spans of yarn, tearing, not cutting, it from the ball. Knotting it under my thumbnail, I pass the end of my needle under and over the yarn. All I have to show for my efforts is a fankle. I try again, with similar results. Frustrated, I tear off another length of yarn and start again under YouTube's disembodied guidance. After half an hour of fierce concentration, I produce a rough circle of twelve stitches, misshapen, loose and wobbly.

Learning to nålebind transports me to my eight-year-old self, first struggling with needles and yarn. I cannot clearly remember the tussle of learning to knit, and my hands now slip automatically through the motions. The how-to part of my brain seems to function at an unconscious level, working so quickly that I cannot catch its individual instructions to my hands. With nålebinding, I am a novice, reverting to those fumbling struggles of childhood. This new craft's necessary discipline shows up my impatient, anxious brain for what it is: quick to take on new ideas, sluggish to learn new ways of doing.

Most knitters learn to knit on the flat, passing their work back and forth between two needles. The assumption is that this is the easiest way to learn to knit, and for practising the formation of basic stitches, this is broadly true. Yet, unlike woven fabric, knitting's unique trick is its ability to flex and fit whatever it surrounds: it is made to cover things that curve. To knit seamlessly on three, four or five needles means never having to stitch together garments from their component parts, but instead constructing tubes of knitting for head, hand, foot, leg or torso.

When were garments first knitted in the round in Europe? An early mediaeval grave from the village of Równina Dolna in northern Poland contains a twelfth- or thirteenth-century example of woollen knitting on thick needles, and knitted peasants' gloves and a cap have been found in Latvia, dating some hundred years later. We cannot know for certain, but it seems that somewhere between the tenth-century Coppergate Sock and thirteenth-century Spanish silk stockings, knitting moved from one needle to two. The reason seems to have been the advent of fine wire manufacturing – though knitting is known to have been done on sticks and the calami of feathers. Certainly by the thirteenth century, knitters across Europe were working intricate designs with fine yarns and needles and forming highly regulated guilds. These were skilled men serving long apprenticeships, and their gloves and stockings commanded high prices, fit for the legs of royalty and the hands of the episcopate. Knitwear formed an important part of the northern Italian city of Mantua's economy from the fourteenth century, and by the sixteenth century Verona, Padua, Lucca, Milan, Genoa and Naples all exported knitted stockings.

The earliest representations of knitting in Europe show needles being worked in the round. A handful of extant mediaeval paintings of the Virgin Mary depict her knitting; she is the *Madonna dell'Umiltà*, the hardworking 'Madonna of Humility'. The phrase usually refers to Madonnas portrayed sitting on the floor or on a cushion in place of the usual ornate chair or throne.[2] Mary has been literally grounded – the Latin *humilis* (humility) contains aural if not semantic echoes of *humus*, meaning earth. Madonnas of Humility are usually shown with the Christ child in their arms or close beside them, and often they are doing physical, useful, domestic tasks. These holy mothers breastfeed (and are referred to as *Madonna del latte* – 'Madonna of the Milk'); they knit, cuddle and soothe, and teach the Christ child to read. Sometimes representations of these 'homely' activities are combined, with a breastfeeding Madonna's knitting needles lying beside her as she suckles her child.

It is not known exactly when and why the Madonnas of Humility first appeared in iconography. By 1358, Vitale da Bologna had painted a Madonna and Child flanked by two virgin martyrs, with Mary knitting a floral pattern in two colours as a rascally Christ child grabs a spool of yarn from a nearby table. Around the same time, Ambrogio Lorenzetti of Siena depicted the Holy Family seated on a floor covered with a rug worked with animal pictures. In this painting, Mary knits in the round beside a rotating tray full of coloured spools of yarn, her young son clinging to her arm as she works with needles against her palms.

Another fourteenth-century native of Siena, Niccolò di Buonaccorso, depicts the Madonna with Jesus on her knee in a triptych, her knitting – stranded colourwork in the round – and multiple spools of coloured yarn set behind her, out of reach of her child's fingers. His fellow Sienese artist and contemporary, Benedetto di Bindo, also included several colourful yarns in his depiction, laid to one side as his Madonna breastfeeds, while Tommaso da Modena's mid-fourteenth century triptych, likely painted in Bologna, contains three images of the Virgin: in one she reads, in another she suckles Jesus, and the third shows her with a plate of carefully wound yarns on her lap, her knitting stretched on a frame and her child beside her.

The most famous of all the knitting Virgins appears on the Benedictine polyptych known as the Buxtehude Altar, painted in the 1390s by Master Bertram of Minden. It shows Mary seated in a richly decorated room – no cushions or bare earth for her – holding her knitting and about to cast off the neck of a shirt or coat. Worked on four needles, the shirt is believed to represent the 'unsewn garment' worn by Christ at his crucifixion, referred to in the Gospel of John: 'now the coat was without seam, woven from the top throughout.'[3]

At first glance the image appears cosy – the Madonna has her basket of yarn and plies her four needles, whilst her son lies before her on his stomach, holding open the pages of a book. But behind him stand the archangels Michael and Gabriel, bearing the *Arma Christi*, the instruments that will later crucify the adult Jesus – a lance, cross, nails, and crown of thorns. Mary's eyes are downcast, on her work, as she prepares this last garment for her son, an act of love so poignant that her refusal to look directly at her child, or at the angels with their arms, seems to be a deed of self-protection. Her knitting stands not for cosy domesticity, but for the sorrows of the world. Christ's crucifixion is prefigured on her knitting needles.[4]

After two days and many YouTube video repeats, I can finally cast on and make an almost-perfect circle of twelve nålebound

Completed Dentdale gloves, 2017.

Fisher lassies at Yarmouth, knitting as they rest against a large pile of 'Yarmouth swills', *c.*1900. Scottish Fisheries Museum, Anstruther.

Author wears her Pussyhat at an anti-Trump demonstration in London, 2017.

Virginia Woolf by Vanessa Bell. Oil on board, 1912. 400 mm × 340 mm. National Portrait Gallery.

Temperature and knitting yarn chart, Marsha Willey, taken at Edinburgh Yar Festival, 2017.

Gairloch stockings from the early twentieth century, Gairloch Museum.

Canach (cottongrass) yarn in 'Corca' (oatmeal), Uist Wool, Grimsay, North Uist, 2017.

Yarn in production at Uist Wool Mill, Grimsay, North Uist, 2017.

Military hose dating from the nineteenth century, Highland Folk Museum.

Knitting frame with certificate of indenture for framework knitter, Ruddington Framework Knitters Museum.

Dubied hand-flat machine at Heriot-Watt School of Textiles and Design, High Mill, Netherdale, Galashiels.

Author models her handmade bikini, Embleton Bay, Northumberland.

Completed child's cricket slipover made from handspun Clun Forest DK yarn and West Yorkshire Spinners Illustrious DK yarn.

Author and friend Elly Murrell with raw fleece.

Nålebound Jorvik sock made using Léttlopi yarn by Álafoss in 'Ax' and Titus yarn by Baa Ram Ewe in 'Viking'.

Jersey spinning wheel on display at Hamptonne Country Life Museum, St Lawrence, Jersey.

Sleeve of a 'grey-belly' jersey and a dyed navy jersey, on display at Hamptonne Country Life Museum, St Lawrence, Jersey.

Display of 1920s knitwear, Shetland Museum, Lerwick, Shetland.

Jumper knitted from handspun yarn dyed with ground elder, Shetland Wool Week, 2017.

Madder dyeing, Julia Billings's workshop, Shetland Wool Week, 2017.

Fair Isle fisherman's kep, Shetland Museum.

Rib and loop of replica Monmouth cap.

Woolcraft: A Practical Guide To Knitting & Crochet With Beehive & White Heather Knitting Wools Beehive Knitting Booklets No 9 New and Enlarged Edition. Published by J & J Baldwin & Partners Ltd, Halifax England, 1925.

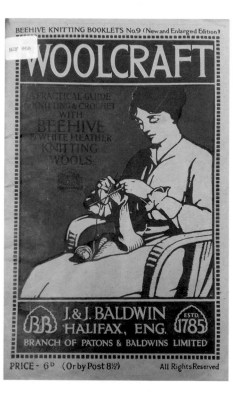

Funeral stockings belonging to Eliza Lewis, St Fagans National Museum of History, Cardiff, Wales.

Lace shawl knitted by Betsy Williamson and displayed at A Happening, Ollaberry, Shetland Wool Week 2017.

Border and edging of baby hap knitted in Blacker Yarns St Kilda Laceweight and Jamieson & Smith 2ply Laceweight yarns.

Detail of completed gansey including 4-stitch cables, 'Tree of Life' and 'railroad' patterns.

Author's father, Michael Rutter, in his gansey.

loops that pull tight to make a toe-point. At first I try to prac-
tise stitches on spare yarn, unconnected to the neat cast-on,
but quickly realize my mistake. Coppergate stitch is unique to
this sock, and only truly works in a continuous shape. Passing
the yarn under two stitches and then back over three, I work
steadily round to form the sock's toe in painstaking circles.
Each metre or two of yarn quickly absorbs itself into the stitch
and I spit-splice one length to the next, rolling the damp,
ragged ends between my palms to bind them. The sock slowly
takes shape as I add a new loop for every other stitch; I keep
poking my big toe into the tip of my nålebinding as I work
round after round of stitches, checking that my stitches mirror
the curve of my feet.

Embarrassed at the messiness of this sock so far, I abandon my
first attempt and begin anew. This time the neat circle of stitches
is tighter and truer, the loops denser and neater. Once I've made
the first toe-circle to my satisfaction, I cast on another. My nålebinding slowly improves, the stitches growing smaller and neater
with practice.

Knitting two socks at once is a method favoured by adept sock
knitters. Using a circular needle and the 'Magic Loop' technique,
whereby the needle's long loop holds two smaller rounds of
stitches side by side, a knitter can work two socks simultaneously
on one wire, thereby avoiding the dread inertia that follows the
flush of satisfaction at completing a sock. Although I've not yet
attempted knitting socks simultaneously, I want to make sure
that my nålebound socks are as similar to each other as possible.
And apathy towards a second sock has undone me before. Many
years ago, I decided to provide my father with hand-knitted socks
for Christmas. That year, I presented him with the fruits of my
labour – a single sock. Such was my reluctance to crack on with
the second that he had to wait an entire year to receive it.

*

People have been making socks at home for centuries, but there is another way of knitting socks: by using a circular hand-powered knitting machine. Whilst traditional flat-bed frames like those commercially used in Hawick, London and Nottingham can only produce flat pieces of fabric requiring seaming, circular knitting machines were designed to create seamless tubes of fabric. Crucial to the development of these circular machines was Pierre Jeandeau's invention in France in 1806 of the latch needle, which had a tongue or sliver of steel to keep yarn from slipping as it was worked. In 1816, Marc Isambard Brunel, father of the engineer Isambard Kingdom Brunel, used these latched needles to make the first machines capable of knitting cylinders of fabric, and in 1856 the American Walter Aiken and his brother Jonas registered the first patent for knitting machines with latched needles.[5] Together with the New Hampshire inventor William H. Pepper, they produced and improved knitting machines for generations of domestic and commercial knitters. In 1878 Henry Griswold was able to add a ribber to the machine, which enabled knitters to make alternate knit and purl stitches to produce a stretchy rib for sock and stocking tops.

Cymbal, Griswold, Harrison, Imperia, the Automatic Knitting Machine Company – all were manufacturers of circular knitting machines for domestic use in Britain from the late nineteenth century until the middle of the twentieth. These machines were also supplied to children's homes and orphanages to encourage their inhabitants to learn profitable skills that they could use to earn their keep. Industry masquerading as benevolence, this attitude was typical of the popular and prevalent Victorian virtue of labour, what Thomas Carlyle termed 'the Gospel of Work': 'Work and therein have wellbeing'. One such institution was the Church of England's Waifs and Strays Society, which ran St Chad's Home Stocking Industry at Far Headingley in

Leeds. They sold cashmere machine-knit stockings at 2*s*. 9*d*. a pair in 1898 – the equivalent of around £12 a pair in 2018.[6] These circular machines are no longer manufactured in Britain, so to learn how to use one to make a complete pair of socks, I must return to school – Anne Drew's Sock School, to be precise.

Anne Drew discovered circular knitting machines during her Textile Management studies at Leeds University, and in 2010 bought her first historic machine – a Cymbal. A year later, she began selling hand-cranked socks at local markets, and then, having acquired a few more antique machines, set up 'Sock School', a day-long course for people keen to learn how to machine-knit socks.

I sign up online and, months later, arrive early one Sunday morning at a community centre in Gloucestershire. A circle of six knitting machines bolted to sturdy iron frames greets me. The one designated mine is an Imperia, made in London. Each machine has a central ring of neat latched needles that lies open like the maw of an obliging shark. Half of them jut out to form a prickly collar; the alternating ones point to the sky, forty-two vicious hooks with their latches open. The horizontal needles are called 'ribbers', the verticals are known as 'cylinders'. One follows the other to form a knit-and-purl rib to grasp an ankle. They are almost identical to the latched needles on the knitting frames in the Framework Knitters Museum, though there are many fewer here and today's machinists do not need to lead-cast their own replacements. My eighty-four-slot cylinder machine includes a tiny brass dial that automatically counts each round of stitches, clicking the measuring finger one slot further on with each push of the yarn carriage. On every machine are four dabs of nail varnish, dubbed 'geography points', equidistant markers to help us navigate our knitting. Above each circle of needles, a heel-spring bobs and quivers, an arc of wire useful when we come to shape the heels of our socks.

As I watch my numbered yarn carrier click on with each swipe of the yarn carriage, I am reminded of Annie 'Nan' Bradley, a sock and stocking knitter who knitted by machine from the age of fifteen until she died just short of her hundredth birthday. Nan's machine did not have numbers printed on its face; instead, raised brass nubbins marked every tenth row. Written numbers were no use to Nan: she had been blind since early childhood. Born in London in 1905, she was trained at school to use a circular machine and at the age of fifteen won a funded place as an apprentice machinist at the Swiss Cottage Workshops for the Blind. Travelling to the workshop in Belsize Crescent by tram and bus each day she learned to make socks on a circular machine, and skirts and jumpers on a small Harrison flat-bed machine.

As a young married woman with small children – bells tied to their shoes so she could locate them – Nan was allowed to start working from home, following an inspection to check that her ground-floor flat was suitable for a loaned Harrison circular machine. Each week, six pounds of wool would be delivered in raw skeins, which Nan then waxed and wound at home. Open-toed socks took Nan an hour to make; closed ones an hour and a half. She was paid at 10*d.* per pair of socks and had to earn a minimum of 10*s.* a week by knitting at least a dozen pairs. Nan's income was then augmented by a further 10*s.* payment from Middlesex County Council.

Nan continued to knit socks and make her returns to the council until compulsory retirement at the age of seventy. It was only upon retiring that the machine that she had used for all those years finally became her own – the council would have sent it for scrap had it been returned. With orders from Sweden, America, Australia, Canada and New Zealand, Nan continued to produce socks for regular private customers. It was only as her sense of touch diminished in her hundredth year that she finally put down her needles. Nan estimated that she produced over 60,000 pairs of socks on that one loyal machine. She died at home in October 2005 and her machine was donated to Ruddington's Framework Knitters Museum.

Busy on my machine with the rib of my first imperfect pair, I crank the handle through thirty careful revolutions, thirty rounds of eighty-four stitches, before giving a gentle tug on the weighted sock end to maintain tension. The machine stands before me like a spinning wheel, and I bend closer to it to see the stitches being formed. 'Legs wide apart,' commands Anne: the 2 lb tension weight will gradually lower as the sock grows, needing space to safely dangle and not drop.

Sarah, Nicola and Anne command the room like jolly midwives, coaxing us through a process they have seen a hundred times before. The room is warm with the robust physical humour of women – 'Take your belts off,' 'Grab your bits,' 'Pop them in like forceps.' The belt is a length of coiled metal, its tension keeping needles in their place. Mattie bustles in from the kitchen to lay out tea and cake. We ask why she isn't helping with the class. 'I once instructed someone to take their belt off, and all their needles fell out,' she says ruefully, 'and after that they haven't let me teach.'

Rib completed, we nervously undo our belts, then painstakingly remove the ribber needles one by one, hooking each out and clumsily replacing them with cylinders to form knit rows. 'Stop,' commands Anne, and leaps in with her two-pronged metal hook. Decked in the white apron of medical and domestic capability, she bends over the still body of my machine. Fierce silent concentration accompanies a few deft flicks and wriggles of her wrist, and my loops are back in line. She moves from midwife to major general in a moment, commanding my unruly yarn, recalcitrant latches and wayward needles into place.

'I've left my mark on your knitting,' she says, stepping away from my machine, 'my own tattoo.' She's right: every knitter's work bears the trace of their workings. At five o'clock, I leave the workshop with a pair of finished socks. Like a mother with her newborn, I cannot stop looking at them, marvelling at their sudden existence. This morning they were not there; now I can hold them in my hand and say, 'I made these today.'

In contrast to the smooth ease of the hand-turned knitting machine, nålebinding makes my wrists ache with the strain of pushing the bulky wooden needle through the sock's small loops. Many modern nålebinders prefer the neatness of a metal embroidery needle to work their stitches so I fish one out and try it. Each stitch is so much smoother and faster than with the wooden needle that I am obliged to give up the beauty of its handmade shaft for the uniform convenience of mass production.

During the nineteenth century the mass production of both knitting needles and woollen yarn saw the craft boom in popularity. The development of the spinning jenny to produce woollen yarn on an industrial scale dramatically changed not only the fortunes but also the landscape of much of West Yorkshire. Keighley, Shipley, Bradford, Halifax – all were mill towns intent on turning fleece from the rural counties of Lincolnshire, Leicestershire, Westmorland, Northumberland, and the North and East Ridings of Yorkshire into yarn. Woollen yarn's boom years came in the nineteenth century; the cotton industry had begun to decline, but the same spinning machines were adapted to produce worsted yarn and by 1879, the West Riding of Yorkshire was the centre of worsted spinning worldwide. In 1852, Dickens travelled to the district and compared it favourably with the cotton-spinning towns of Lancashire: 'You need not inquire when you are beyond Lancashire and into the confines of the West Riding: you can detect the locality by your nose. There is nothing but wool, and oil, and water, being knocked about, and mixed up, and torn asunder, and broken on savage, unrelenting wheels, and drawn out into "slivers", and scalded in hot soap-suds all day long, and all the year long. It may rain, hail, thunder, or anything else it pleases but it's all the same to the Yorkshire folk: there's no peace for the wool. The whole county smells fusty, frowsy, and moist: the length and breadth of the West Riding must be full of damp great-coats and wretchedly wet trousers, or I am much mistaken.'[7]

One of the largest sock-yarn producers in Britain today is West Yorkshire Spinners, and it is on a monsoon-wet summer morning that I make a pilgrimage to their factory in Keighley. Leaving Leeds as the city's central station swarms with the morning's commuters, I climb aboard a battered Northern train, empty save for a couple of older men well-wrapped in sensible waterproofs. Heading west, we pass balconied high-rises, print workshops and brick warehouses before diving into the dark of a long and smutted tunnel. Beside us run the ghosts of industrial train lines that once connected West Yorkshire with the provinces that supplied its woollen mills and the Leeds and Liverpool canal, another important route for transporting woollen goods to and from the city.

The canal accompanies the train as far as Saltaire, where a huge 'Palace of Industry' stands by the railway line, splendid in sandstone. Named for its founder, the visionary industrialist Titus Salt (1803–1876), Saltaire was built in the middle of the nineteenth century to house the workers of Salt's Mill. Born the son of a wool-stapler who traded in fleece in Leeds, Salt made his money in the worsted textile trade, owning five mills in nearby Bradford (dubbed 'the City of Sheep') and becoming the city's largest employer and its mayor in 1848.

Salt was jokingly known in his lifetime as the 'Great Yorkshire Llama'. When inspecting consignments on Liverpool docks in 1833, he came across bales of alpaca fleece from South America. Although pure alpaca yarn was difficult to work with, Salt immediately saw the potential of blending this soft fleece with other fibres to make superb yarn and cloth. By 1836, Salt was successfully combining alpaca and mohair with silks and cottons to make soft, warm, hard-wearing cloth, alpaca on the weft and cotton or silk on the warp. He became one of the richest men of his generation, not just in Yorkshire but across Britain.

Salt was a philanthropic paternalist who cared deeply about his many employees. When mayor of Bradford, he tried to pass legislation to tackle the problems of urban air pollution, and introduced the ten-hour day – long by modern standards but a huge improvement on the fifteen to eighteen hours common at the time. Alas, these measures were largely opposed by other mill owners in the city, wary of a loss of profit or unconcerned with workers' welfare.

Frustrated by the limits to the good he could do in Bradford, in 1850 Salt announced a bold new vision: he would build a thoroughly modern mill with 'ventilation, convenience and general comfort' 3 miles outside the city. His dream was for a mill where noise and air pollution would be dramatically reduced, with deafening machine shafts hidden away underground and the factory's chimneys fitted with Rodda Smoke Burners, devices Salt had unsuccessfully tried to enforce in Bradford's mills. His vast, visionary mill was completed in 1853, and in 2001 was designated a UNESCO World Heritage site for its architecture, its influence on the 'garden city' movement, and 'the important role played by the textile industry in economic and social development'.[8]

Salt's Mill employed 3,500 workers, most of whom commuted from Bradford. But Salt's dream was to house them at Saltaire, and over the next twenty years 850 houses and attendant shops, a school, church, park and library were built by the banks of the River Aire. Unlike many workers' houses in the mid-nineteenth century, Saltaire homes had running water, outside flush toilets, gas for heating and lighting, and public baths available to all. Salt's aim of ensuring that his workers had unfettered access to 'fresh air, pure water and cleanliness' was realized.

So enduring was Yorkshire's reputation for worsted spinning that in the 1920s, Ernst Gylfe, a Finn who saw the potential for high-quality worsted yarn in his native country, made a pilgrimage to Bradford to learn the nuances of worsted spinning. On returning to Helsinki, he set up a new business in 1928, which went on to become Novita, the largest yarn company in Scandinavia, a position it still holds today.

I arrive in Keighley in the continuing downpour, and strike out for the industrial estate where West Yorkshire Spinners turn wool from across Britain into hand-knitting yarn. Founded by another Ernst Gylfe, grandson of the Finn who had come to Bradford in the 1920s, and Yorkshireman Peter Longbottom in 1997, West Yorkshire Spinners is one of very few British mills that spin wool in large quantities. Longbottom began his apprenticeship with

Hayfield Textiles in 1964 and spent years working in the mills and studying commercial textiles. But by the end of the 1980s, knitting was beginning to go out of fashion in Britain – though not in Gylfe's homeland of Finland.

Come the 1990s, the hand-knitting market in Britain suffered a serious downturn; areas that were built and reliant on textile manufacturing were going to the wall as cheaper imports of yarn from Turkey and China were coming onto the market. Many of Yorkshire's spinning mills were closing down or had already become derelict; only a tiny number of small-scale mills still spun yarn, and much of this once-dominant industry's workforce was retired or out of work. Longbottom, who had worked with Gylfe at Hayfield Textiles, got in touch with his Finnish colleague at Novita to see what could be done. Both men were driven by the knowledge that if they didn't act, Yorkshire's yarn-spinning skills and heritage could be lost for ever.

So, in 1997, they set up West Yorkshire Spinners in a mill in the small village of Oxenhope, employing a modest staff of five. People told them they were crazy to open a textiles production unit when so many were closing down, but Longbottom and Gylfe proved them wrong. They began by spinning yarn for Novita and on commission for other companies, but soon found that they were outgrowing their small traditional factory. Twenty-one years after it was founded, West Yorkshire Spinners has moved premises twice, employs seventy people and champions British wool around the world. In 2013, they launched their own WYS-brand yarn, spun in Keighley from natural fibres, and have gone on to win countless awards for their yarn, including Best Brand for British Yarn every year from 2014 to 2017 at the British Knitting and Crochet Awards.

West Yorkshire Spinners have also worked closely with other like-minded local companies to help them to produce and develop their own yarn. One of these is Baa Ram Ewe in Leeds, who pride themselves on their Yorkshire heritage – and that of their yarns. Named for the Great Yorkshire Llama, Titus Salt, their signature yarn, Titus, is spun from Wensleydale Longwool, Bluefaced Leicester and alpaca, all grown in Britain. Launched along with their company on Yorkshire Day in 2012, the first commercial batch of Titus was spun by West Yorkshire Spinners, and the yarn's bright, vibrant colours are named for all things Yorkshire: Aire, Heathcliff, Parkin, Filey, White Rose. A bright orange-red shade has been dubbed 'Viking', and as soon as my eyes alight on this colour I know just what to do with it.

The Coppergate Sock stops with a line of red yarn at the ankle. We do not know if this colour continued up the wearer's leg, or whether this little sock simply ended with a bright accent, added as a flourish by its knitter. Back home, I lay the skein of 'Viking' across my lap and break off a metre length, and then another. The four-ply is so fine compared to the Léttlopi that I need to double it up. Taking up my needle for the last time, I join Yorkshire Titus to his Icelandic cousin. The circle, and the sock, is complete.

I pull the finished item on my foot. It takes no little effort: without the stretchiness of knitting, this Jorvik replica is more like a close-fitting slipper than a softly flexible sock. The stitches are dense and, though warm, quite stiff. It is also very thick: there is no way of squeezing my nålebound foot inside a shoe. I imagine the Norsemen wearing these as they went about their lives on Coppergate. There are a thousand years of Yorkshire's human history wrapped around my foot.

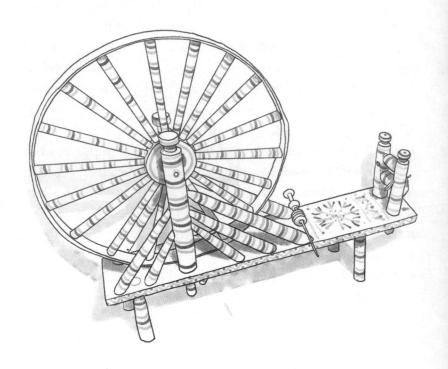

8

Knit-frocks,
Guernseys and Jerseys

As August greens under summer showers, I continue to work on Dad's gansey. Having completed the broad swathe of stocking stitch from waist to ribcage, it's now time to pattern the gansey's chest and yoke, shaping 'tree of life', 'ridge and furrow', cables and 'railroad' motifs. Though I love their twisting form, cables make me tense, nervous of their stitch-sliding trickery. Knitting too tightly tugs them into knots in place of even columns, so I try to relax my hands and give the cables the room they need to form. The wool is so dark that, as I work the first few rounds, I can't immediately pick out new patterns. Eye-blind, I rely instead on my fingertips, checking the rise and fall of the stitches with my hands as I count six blocks of fifty stitches. Knit one, purl one, cable, purl one, knit one.

August is a time for summer holidays, and in this month's stickiness I follow the knitwear trail as far south as it is possible to go on the British mainland. I pack gansey, yarn and needles into a thick canvas rucksack, the only bag through which the steel pins do not poke. My suitcase snaps at my heels as I board the southbound train: my destination is Penzance, Cornwall, where England dips her toe into the Atlantic. I have long loved England's far-west counties, with their high cliffs and deep mines.

A clutch of cousins used to live in neighbouring Devon, and we often holidayed with them, running down to sandy Mothecombe beach before throwing ourselves into surf-topped waves rolling in from the ocean.

With a coastline measured by the Ordnance Survey of over 1,000 kilometres, Cornwall is an intrinsically seafaring county. For hundreds if not thousands of years, pilchards and mackerel, skate and sardines have been landed here, fattened in the ocean's deep waters. When Richard Carew compiled the first *Survey of Cornwall* in 1602, the area's fishing industry was of national importance, and it continues thus today. And wherever you find sailors, knit-frocks will not be far away.

'Knit-frock' is Cornwall's old word for a fisherman's gansey. More particular than that: it is Polperro's word. In Newlyn, 50 miles to the north-east, they were called 'worsted frocks', their tight, smooth yarn plied from five strands. Today, 'frocks' are women's dresses, the word reminiscent of tea parties and supper dances. Yet a hundred years ago, a frock was a man's garment – the frock of frock-coats and a clergyman's de-frocking. In its earliest form, *froc* was a twelfth-century French loanword for a monk's long-sleeved habit. Mary Wright, author of *Cornish Guernseys and Knit-Frocks* (1979), notes that by the nineteenth century, a frock was 'a man's knitted garment as opposed to a sewn one' and that frock was 'often tacked on to another word for greater emphasis':[1] frock-shirts, smock-frocks, knit-frock.

For eight years in the 1970s, Mary Wright searched the parish records and fishing villages from Tamar to Land's End on the hunt for Cornwall's traditional knit-frocks. She found that almost all men wore them, from the county's many fishermen to Morwenstow's eccentric vicar, Robert Stephen Hawker (1803–1875), who paired his long Georgian coat with a blue guernsey to demonstrate his role as 'a fisher of men'. Wright had been challenged not to write a book but to knit a fisherman's jersey, copied from an old photograph, for the Royal Cornwall Show. But how had these knit-frocks traditionally been made? This quest sent her to archives and museums, to the houses and pubs of fishermen. The art seemed to have vanished from Cornwall; she was warned that she 'had started twenty years too late'.

But it wasn't too late – not quite. 'Memories have proved surprisingly vivid,' Wright noted, particularly among the older fishing communities, 'where grandmothers knitted frocks for their sons and grandsons, working in pockets for watches as "they work better when they're warm".'[2] Wright also scoured the nineteenth-century photographs taken by the Cornishman Lewis Harding, who recorded the lives and faces of Cornwall's fishing communities as they began to disappear under modernity's lure and pressure, to find patterns and designs that she used to connect people to places. Wright found no Cornish tradition of bodies being identified by their knit-frocks, though she does recall one woman picking out her grandson's jumper in a crowd, on the body of the thief who stole it. As I have done for Dad, she had worked his initials into the jumper, and was able to thereby identify and proudly claim it back.

The sun begins to dip below the horizon by the time I reach Penzance. England's westernmost end curves away along Mount's Bay as we slow to a shuddered stop after thirteen hours on the rails. Lights shine along the prom, and the dark hulk of St Michael's Mount is visible to the east. Since leaving Edinburgh this morning, the entire length of England has passed in a Dopplered blur. With the last of the day's sun staining the sky pink, I take a coatless walk in the mild evening air, which is full of the same sound of seagulls as the familiar harbour at St Andrews.

The next morning I wake to the brightest of late summer days and head east along the south Cornish coast, bound for Polperro. On my way, I pass through St Blazey, a village on St Austell Bay whose buildings cluster round the parish church of St Blaise. Perched high above roads and houses, the church looms like a marooned ship, washed up on a high tide centuries ago. The wall that borders the churchyard was built to keep out the sea: when the oldest parts of the church were constructed in the fifteenth century, spring tides lapped against this wall. The village's older, Cornish, name was Landreath, meaning 'holy place upon the sands'; only in the woollen boom of the sixteenth century did the village change its name to St Blazey. The name links it to Bishop Blaise (c. 289–316 CE), the patron saint of wool-combers.

During the fourth century, Blaise was Bishop of Sebaste, in historical Armenia, today part of Turkey. Around 312 CE, the Cappadocian governor Agricolaus began persecuting Christians; one of his victims was Blaise, who, according to legend, was tortured with iron hooks. Early icons of St Blaise portray him holding hooks not dissimilar to the hard 'heckles' used to tease out woollen fibres. Turkey was known for its manufacture of textiles from wool and silk, and some historians claim that persecutors like Agricolaus repurposed the wool combs used in this industry as instruments of torture.

At the time of the Crusades, the cult of St Blaise swept through Europe. In Italy, he was known as San Biagio and elsewhere as St Blasius; his saint's day was widely celebrated on 3 February in the Latin Church, and on 11 February in the Greek. The Crusades coincided with the growth of the English wool trade, and St Blazey is not the only place in England with a church dedicated to Blaise. The twelfth-century priory church of St Mary and St Blaise at Boxgrove in West Sussex bears his name, as do two other parish churches: the thirteenth-century collegiate chapel of St Blaise in Haccombe, Devon; and the church of St Blaise in Milton, Berkshire, where the wool staplers' mark can still be made out on a fragment of ancient glass.

*

The narrow lanes of Polperro, a port since the fourteenth century, now bustle with tourists. The small harbour is guarded by tall stone walls, nicked to allow boats to pass through into safety. Above them rise the cliffs and rocks of the natural waterfront, and, nestling on Peak Rock, is the Net Loft, a long stone building roofed in slate that saw service both as a chapel and a store for pilchard nets. It is a still late-summer morning when I climb the steep cliff path by the Blue Peter Inn, the sea twinkling benignly below. Today, there is no hint that waves crash over the top of the Net Loft in winter storms.

Clinging to the northern edge of Polperro's harbour is a low stone building, thickly walled to keep out the wildest weather. Once a pilchard factory, it is the home of the Polperro Heritage Museum of Smuggling and Fishing, containing the only permanent exhibition of Cornish knit-frocks. Sandwiched between glass-fronted cases filled with smuggling paraphernalia – including nappies stuffed with replica drugs and swags of ropes and nets – is a vitrine of knitwear and its attendant tools.

Hand-written labels in faded ink tell the knit-frocks' story. Old knitting wires, curved with use like those of the Daleswomen, sit beside knitting sticks and guards, known as 'knitting fish' in St Ives and 'knitting shades' in Polperro. S. Winifred Paynter's *Old St Ives* (1927) notes that in the 1920s a St Ives knitter had 'tied round her waist a wooden fish, in the open mouth of which the end of one of her needles rested'.[3] Around 20 centimetres long and curved to mirror the wearer's torso, it would hold the working needle upright so that the knitter could 'strike the loop faster than the eye could see', reaching a speed of some 200 stitches a minute. Today, the record stands at 262 stitches per minute from the flicker-fast fingers of Shetland's Hazel Tindall. The simplest of these knitting sticks is a stick of elder stripped of its spongey pith. The most ornate was carved from the wood from the wreck of the *HMS Nelson* in 1926.

Beside the sticks are samples of the knitting stitches that Wright translated from historic photographs. The patterns are named after the man on whose chest they appear: John Northcott, five generations of Charles Jolliffs, Richard Searle. Men who would be long forgotten, were it not for Mary Wright's keen eye, are recalled in stitches. Each pattern stands for a person. Some names are not known, as in a photograph entitled 'The Boy Musicians', but 'musicians' is a pattern featuring the same arrows as those on the squeeze-box-player's chest. Like Gladys Thompson in her *Patterns for Guernseys, Jerseys and Arans* in northern England and Scotland, Wright named the patterns retrospectively.

Most knit-frocks were of local make. Many of the museum's photographs show Cornish girls and women knitting, huge part-finished guernseys hanging by their waists and balls of yarn pinned to their skirts or placed in baskets. In the case of Jane Jolliff, captured knitting by Polperro's Peak Rock in 1904, her yarn is spiked on the cliff path's iron railings. Throughout the industrial boom years of the nineteenth century, when many sought new lives in North America and the Antipodes, Cornwall's female knitters turned to their pins to support themselves. Usually the women were contracted to knit for a local agent, who supplied the yarn they turned into finished knit-frocks, paying them on completion and then selling their work on to merchants and wholesalers. In 1859, the Liskeard draper J. Eliot wanted 'immediately, 100 Hands to Knit Frocks', with the caveat that 'They must be quite competent to undertake the work.' Ten years later, Looe's drapers placed a similar advertisement for '500 good frock knitters', promising 'constant employment'.[4]

From Looe, knitters would transport their wares to Plymouth, carrying eight to ten finished guernseys on their backs as they walked to W. Johns and Co., drapers in Old Town Street. With wooden overshoes known as 'pattens' on their feet, the women knitted as they walked, sometimes pinning a spare skein of yarn to their skirts 'so they would never run out'.[5] Their time was not paid, and they would return with packs stuffed with yarn for the next consignment. The system was open to abuse, as shopkeepers got to decide the value of the goods exchanged in payment. One Looe shopkeeper 'insisted that all her knitters were paid with goods from the shop and absolutely refused to make cash payments'.[6]

I leave Cornwall as night falls, travelling north-east under cloudy skies. As the train hurtles on and the countryside disappears under thick banks of mist, I take out my gansey and work its yoke, wielding the needles carefully in my seat. I am bound for Portsmouth, where, after a too-short night in a portside Travelodge, I will climb aboard a ferry heading south. Next stop is Jersey, twelve hours away across the Channel.

The Bailiwick of Jersey is the largest Crown dependency in the Channel Islands, a cluster of seven inhabited, and some thirteen smaller uninhabited, islands and islets. Like its sister bailiwick, Guernsey, Jersey was once part of the Duchy of Normandy. Though England's mainland Norman territories are long gone, to this day the British Crown appoints the islands' Lieutenant Governor and Bailiff to rule in the monarch's stead, but the islands do have their own parliaments, known as the States, and issue their own coins and banknotes.

Guernsey and Jersey have long been associated with the craft of knitting. Whilst 'ganseys' might be 'garnseys' for some, the name 'guernsey' for a sailor's knitted jumper persists. Though today 'jersey' refers to sweaters or fabric, the word was first used to describe an especially fine type of worsted yarn.[7] In 1662, Jean Poingdestre (1609–91) recorded in *Cæsarea*, his history of Jersey, that there were three methods of spinning wool on the islands: one used the treadless 'Great Wheel' to produce woollen-spun yarn; another the 'small wheel' for what is termed Guernsey or Jersey yarn ('because that manner of spinning was first practised in these isles');[8] the third was the drop spindle for spinning worsted, which Jersey folk termed 'upon the rock'. As late as 1882, Samuel William Beck wrote in *The Draper's Dictionary* that 'Jarsey is still the local name for worsted in Lancashire'.[9]

'Jersey' also had another meaning in the seventeenth and eighteenth centuries: it was used to refer to combed wool ready for spinning. Tradesmen from London and Canterbury were registered variously as 'jersey-weavers' and 'jersey-combers' from the sixteenth century onwards, and in 1657 it was noted that 'the finest sorts of wools [are] ready combed into jarsies for worke'.[10] The earliest written usage of 'jersey' to mean a fitted jumper or upper garment dates from 1837.

The crossing from Portsmouth to Jersey takes all day. On departure the remains of yesterday's haze linger in the Solent, but as we pull out into open water, the sky clears and all is sunny-still.

I wedge myself into a corner of the viewing deck and watch England slip away. In the bar next door, truckers knock back pints of lager, and out on deck a brave few nurse cigarettes. Needles out, I work away at Dad's gansey, patterning the chest with rows of knit and purl.

The boat, delayed by high winds off Alderney, docks in Jersey's capital as the sun begins to set. St Helier's modern harbour is a mass of luxury yachts and shipping containers, flanked by a backdrop of tower blocks and glassy modern buildings. Walking from the port into town, I catch sight of a trace of the island's knitting history. Beside the harbour stands a bigger-than-life-size statue of a sailor, hauling on a heavy rope attached to some imagined ship. With a cap low on his forehead, he wears a jersey, with an anchor in relief across the chest. I run my fingers along his knitted metal arm, and feel the rise of every stitch realized in steel.

Yet it was stockings, not jumpers, that first brought Jersey's knitting to international attention. In 1586, William Camden's chorographical survey *Britannia* recorded that 'Their woman gain by knitting stockings which we call Jersey stockings.'[11] Best known of all knitted Jersey-wear is a pair of woollen hose worn underneath worsted stockings by Mary Queen of Scots at her execution in 1587: 'nether stocke of worsted coloured watchett clocked with silver and edged on the topps with silver and next her legges a paire of Jersey hose white'.[12] Queen Elizabeth, who ordered Mary's execution, gave Jersey stockings a second, and more enduring, royal endorsement. In 1601, having been presented with a pair of 'Jarsey stockes' by the governor of Jersey, Sir Walter Raleigh, she granted a licence to the islanders 'to trade freely in knitted woollen articles with the English mainland in perpetuity'.[13] This ancient right was last invoked on the island in 1962, when the British government introduced levies on imports to the UK. Negotiators from Jersey's one remaining knitwear

manufacturer, the Channel Island Knitwear Company, were able to claim exemption by virtue of Elizabeth I's charter.

By the first decade of the seventeenth century, knitted stockings had become Jersey's main export, with nearly half the population knitting items for sale. But 'too many hale and strong persons' preferred knitting to manual labour, and as a result agriculture on Jersey began to suffer. In 1608, the States passed an Act forbidding anyone over the age of fifteen from knitting at harvest time and when the *vraic* – pronounced 'wrack' – was gathered from the shore to be used as a fertilizer; the penalty for so doing was imprisonment on bread and water, or sitting in the stocks. This Act had little effect and, nine years later, the States tried a different tack to control the burgeoning stocking industry: introducing inspections of stockings for quality, with the threat of fines hanging over anyone found to be knitting with inferior wool.

In 1637, a report of the Privy Council recorded knitters in Jersey making 6,000 pairs of stockings, using 100 tods of uncombed wool; 100 tods weighed 200 stone, or a little over 1 metric ton. Jersey's sheep alone could not supply all this fleece, and additional wool had to be imported from England. Throughout the seventeenth century, the trade continued to grow and in 1662, Poingdestre noted that there were 'many houses where man, wife and children, beginning at the age of five or six [...] make everyone a pair of stockings every week, which must come to more than 10,000 pairs weekly'.[14]

Come the end of the eighteenth century, the French Revolutionary Wars caused a great scarcity of wool on the island, which 'hampered growth of exports, and eventually knitters were rationed with a small quantity of wool each and penalties were imposed for those hoarding supplies.'[15] But, despite fluctuations in the supply of wool from England to Jersey, knitting continued to be a part of island life. In 1809, J. Stead observed in his illustrated travelogue *A Picture of Jersey: Or, A Stranger's Companion Through That Island* that 'Stockings, gloves, and various other Articles of Dress' were being made from 4,000 tods of wool imported into the island. By this time, most men had relinquished the needles; 'This is the Chief Employment of the Women', he writes, and, with admiration: 'The Dexterity and Expedition with which they dispatch a Pair of Stockings are almost incredible. To them Light and Darkness are indifferent.' Like women knitting ganseys in the dark of a Scottish winter, Jersey's knitters could knit by touch alone.

The importance of knitting to the island economy is borne out in Jersey's historic tongue, Jèrriais. Combining Norman French, Norse, English and Breton influences, Jèrriais was the first language of most of the island until the end of the nineteenth century; English was only allowed in debate in the chamber of the States from 1900. Until the Second World War, Jèrriais was still spoken by half the island's population, but with the disruption of the evacuation and occupation, it ceased to be the island's main language. However, when I arrive, I catch a taste of it: stepping off the ferry, I am greeted with the words *Séyiz les beinv'nus*; and on the street, rubbish bins offer me the choice of *Papi*, *Tinnes* or *Tés* for my waste.

Jersey knitters used a specific vocabulary for their trade. 'To knit' in Jèrriais was not *tricoter*, as in French, but *ouvrer*, meaning 'to work'. Jersey's stocking knitters were *ouvreux* and *ouvreuses*, men and women respectively. Knitting was vital in Jersey – in the words of J. Stead, 'so attached are they to this employment that they have appropriated to knitting the Name of Work'.[16]

The following day dawns, a mild, damp morning, I head into the island's heart, catching a bus bound for La Hougue Bie. Stepping off at a crossroads by a small garage, I turn down quiet lanes overhung with trees and fringed by fields. There is no one else about, though I hear a tractor's rumble in the distance. Three hundred years ago, the lanes of Jersey would have been thronged not only with travellers but also with groups of local women. In warmer weather, women would 'assemble in large Numbers, and sit in a Ring under the Trees, which make of all the Roads a continued Avenue'.[17] In the breezy shade, they sat and spun or knitted, chatting and singing as they worked. As in other communities in Britain where knitting constituted a major part of the economy, judgement of the 'hand idle' could be fearsome. Stead describes it in these unequivocal terms: 'A Woman seen Walking without a Stocking in her Hand is stigmatized with idleness'.[18]

I arrive at Hamptonne Country Life Museum as the drizzle turns to rain, and take shelter in the knot of mediaeval farm buildings clustered round a courtyard. Climbing broad wooden stairs, I enter the parlour, a large room where the wealthy Langlois family and their friends would spend their evenings. Inside stands a short spinning wheel on three legs. Narrow in the beam, its wheel has broad spindles, its shaft held by five tapering poles called 'stays'. Turned to a smooth finish, it is a thing of beauty. Unlike most other spinning wheels I have seen, Jersey Wheels can be brightly patterned in stripes and dots of red, black and gold. Like the Great Wheel it has no treadle, but instead a small hand-crank demanding to be turned. In Jèrriais, a spinning wheel is *lé rouet* and wool *la trème*. A Jersey saying, '*lé cat file sa trème*', describes the rhythmic sound of a cat's purr to perfection: 'the cat spinning its wool'.[19]

In the corner of the room is a kind of raised settle, like a chaise longue with two enclosed sides. This is a *jontchéthe*, its seat stuffed with rushes or gorse. Come September, the outdoor gatherings in Jersey's lanes would move inside, the shady arbour of the roads grown cold with the changing seasons. These meetings were known as *les veilles*, 'the evenings', with the year's first session dubbed *L'Assise dé Veille* – 'the evening sitting'.

At *les veilles*, held from sunset until midnight, women would comb or card their day's provision of wool, and as they worked they would 'indulge their native Mirth in innocent recreation, and the Song of Festivity forbids the Intrusion of Melancholy'. And it wasn't just women: 'The young Men, returned from their more hardy Occupations of the Day, repair to these cheerful Meetings.'[20] On the evening of 23 December, folk gathered for *la longue veille*, an evening spent completing knitted wares to sell at the market on Christmas Eve. Women decorated the room with greenery, furze, palm leaves and a *mênagiéthe* – a festive wreath 'made of wickerwork covered with coloured papers'.[21] At the market the following day, knitters sold their garments alongside farmers selling crops and animals, and the money raised was then used to buy Christmas fare and presents.[22]

By the mid-nineteenth century, Jersey's hand-knitting industry was on the wane. In 1837, Jersey historian Edward Durell (1781–1848) lamented that 'the knitting of stockings declined by degrees and has now ceased altogether as a branch of trade'.[23] People still knitted for personal use in what Durell dubbed 'the land of knitter', and these knitters – like the Herring Girls – were public in their work: 'Strangers may remark it as a peculiar feature in the character of the people, to see females of the humbler classes, knitting as they move leisurely along the lanes in the country.'[24] The 1842 edition of *A Guide to the Island of Jersey* shows that industrialization was in part to blame: 'Some [stockings] are made, though to a very small extent: the use of machinery in the making of this article in England has caused the Jersey-made stockings to be confined to a limited home demand'.[25] Where once 6,000 pairs a week were sold, now 'the export [is] not exceeding 1000 pair annually, and these for the use of persons on the fishing stations in British North America'.[26]

In 1851, Jersey sent examples of its fine woollen goods to the Great Exhibition at the Crystal Palace in Hyde Park in London; the island's newspaper noted with pride that this included 'twelve pairs of knit stockings the manufacture of various parts of the Island, and showing the high perfection to which this art was formerly brought in Jersey.'[27] Other items included a 'Purse of chaste and intricate design, fringed and skilfully knit of pure coloured silk, by a lady aged 83', and, perhaps even more remarkably, a 'pair of ordinary grey worsted socks, knitted in the Jersey style, by a lady aged 93 without the aid of glasses'.[28]

How did knitting come to be such an important part of Jersey life? In part it is due to the island's pastoral past: long before Jersey cows became famous for their rich milk, the Channel Islands were a predominantly sheep-farming archipelago. Sheep have lived on Jersey for at least six millennia: Neolithic sheep remains have been found at Pinnacle Rock and St Ouen in the north-west, and at La Hougue Bie in the south-east. Ovine bones were also buried at sacred sites by the island's dolmens, indicating that sheep were held in high regard by Stone Age Jersey people. Wool was being worked here then too, and by the dolmens of Grantez and Geonnais, pierced stone spindles used for spinning thread have been found.[29]

What were these early Jersey sheep like? Seventeenth-century chroniclers describe them as an abundantly horned breed, small, dark and hardy: 'The wool is fine but generally black or dark coloured and the lamb is in high repute for its delicious flavour.'[30] Like Soays and Manx Loaghtans, Jersey sheep were resilient, 'cropping the scanty herbage growing along the cliffs on the north and west coasts of the Island, in places and in pastures where no other live stock could exist'.[31] They were also in possession of multiple horns; Poingdestre notes that ewes most commonly had four horns, and rams six: 'that is three of each side whereof two made a circle towards the nose, two others another circle backwards towards the ears and two stood upright between them, which kind was of small size'.[32] This peculiarity is also referred to in the jaunty couplets of Michael Drayton's 1612 rhyming journey through the British Isles, *Poly-Olbion*:

> *Faire Jersey, first of these heere scattred in the Deepe,*
> *Peculiarlie that boast'st thy double-horned sheepe.*[33]

But even in 1662, the old Jersey breed was already in decline: 'almost abolished by the substitution of a large kind like those on Salisbury plain'.[34]

The Jersey custom of *lé banon* meant that flocks could graze freely across unenclosed land from September's harvest time until new crops were sown in spring. Wheat stubble, heathlands and grasslands were used for rough pasture; during the spring and summer crop seasons, flocks were kept in pens or pounds known as *vergs*. Although abolished by statute in 1771, *lé banon* continued unofficially until the beginning of the nineteenth century. In 1791, Jersey had around ten thousand sheep, at that time outnumbering cows. Once *lé banon* ceased, sheep were grazed in sheep runs, and by the early years of the twentieth century, sheep farming had all but disappeared in favour of cattle, although the north-west, around St Ouen, continued its connection to sheep longer than did other parts of the island. A different type of sheep seems to have been farmed here, a fact that is reflected in the Jèrriais terms for sheep. The linguist and historian Frank Le Maistre (1910–2002) notes that '*bèrcas*' was used to mean sheep in general, but '*du bèrcas d'falaise*' (meaning 'of the cliffs') referred to beasts grazed on the island's north and west coasts, regarded as inferior stock. The expression was then applied pejoratively to people to imply a lack of refinement.

Men from St Ouen were known as *les gris-ventres*, or 'grey-bellies', the name derived from the close-fitting jerseys they wore, knitted from the wool of their own sheep – to this day, *les gris-ventres* is a nickname for one born or living in the parish of St Ouen. In contrast, Jersey fishermen from other parishes wore the dyed indigo jumpers found from Lerwick in Shetland to the Netherlands. Not only did Jersey's fishermen wear jerseys, they also knitted them. A nineteenth-century visitor from Barfleur in Normandy wrote with surprise that 'The fishermen of Jersey were all knitting! They carried their knitting in a clean bag ... while waiting to haul, they washed their hands [...] and began to knit.'[35]

In modern times, Jersey's north-west coast has become home to another breed of sheep. In 2012, the National Trust for Jersey resettled a herd of twenty Manx Loaghtans there as part of a controlled grazing programme, this hardy horned breed chosen for their dark-fleeced similarity to the island's native breed. Since then they have flourished, and within five years increased their number to two hundred.

As with the Scottish islands, where knitting traditions thrived thanks to their sea-borne connections with other cultures, throughout the mediaeval and early modern period the Channel Islands welcomed sailors and merchants from across the known world. Spain and France had a booming trade in knitwear and Protestant refugees sought succour and freedom from religious persecution on the islands, as seen in the old tales told at *les veilles*. Durell noted that as well as telling 'the strange stories of olden times: – of ghosts, of witchcraft', the knitters also talked 'of the dreadful Persecutions, which drove so many French Protestants to such an asylum on our friendly shores'.[36] Some may have been members of the Parisian guilds, whose master craftsmen had been making intricate and expensive stockings in the French capital since the sixteenth century. Others were Huguenot spinners, like those who ended up in Norfolk and Suffolk.

There is, however, one further theory about the genesis of the Channel Islanders' dexterity with yarn. In Halifax, West Yorkshire's great wool town, I found mention of Bishop Blaise and his skill with wool. When a new town hall was built there in 1779, the following ode was composed in celebration, championing Blaise and his connection to Jersey:

Oh, let us not forget the good
The worthy Bishop Blaize
Who came from Jersey here to us
As ancient Hist'ry says

He taught us how to Comb our Wool
The Source of all our Wealth,
Then let us still remember him,
While we have Life and Health.

In the 1950s, the historian T. F. Priaulx suggested St Blaise was not beheaded or flayed to death as per the hagiography, but instead fled to Caesarea (the Roman name for Jersey), where he taught the inhabitants to comb wool. In 1959, the magazine of the Jersey Society in London developed the theory further: 'It was known from earliest times that Jersey was a Christian settlement and [St Blaise] may well have wished to return to so remote a spot, as far from his tormentors as possible. He may also have taken with him a knowledge of wool manufacture as practised in the East and later gone over to England and taught them the secrets of wool-combing.'[37]

But I have my doubts. There were three places in the Roman world known by the name Caesarea: Jersey, a place in Judea, and another in Cappadocia. The chances of St Blaise fleeing to the Channel Islands seem far less likely than him travelling to either modern-day Israel or Turkey. To my mind, this is a false linguistic friend translated into folklore.

The following day, I head to nearby Guernsey. After a two-hour ferry hop, where I work my way through a few more gansey rows, I arrive at St Peter Port. Unlike bold St Helier, with its modern marina, Guernsey greets me with a few lights twinkling in the darkness behind a battered shipping port. The islands have a long-held rivalry and consider themselves quite different and distinct. Where Jersey is sleek and busy, Guernsey seems to me an island operating on a different time.

Guernsey's earliest written references to knitting date from the sixteenth century. On New Year's Day 1556, Sir Leonard

Chamberlain, Governor of Guernsey, gave Queen Mary Tudor four waistcoats, four pairs of sleeves and four pairs of hose, all Guernsey-made. Priaulx notes that in Guernésiais, the island's ancient language, waistcoats are *'corsets d'oeuvre'* or 'knitted corsets'[38] and were possibly similar to a modern jumper or a fitted undergarment known as a 'spencer'.[39] An inventory of the royal wardrobe in 1578 during the reign of James VI of Scotland details three pairs of worsted hose and six pairs of gloves of Guernsey manufacture. Elizabeth I's wardrobe also included Guernsey stockings. The Crown accounts of 1586 record 'a payment of twenty shillings for a pair of knitted Guernsey stockings – *caligarum nexat de factura Garneseie'*[40] – with their tops and 'clocks' (decorative patterns worn on the shin) worked in silk.

In 1581, Guernsey wool-combers were being paid a groat (four pennies) a day,[41] and by the early years of the seventeenth century, Guernsey's knitting industries were well established. In 1605, the royal court ordered that combed wool must be cleaned and washed for sale, and set the wool-combers' wages at ten *derniers* (pence) a day for those who worked for themselves. This was the same rate of pay as for carpenters, stonecutters, masons and slaters, far more than a labourer earned. In 1611, the sale of all knitted waistcoats, blankets and stockings was regulated by court decree, stating that three-ply wool must be used to ensure quality.

As on Jersey, much of Guernsey's wool for knitting was imported from England. In 1616, the States of Guernsey, the island's parliament, gave their permission for Peter De Beauvoir, a London-based Guernseyman, to apply for a licence from the Privy Council to import 500 tods – some 6 tonnes – of wool to the island. By 1622, the licence had been granted, though its wording demonstrates that the export of wool from England to Guernsey was a matter of some long standing: it was granted 'for the continuance of the like favour as hath anciently afforded unto them'. The licence also made clear that this wool was intended to benefit the knitters of Guernsey, 'who are chiefly employed in converting wool into stockings and other knitt ware'. Knitted 'wares', meaning goods for sale, long predates the modern compound 'knitwear' (knitted things that are worn), which did not appear in English until the 1920s.[42]

Guernsey benefitted too from its proximity to France, where the island's stockings commanded high prices and aristocratic patronage. The Anglo-French War of 1627–9 disrupted this trade, though the 1483 Papal Bull of Neutrality ensured that some measure of commerce could continue locally.[43] The States recorded that there was 'sufficient interruption to cause distress among the poorer people in Guernsey' and took control of the trade; in 1629, they even gave Colonel Piperell, who oversaw works in the island during the war, a knitted camisole in gratitude for his labours in repairing defences.[44] Until the reign of Louis XIV (1643–1715), French traders continued to come to the Channel Islands to buy stockings: 'the knitted goods of Guernsey bore so high a reputation that they were thought worthy of being offered to princes as presents'.[45]

This tradition of giving Guernsey-knitted goods to royalty continued into the twentieth century. When Queen Elizabeth and the royal family made a trip to Guernsey in 1957, members of the island's Federation of Women's Institutes knitted guernseys for their visit. Nimble hands from St Saviour made the Queen's, the parish of St Peter turned out Prince Philip's, Fermain's knitters made one for the young Prince Charles, and St Peter Port made the smallest guernsey, for six-year-old Princess Anne.[46]

Guernsey continues to produce and sell island-made knitwear to this day. In 1965, Robert MacDougall set up Le Tricoteur ('The Knitter') on the island. Buying up industrial knitting machines from Yorkshire, he developed a workshop that churned out thousands of flat-knitted pieces ready to be turned into guernseys by six hand-knitters. By 1993, Le Tricoteur used three industrial knitting machines and employed over a hundred hand-knitters. In

2017, it remains the only working manufactory of guernseys on the island, employing five factory workers and over thirty piecework knitters to make several thousand guernseys every year.

I take the bus round the island's coast and we pass endless low houses, brightly painted, many with palms in the gardens. The sea rolls over the rocks at Rocquaine Bay as the bus draws up by a small industrial estate, where Le Tricoteur's long, low workshops face the sea. By the door are a row of paper potato-sacks, each emblazoned with a knitter's name. The knitted pieces, made from yarn worsted-spun in Yorkshire, come off the factory's Stoll machines and are placed in the sacks before being delivered to the home knitters once a week, for them to knit shoulders, necks and underarm gussets. Most of Le Tricoteur's knitters are elderly and work from home. This is not a subsistence occupation – many do it for the pleasure and the pride in making guernseys on Guernsey.

During the eighteenth and nineteenth centuries, Guernsey's Town Hospital in St Peter Port – comprising hospital, workhouse, orphanage and asylum, the largest institution on the island – started to put its inhabitants to work in the production of various textiles, including linen and knitted goods. Whole families lived there and children would be apprenticed to trades deemed suitable for their station. In 1808, a School of Industry was set up in the Town Hospital, run by local women. Knitting and spinning were added at the suggestion of the hospital board in 1817, which reported that 'girls to the number of about sixty knew no other means of earning their living than by the use of the needle'.[47]

The School of Industry was not the only charity-supported knitting manufactory in the Channel Islands. In 1901, Father Leon Le Grand and his sister Maria Le Grand, Mother General of the Sacré Coeur order in Amiens, arrived on Jersey and founded the Sacré Coeur Orphanage at Summerland, a large site on the outskirts of St Helier. From the first, it trained the female orphans in clothing and textile work. Early projects for Jersey's orphans included hand-sewn and knitted garments, hand-machined socks, and loom-made carpets. Production of knitwear on a more commercial scale started in 1905 at the *ouvroir* – Jèrriais for 'knittery' – at Summerland. Under the direction of Louis Jules Sangan, a Jersey-born tailor trained in Paris, who was awarded the Gold Medal for Haute Couture, large-scale manufacturing machinery was introduced and a purpose-built factory constructed.

By the 1930s, the Summerland knitwear factory was employing people from outside the orphanage, though the influence of the nuns remained. The working day started and ended with prayer, to 'bring upon their work the blessings of God'. Regulations were strict: workers arriving after 8 a.m. were locked out until the mid-morning break, with loss of pay. Talking at work was punished with a fine, and girls were forbidden to roll up their sleeves above the elbow as they laboured.

Jersey's proximity to mainland Europe had been its trading strength in the seventeenth century; in 1939, it became a hazard. Deemed too close to France to be defensible, the Channel Islands were left without military support from mainland Britain. On 1 July 1940, Germany invaded Jersey. The factory at Summerland closed soon after, as its manager, Robert Sangan, was arrested for refusing to use the factory to manufacture German army uniforms.[48] However, Sangan was soon released, and on 21 October 1940 Summerland was nationalized by the States to provide employment and to coordinate the production, purchasing and supply of clothing for the entire island. The States Textile Department ordered 10,000 pounds of underwear wool, 200 pounds of white sewing cotton, 500 yards of facing materials, and 200 Singer sewing machine needles from France. As they could not import wool from England, they also unpicked wool from old garments, rewound it, and made it into new clothes.

Around a hundred children lived with the sisters at Summerland during the Second World War. One of these orphans became a nun herself: Sister Peter, born in Guernsey, and brought to Summerland as a teenage worker. Sister Peter took delight in small acts of patriotic defiance, and became notorious for wearing French Tricolor and Union Jack decorations to work. This was not encouraged by the management, as the orphanage and factory were regularly inspected by the Germans. In an interview in 1994, Sister Peter gleefully recalled that 'immediately before the official German tour of inspection' she deliberately put red, white and blue yarn in her machine. Robert Sangan, reinstated as the factory manager, 'suggested that discretion might, in this case, be preferable to valour, and suggested that she remove the patriotic but politically incorrect material'.[49] Other workers remember extra young people being employed at Summerland, simply to avoid being deported.

By January 1942, the company was running out of raw materials, and the whole island was faced with chronic clothing shortages. The Bailiff of Jersey was appealed to – the shortage of finer wool for use in the manufacture of undergarments was a matter 'of vital importance, as up to the present moment only 200 lbs of underwear wool had been received'. By 1944, the situation had deteriorated further. The Allied D-Day landings in Normandy on 6 June 1944 left the island unable to import supplies from France. Come March 1945, the factory could no longer operate, as 'the shortage of raw materials was becoming very acute. After much discussion, it was decided that the factory would officially close on 28 April 1945.'[50] Less than two weeks later, on 9 May, the German garrison surrendered – Liberation Day for Jersey.

Post-war Summerland was a different place. There were no more compulsory prayers before work or the strict silence enforced by the nuns. Music had been introduced by the workers during the war: 'Just before Christmas 1943, the girls clubbed together to raise £7 towards the cost of installing a gramophone and amplifier to get "music while they worked".' In April 1944, the social committee made an appeal for gramophone needles as another wartime shortage temporarily silenced the music.[51] But the Church's influence still prevailed: it was not until 1975 that the nuns applied for a papal dispensation so that Catholic staff no longer had to stop working on Holy Days of Obligation. Even when the factory finally closed in the 1990s, a French-speaking nun was still employed in the company's quality control department, and 'a Vatican appointee still sat on the Board in the shape of a Jesuit accountant'.[52]

In 1964, Summerland became the Channel Islands Knitwear Co., and to celebrate its relaunch it revived a Channel Islands tradition – the fisherman's jersey. In the attic of a house in St Martin, 'an ancient Jersey' was unearthed, apparently 'some sixty years old, but still in perfect condition'.[53] The garment's main feature was the 'distinctive parish shield knitted into the front of the garment', believed to denote the fishing village from which its owner hailed – an anchor, the emblem of St Clements, a fishing parish on the south coast with long connections with the sea.

The company began to reproduce copies of this old jersey, the prototype for what became a sailing garment recognizable worldwide, proudly announcing that theirs were the first genuine jerseys to be machine-knitted on the island. Produced in navy blue and sold at 82*s*. 6*d*. (about £72 in 2017)[54], 'the slimline appearance makes the Jersey intrinsically more fashionable than its close relative, the Guernsey'.[55] With gussets at the neck and sleeves, it was advertised as 'the ultimate practical garment'; after the navy blue, the company brought out the 'natural' undyed jersey – a modern homage to the 'grey-bellies'.

Throughout the 1960s and 1970s, the Channel Islands Knitwear Co. became known worldwide for its Pierre Sangan range, named for the grandson of the company's founder and marketed to businessmen and yacht-owners from Jersey to the Caribbean. The company was quick to see the potential of product placement as advertising; when Chris Bonington led the 1975 British Mount Everest South west Face expedition, the team was clad in Channel Island jerseys. Peter Sangan then capitalized on this exceptional publicity by planning a new range for the American market, grandly titled 'Sheer Knit 29,000' – the summit of Everest being 29,000 feet (8,839 metres) above sea level.

But Jersey's modern connection with the knitted jersey was short-lived. By 1979, the Channel Islands Knitwear Co. was in recession; in 1981, it sold its Summerland premises and the business was dissolved in the 1990s. Jersey had maintained a commercial knitwear industry almost continuously from the sixteenth to the twentieth century – but no longer.

Leaving the islands on the ferry, I pick up Dad's gansey to continue my own knitted endeavour. I calculate that I have spent more than a hundred hours knitting it already, and it is still far from finished. But I do not have the time to complete it as I work my way north – another project, and another month, is calling.

9

Shetland Stitches

After a few restorative days at home in Fife, it is a crisp clear autumn morning when I head north once more. Some fields still sway golden in the sun, their crops yet to be cut, but most are carpeted with stubble, studded with round cakes of straw or squat bales of hay. A few have already been turned back to earth in hasty labour for a winter crop, and still more remain green with grass and speckled with thistles and rosebay willowherb. The train trundles across the long rail bridge as it curves over the Tay and into Dundee, sunlight flickering through the girders arched above. The autumn sunlight keeps me company as we push on to Aberdeen, bound for Britain's most northerly isles.

I am on my way to Shetland Wool Week, highlight of the serious knitter's calendar. Eight days of workshops, talks, walks and plenty of knitting, Shetland Wool Week began in 2010 and the islands now welcome over six hundred knitters from across the world for one intense week in early autumn. Run by the Shetland Amenity Trust in partnership with businesses, charities and knitters across the islands, Shetland Wool Week is a joyous festival of all things woollen. In these last eight months of knitting daily, my speed and technique have improved, but still I shrink from turning my hand to knitting lace, from the terror of steeking – the brutal necessity of cutting a piece of knitwear, in order to, say, turn a jumper into a cardigan. During this busy week, I will take part in workshops on dyeing, colour blending and lace knitting, putting myself on a knitting crash course.

An archipelago of some sixteen inhabited and more than eighty uninhabited islands, Shetland lies some 50 miles north-east of Orkney, closer to Bergen in Norway than to my ferry's departure port of Aberdeen. In the bright September sunshine, I drag my suitcase between seagulls and containers, cars and lorries. The NorthLink ferry's bulk glints in the dock. At the stroke of five, we slowly pull away from the harbour, the sea rippling gently and endlessly, millions of minute murmurs of motion. Over the tannoy, the captain reassuringly announces that we're due a calm crossing.

Beneath me, the boat rises and falls, regular as breathing. The swish of the ferry, of hull through the sea, is like the steady rush of arterial blood. Outside, the horizon has faded to a limey yellow and the sea has darkened. Its surface remains glassily calm and not a single white horse rides beside us. As we trundle north, a smoke-grey *smirr* of cloud drapes itself like a shawl across the sky, the sunset's final golden flash bookended between it and the heavy dark mass of the mainland. Birds fly past, their small black silhouettes determinedly outpacing us.

I make my way into the ferry's heart. The quiet of the main cabin is occasionally broken by a snore or a snuffle, or the rustle of feet on the floor. Outside the shop, a little girl, not more than three, chatters nonsense to her parents, who are draped over adjacent leather-covered benches, trying to sleep. Too excited to drift off myself, I pick up an embroidery needle to put the finishing touches to my 'Bousta Beanie'. Designed by Shetland-born designer Gudrun Johnston, this is a hat with a purpose and a pedigree: it is the official pattern for the 2017 Shetland Wool Week. I knitted mine from scraps of Shetland yarn left over from my Dentdale gloves and it is nearly complete, a warm guddle of soft, sheepy-scented stitches. In the ferry's dim light, I concentrate on working in the yarn ends, and finish the hat's last stitch as the ferry stops to take in one more glut of passengers at Orkney.

Shetland has long been famous for its knitting, a staple of the island's economy since the sixteenth century. In the 1580s, fishing vessels from continental Europe visited Shetland in their hundreds, and Dutch, Flemish and German sailors traded with locals for knitted stockings and mittens. Each June, ships anchored in the Sound of Bressay, the stretch of water linking Lerwick with the isle of Bressay, and the Johnsmas Fair at midsummer became the primary market for these knitted goods.[1] Shetland's women sold their knitted wares directly to the sailors, and before long, rumours began to circulate that trade between the two did not stop at knitwear. In 1615, a Shetland woman was sexually assaulted and mortally injured when selling stockings to the sailors, and in 1625 the Shetland authorities issued a decree that the Dutch sailors' shacks at Lerwick should be 'utterly demolished and down cast to the ground', along with the imperative that the knitters' husbands and sons should do business in their stead.[2]

By the eighteenth century, the industry had grown, involving middlemen and merchants who sold on behalf of the knitters. In 1711, almost four thousand pairs of stockings were exported by just a single Lerwick merchant, and in 1724 a Shetland landowner drew up a contact for his tenants to provide several hundred pairs of stockings for sale. The Shetland archivist Brian Smith suggests that the tenants supplied knitted stockings as part of their rent, along with fish. Shetland knitwear ended up in far-flung places – in 1736, eight hundred pairs of stockings were shipped to Oporto in Portugal, and ten years later 1,590 pairs made their way to Hamburg in Germany. In 1818, Lawrence Levenson opened a knitwear shop in Lerwick, the first hosiery warehouse in Shetland, whose purpose was to work directly with knitters and export their knitted goods south to the rest of Britain.[3]

After a night spent half-upright, I arrive in Shetland in the blazing sunshine of a still September morning. The MV *Hjaltland* docks just after seven and the sea by Lerwick harbour shimmers glass-bright as my suitcase and I rattle our way along the quay. It is brighter than the mainland here, the sun reflecting off the sea. A fish jumps noisily from the water, and ducks and gulls bob in the low-tide soup. Boats loll and slap against walls and chains, and one sailor bails out his boat with a bowl. Each dish of liquid disturbs the water's glossy surface, making him the centre of his own small world of ripples.

This early Shetland morning, with its perfect weather and sun-bright seafront, has a daydream feel. My inner ear rocking from the ferry, I wobble round Shetland Museum in a daze. It is quiet here too, but gently dark. I pass through three thousand years of Shetland history in an hour, following its early settlers and its mediaeval fishermen, its crofters and its store-keepers.

Most of all, I follow centuries of Shetland knitting, and millennia of Shetland sheep.

Sheep have grazed in Shetland for over five thousand years; ancient ovine remains have been identified at Jarlshof, near the southern tip of Mainland, and, like those found at Skara Brae on Orkney, were from animals rather larger than today's Shetland breed. More like the wild Soay sheep of St Kilda, they predate the *villsau* brought to Shetland around the ninth century by the Vikings.[4] They also had coats that combined more than one type of fibre – not quite the double coat of the *villsau*, with their soft inner and coarse outer hairs, but heterotype fibres, broad at the follicle and narrow at the tip. This genetic diversity means that there are two types of Shetland sheep, first described by John Shirreff in 1814 as 'a kindly breed, and another breed with wool that is particularly coarse'.[5]

Whilst they are the sister sheep of other North Atlantic short-tailed sheep, Shetland sheep have fleeces with more soft under-wool and fewer coarse guard hairs than their Icelandic or Norwegian cousins. Wool has been a vital part of the North Atlantic economy since at least the fourteenth century, when records show that in Shetland rent and tithes were paid in *wadmal*, the coarse dense cloth woven by the islanders and fulled at the shoreline, using the waves' power to bind its fibres: 'they fasten a web of cloth, the one end upon the rock and the other upon the land, and the sea by its motion makes the cloth very thick'.[6] In Iceland, Greenland, Norway, Sweden and the Orkneys, *vaðmál* (literally 'cloth measure') was used as a currency in its own right and sold by the *ell*, a unit most commonly measured from a person's elbow to their fingertip – though Shetland defined its ell as a slightly longer measure.

Walking round the museum, I spy a brightly coloured piece of knitting, clasped in a glass case. This is possibly the oldest surviving piece of Shetland knitwear, dating from the early nineteenth century. Long and tapered like a fairy-tale nightcap, it is a *haaf* – an ocean fisherman's hat – knitted using the islands' classic two-stranded technique in bold blues and reds, brown, cream and gold.

Colourwork is the defining feature of what is widely described as 'Fair Isle knitting', Shetland's best-known export. Where gansey patterns are created through texture, thick ropes of cable and lines of flags dancing in relief, the patterns in 'Fair Isle' stranded colourwork are made from contrasting colours of yarn, traditionally two in every round or row. Written records indicate that colourwork, in particular, colourful knitted caps, has been part of Shetland' economy and culture since at least the seventeenth century. In 1822, the travel writer Samuel Hibbert observed that the Shetland fishermen wore striking 'boat dress', including a 'worsted covering for the head [...] dyed with so many colours that its bold tint is recognizable at a considerable distance, like the stripes of a signal flag.'[7] The islands' colourful caps were traded with sailors from across the known world who broke their crossings of the North Atlantic on this archipelago. Shetland Wool Week's Bousta Beanie is the latest in a line of colourful Shetlandic headgear.

Although far fewer in number following the Napoleonic Wars, Dutch fishermen continued to visit Shetland during the nineteenth century. In 1814, that great observer Sir Walter Scott noted, 'In general they are extremely quiet and employ themselves in bartering their little merchandise of gin and gingerbread for Zetland hose and night-caps.'[8] Whereas Sir Walter Raleigh gave Elizabeth I pairs of Guernsey stockings when governor of Jersey, the botanist and explorer Sir Joseph Banks gave George III a gift of Shetland stockings, and this royal patronage helped to create a buoyant English market for Shetland knitwear. Royal patronage continued to be important to Shetland's hosiery industry: Queen Victoria wore black knitted mourning shawls from Shetland, while in the 1920s her great-grandson Edward, then Prince of Wales, popularized Fair Isle jumpers and knee-length stockings as the perfect attire for golf.

Now I'm here in Shetland, my fingers itch to make a piece of knitwear symbolic of my experience of the place. The beanie has whetted my appetite for colourwork, and I want to knit something that will reflect not only the history of these islands but also my time on them. What could I make that would tell the story of this journey, this learning, this trip to Shetland?

Examining case after case of beautiful knitwear in the museum, I spot a beautifully patterned scarf knitted in a rainbow of Shetland yarn. The label tells me that the knitter made it using every shade of yarn available to them, and that the range of patterns and motifs demonstrates the knitter's considerable skill. It is a kind of sampler or showcase piece, a bold display of what is possible with a given palette. During Shetland Wool Week, I plan to take a variety of classes to learn different styles and techniques of knitting: what better way to combine this learning than with a scarf that brings them all together?

I leave the museum with a copy of *A Shetlander's Fair Isle Graph Book*, a publication that reprints patterns found in two notebooks belonging to Bill Henry, born on Yell in 1902 and long-time head of the Hosiery (Knitwear) department at Anderson & Co. Founded in 1873, Anderson & Co. has been trading from its Market Cross premises in Lerwick since 1883, buying finished garments from knitters and selling them on to merchants, fishermen and tourists, thereby providing an essential nexus between producer and consumer.

From the 1930s, Henry was the lynchpin for these transactions. As they worked 'freelance', knitters had the freedom to develop their own colour schemes and patterns, which Henry would then buy on behalf of Anderson & Co. Often the relationship between

Anderson's and an individual knitter might go back decades: two sisters living on a croft at Mouswell near Tingwall, Mainland, specialized in knitting gloves, and supplied Anderson's with garments for decades – Charlotte until her death at the age of eighty-eight, with Mary Ann reaching the age of 102.[9]

Anderson & Co. is the last survivor of a host of knitwear shops that flourished in Shetland throughout the nineteenth century. The increase in demand did not, however, mean that knitters themselves were well paid for their work. As in Cornwall, many knitters were exploited through the notorious 'truck system', whereby they would exchange their knitted items for goods from particular shops, the price of which was set by the merchant and often grossly inflated. To 'truck' was to barter, a word common across Britain until the nineteenth century; it now lingers on solely in our phrase 'to have no truck with': to resist association or dealings with a given person or idea. Knitters were often utterly at the mercy of the merchant, who could decide whether a pair of stockings was worth a certain length of ribbon or quantity of sugar. Many times, knitters were restricted to buying 'fancy goods' like these in lieu of basic foodstuffs. This led to the creation of a thriving underground market, with knitters bartering for potatoes and other staples from their neighbours.

The first government commission to investigate the truck system was in 1870; on the whole, it sided with the knitters, but not much was done to enforce its recommendations. In their early days, Anderson & Co. paid their knitters in sugar and flour,[10] and later in tea. The knitter and entrepreneur Jeannie Jarmson recalled that if she accepted payment in tea instead of money, she got 'extra'.[11] It took the Second World War to change things: servicemen stationed in Shetland wanted to buy knitted items to send home as presents – and were prepared to pay hard cash. By the time Bill Henry worked for Anderson & Co., knitters were being paid in cash for their work. Henry decided to note down some of the beautiful and intricate patterns that passed through his hands, pencilling them in bright colours onto graph paper. In 2016, the Shetland Guild of Spinners, Knitters, Weavers and Dyers published these patterns for the first time, making a rainbow of mid-twentieth-century knitwear designs, previously hidden within two slender notebooks, available to the wider world.

I peruse the patterns closely, noting the echoes in shape and design between these mid-century designs and earlier patterns I saw in the museum. Common to both are the 'OXO' motif, combining circles and crosses; in the museum, I also saw swastikas knitted into garments – an innocent symbol of good fortune before their chilling ubiquity in the 1930s and 1940s. Another wartime motif is the 'Churchill pattern', a medallion surrounded by arrows pointing downward, similar in style to a design from Selbu in Norway, famous for its 'Selbuvotter', or decorated mittens. The 'Churchill pattern' was devised by Mary Slater of Burra,

Shetland, who was an ardent supporter of Winston Churchill; during the war, her village was at the heart of the 'Shetland Bus' operations, which transported resistance fighters from German-occupied Norway to Britain. For Churchill's eightieth birthday in November 1954, Mary knitted him a slipover with her 'Churchill patterns' all over.[12] I decide to include the 'OXO' motif and a Churchill pattern in my sample scarf. But before I can begin to knit, I need some yarn.

On Lerwick's northern edge stands a small shop next to a grey pebble-dashed warehouse. In the window is a picnic basket full of yarn. The warehouse, with a bright green sliding door, used to be a United Free Church, built to serve the herring workers who gutted and salted the 'silver darlings' in the quayside fishing stations. For many knitting pilgrims to Shetland, this is a holy place for yarn – for 90 North Road is the home of Jamieson & Smith (Shetland Wool Brokers Ltd). Whilst not the only wool merchants on the island, Jamieson & Smith is the best known, in operation since the 1930s and championed today by some of the most popular knitwear designers in the world. Those who are famed for their colourwork designs – Kaffe Fassett, Alice Starmore, Kate Davies – all delight in yarn from J&S.

Standing in the tiny wood-lined shop, my senses are overwhelmed. The air is thick with the smell of yarn, simultaneously dry and oily, and the walls are an artist's palette of colour: block after block of reds and blues, oranges and purples, creams and chocolate brown. Bar the Heritage yarns, the skeins are numbered, not named, and some designers can recite the codes of their favourite shades by heart. To the casual observer, there is no obvious magic in FC50, 9113, 82 mix, but to the knitter there is beauty potent in each number.

The shop's clock strikes the hour, and a man in a grubby boiler suit emerges from a small door at the back of the shop. Bright eyes twinkle above a soft curling beard, and, in the soft tones of a born Shetlander, he welcomes the throng of knitters who now fill the shop, eager to join his tour into the heart of the business. They have come from as far away as Australia to visit the shop, and he is Oliver Henry, wool-grader extraordinary and author of *Jamieson & Smith: A Shetland Story* (2017).

Oliver Henry began working for J&S in the 1960s and has been there ever since. Wool is his life; as our guide, he talks us through fleece after fleece, from the finest quality – the 'kindliest' – to the coarsest. We stroke and sniff, coo and exclaim. Oliver's obvious delight as high priest of Wool Week is made all the more poignant by a recent cancer diagnosis. Lying in his hospital bed, he realized that he was the only person who truly knew the company's history, and the possibility that it might be lost inspired him to begin writing it down. Producing the book saw Oliver through his successful treatment.

Jamieson & Smith takes its name from John 'Sheepie' Smith, a crofter and livestock dealer from Sandwick, and James Jamieson, another Shetland wool buyer. Sheepie farmed at Berry Farm in Scalloway, on the west coast of Mainland. A dealer in livestock from a young age, he started to specialize in buying wool. Soon he was dealing in up to 200 tonnes of fleece a year, almost three quarters of Shetland's total clip. In the winter, when the farm was quieter, the raw fleece would be graded in the sheds at Berry Farm and sent to be spun and knitted on the mainland. At this time, anything other than hand-spinning was not viable in Shetland: the large investment costs of setting up a mill were too risky when the wool market could be so volatile.

T. M. Hunter of Brora, Patons & Baldwins at Alloa, and Stewart Brothers of Galashiels all processed Shetland wool. Oliver says that as far back as 1901, Shetlanders were sending their wool to be spun on the mainland.[13] In 1950, the British Wool Marketing Board (BWMB) was set up to sell the UK's entire wool clip at annual auction. At the time, this kind of government-mandated marketing board was not unusual. During the Great Depression of the 1930s, when malnutrition was a real and vivid threat, the British government took over the sale and marketing of milk and potatoes, across the whole country, guaranteeing farmers a minimum price for their produce. Marketing boards were set up to coordinate the sale of pigs and bacon, and, in 1956, eggs.

The BWMB still dominates the sale of British wool today. Owners of all but the smallest flocks must register with the board, which then buys and collects the clip each year. Only what are termed 'artisan mills' – small-scale operations such as Uist Wool – can buy fleece direct from farmers. Prices vary depending on the world fibre market, of which wool comprises only 1.5 per cent; all-time lows of less than 10 pence per fleece meant that it has cost more to pay someone to shear the sheep than the fleece would sell for.

Shetlanders declined to join the BWMB. Along with the Isle of Man, Shetland remains the only part of the UK where it is not a legal requirement to sell wool through the board. Instead, Shetlanders trade directly with merchants, mills and knitting factories. In the heyday of the 1950s, twelve Shetland knitwear companies existed, including T. M. Adie of Voe, who produced jumpers for the 1953 British Mount Everest expedition. Today, only Anderson & Co., Jamieson's and Jamieson & Smith still sell their own knitwear. Shetland Organics provides Jamieson's sough-after organic-certified yarn.

In the beginning, J&S sorted and sold raw Shetland wool. But by the 1960s, the firm's enterprising manager, Gilbert Johnston, realized that there was the potential for a boom in business as Shetland's hand-knitters were looking for high-quality local yarn in a kaleidoscope of colours. Working with Hunters of Brora, the company developed a two-ply range, starting with pale-brown 'Fawn' in 1967.

It wasn't only Shetlanders who wanted Shetland yarn – from the nineteenth century, migrant herring gutters worked the North Road's curing sheds each summer, developing their knitting alongside the Shetland women with whom they worked. They too bought yarn from J&S, its premises handily situated close to the huts in which they stayed. From 1968, they clamoured for a mail-order service so they could continue to buy Shetland yarn when they returned home. Ever since, J&S has shipped its yarn worldwide. It also delivered yarn daily to the herring drifters from Whalsay berthed at Lerwick: the knitters of Whalsay, the island east of Mainland, were famed for the intricate colourwork of their Fair Isle jumpers.[14]

Today, the company offers a rainbow of colours in its Shetland Heritage range, a worsted-spun light four-ply yarn developed in direct consultation with the Shetland Museum and Archives. Since 2011, the team has carefully replicated the colours and yarn weights used in historic keps (hats), cardigans and jumpers from across the islands.

After more than an hour of gasping and grasping at fleeces, the audience of wool-clad women dissolves, and I head back into the shop to choose yarn for my Shetland scarf. Remembering the museum's indigo, madder-red and golden-yellow keps, I add those colours, and throw in a skein of peat-brown yarn. As I go to leave, I press my hand into Oliver's to thank him. It is as soft as butter, smooth from fifty years of lanolin.

Walking into the centre of Lerwick from North Road, I stop at a brightly coloured shopfront, the woodwork round its window frames and doors painted russet-red and cream. This is the premises of Anderson & Co., where Bill Henry worked. One of Shetland's biggest woollen businesses, its shop on Commercial Street is full of locally made jumpers, gloves, hats and cardigans, as it has been for over a hundred years. Across the road is Jamieson's of Shetland, its window bright with yarn of every

hue. Unlike its rival Jamieson & Smith, Jamieson's yarn is spun in the company's own small mill, at Sandness in west Mainland. Its two-ply Spindrift yarn, equivalent to a traditional four-ply, is available in more than two hundred colours. With images of last night's sunset whirling in my head, I pick out an autumn rainbow of oranges and pinks, pale blues and browns, warm yellows and creams, to add to my J&S yarn. The light is different this far north, and colours are important.

Now I have my woollen palette, it is time to start knitting. The sampler scarf I saw in the museum is double-sided, knitted in the round and warmly thick. I cast on 120 stitches on 3.25 mm circular needles, using the last of the dark brown yarn from my Bousta Beanie, and start at the beginning of *A Shetlander's Fair Isle Graph Book*. The pages are full of simple two-colour patterns worked over five or seven rounds, and, sitting in the airy cafe of the Shetland Museum, I begin knitting the first in autumnal shades of red and brown. The two strands cling to each other as I work, threatening to ply themselves into a single thread, so I keep them apart by holding the red strand in my right hand, the brown in my left.

As the clock ticks towards six, I head to Lerwick's tiny bus station. From this string of storm shelters round a turning circle, I catch a bus south to Sumburgh. The sun begins to set, and the Mainland of Shetland expands before me as my hands work on the scarf. It is a rolling landscape, where high places fall away down sharp cliffs and fields are scored where turf has been cut, the earth the same rich colour as the chocolate-brown yarn in my hands. The sun is low and dazzling, throwing long shadows from the farms and houses we pass. Their names sound strange to southern ears: Gulberwick, Quarff, Fladdabister, Aithsetter, Levenwick, Dunrossness. The Nordic tang lingers on the tongue.

We drive straight over Sumburgh airport's tiny runway before the bus lurches to a halt at the roadside. I drag myself and my suitcase onto the track and I see two low round buildings, Iron Age brochs that housed Shetlanders over two thousand years ago. Beside them is a single-storey dwelling hugging this windy promontory. With thick stone walls beneath a felted, lichen-marked roof, it looks more like a shed than a house. I've arrived at Betty Mouat's *böd*, my home for the next ten days.

Inside is a glowing peat stove that roars when the wind is in the chimney. This *böd* – Shetlandic kin to 'booth' and 'bothy' – is a small four-roomed building with a kitchen, a two-bunk bedroom, a toilet and shower, and a living room with three bunks at one end. The mattresses are wipe-clean and have held many sleeping bodies. There is no bedding, and, unprepared, I have to beg a sleeping bag from the warden. There is one pillow provided for anyone who needs it, torn in half and its ends knotted closed.

The fire is made of peats, cut by hand and bought by the sackful from the *böd* warden. Each is a deep-brown fibrous brick, a solid clod so dark as to be almost black. Unlike coal, it leaves no oily smudges as I pick one up, just a dusty print of earth upon my palm. Stepping outside to see the night, I see the smear of the Milky Way above me and the stars, too numerous to count, glitter out.

Since at least the nineteenth century, this booth belonged to the Mouat family. Its best-kent member, Betty Mouat, still keeps watch over its visitors. A photographic portrait above the peat stove shows Betty in a dark fitted dress, her gaze steady beneath a bonnet edged in frills. Her mouth twists into a half-smile, her hands holding knitting needles and yarn, her elbows angled out to knit. Betty is a knitting hero, survivor of misadventure.

Born in nearby Levenwick in 1825, Elizabeth was the only child of Thomas Mouat, a shoemaker and fisherman, and his wife, Margaret Harper. Thomas was lost at sea when Betty was still a child, and her mother moved back to her family home adjacent to the Iron Age brochs at Scatness, at the southernmost tip of Shetland Mainland. Like many Shetland women of her generation in Shetland, Betty was a proficient hand-spinner and knitter who earned money from her work. Yet at the age of sixty-one, an unexpected adventure pitched her into sudden celebrity.

As an unmarried woman without family responsibilities, she was able to courier knitwear made on the crofts around Scatness up to Lerwick for sale. Today, the bus covers the 22

miles between the two in fifty minutes, but in the late nineteenth century it was quicker to sail than travel overland. With
a prevailing southerly wind, it should have been not more than a
three-hour trip.

It was late January 1886 when Betty set out from Grutness
Voe for Lerwick on the *Columbine*. The sea around Shetland
is notorious for high winds and fast tides, and, 3 miles into the
voyage, storm gusts jerked the boom, breaking the main sheet
and leaving the boom swinging freely in the wind. Skipper
James Jamieson and the mate tried to repair the broken sail but,
with the sea heaving and the wind howling, the sheet slipped
and both were cast into the sea. The mate kept his grasp on the
main sheet and hauled himself back on board; together with
the remaining crew they launched a small boat to try and save
the skipper. It was too late: the sea had claimed him. The crew
tried to return to their boat, but the *Columbine* was drifting and
in high seas they could not reach her, so they were forced to
return to Shetland.

On board the *Columbine*, Betty was now alone, with nothing
more than her cargo of knitwear for company. The boat drifted
on the currents, heading north-east. After eight days adrift at sea,
never leaving the cabin, and with only a quart of milk and two
hard biscuits to sustain her, Betty reached the island of Lepsøya,
near Ålesund in Norway. Knut Veblungsnaes, a local fisherman,
rescued her on 7 February 1886.

Betty returned to Scotland a hero, feted in newspapers from
Lerwick to London. She arrived in Edinburgh three weeks after
her rescue, and from there her story captured the popular imagination – songs, poems and highly dramatized stories all emerged,
featuring her as their unlikely heroine. Some deliberately trans-
formed her identity from that of an older woman to a younger, far
more glamorous creature. For the next thirty years, visitors would
come to her house in Scatness to hear the tale of her adventure.

Many years after her death, the Shetland Amenities Trust
renovated her home and opened it as a camping *böd*, providing
low-cost accommodation to visitors seeking shelter.

Waking at six the following morning, I dress in the dark and wait
for the first bus of the day as the sun begins to rise. Like a drop
of ink in water, the dawn spreads slow and limpid across the sky.
The wind rattles and buckles the bus shelter, and I bury my chin
deep in the soft warmth of my scarf.

I'm on my way to Tingwall for the first morning flight to Fair
Isle. Six of us in Bousta Beanies congregate at the bus terminal:
a German couple from Mainz, two Americans from Michigan
and Indiana, Sara from Sweden, and me – all in matching hats,
the badge of our clan. Someone voices a hope that our headgear
will prove to be a lucky charm, for the forecast for Fair Isle is not
promising. The tiny eight-seater twin-prop plane can only land
on calm days, and calm, mist-free days at that. In late September,
the odds of us reaching Fair Isle are less than favourable: in an
average year, sixty-four days see winds reaching more than 34
knots, with hurricane-force gusts of over 64 knots a feature of life
from September through to March.[15]

Midway between Shetland and Orkney and home to around
fifty people, Fair Isle punches above its weight in terms of knitting. Nowadays, 'Fair Isle' generally refers to any patterned
fabric that features the angular geometry of two-tone stranded
colourwork. Unlike Harris Tweed, Fair Isle knitwear has no
protective patent – the term is now used indiscriminately to
describe geometric coloured knitted patterns. Attempts have
been made to patent the name: as early as 1924, the island's
postmaster, Jerome Stout, made a case for this to the London
Board of Trade, but was only able to secure the assurance
that for island-made goods, the Shetland trademark would be
overprinted with 'made in Fair Isle'.[16] Yet 'Fair Isle' knitting

has commanded interest and respect since at least the Great Exhibition of 1851, which included 'Fair Isle socks, gloves, vest piece, comforter, and cap';[17] by the exhibition of 1886, it was considered 'of a very distinctive type, and may be known by its bright and varied colours with chequered patterns'.[18] How did this tiny scrap of land in the middle of the wild North Sea come to be known the world over for its knitting?

Whilst it is tempting to think of Fair Isle as remote, to a seafaring society, the island is extremely accessible, a stopping point on many trans-European routes. The Vikings, those kings of the waves, sailed here in open wooden boats powered by woollen sails, the precursors of the square-sailed Fair Isle *yoles* used until the Second World War. The first written record of Fair Isle dates from the thirteenth-century saga of Burnt Njal, in which two Vikings, Kari and Kolbein, land on Fair Isle on their way from Iceland: 'the first land they made was the Fair Isle [...] there that man whose name was David the White took Kari into his house [...] and Kari stayed with him for the winter.'[19]

With Norway, also known for its colourful knitting, to the east, mainland Shetland to the north, and the rest of Britain to the south, Fair Isle has long offered shelter in the midst of the North Sea. The island's connection with other cultures was part of its identity and economy: when Alexander Selkirk (better known in his fictionalized form as Robinson Crusoe) was becalmed close to the island in 1711, the islanders rowed out to his ship offering to sell provisions.[20] Sir Walter Scott, who visited Shetland in 1814, remarked in a letter home: 'The women [of Fair Isle] knit worsted stockings, nightcaps and similar trifles, which they exchange with any merchant vessels that approach their lonely isle.'[21] The men of Fair Isle would set out in *yoles* to barter these goods with passing boats – until the mid-twentieth century, the island had no port deep enough for a large ship.

These endeavours were fraught with danger: in September 1897, four boats set out to trade with fifteen sailing vessels passing to the east of the island; a north-westerly storm blew in, and in the morning only two of Fair Isle's boats returned. Another was later found with over half its crew of seven dead; of the fourth, nothing more was ever seen. Four widows and twenty-seven dependents were left in the island's care.[22]

The way of life on Fair Isle has long been a diversely skilful one. As well as bartering, hunting wild birds, fishing, beach-combing, smuggling and farming all helped to support the inhabitants, with most households diversifying as seasons and demand fluctuated. The island's population has fluctuated greatly over time, from a peak of 380 in 1861 to a low of forty-two in 1973.[23] For centuries, knitting has brought income to the island: in 1769, James Robertson recorded 'that the women were continually employed in knitting stockings or gloves and spinning woollen yarn'.[24]

In the census of 1851, only four of the forty-one Fair Isle households did not name spinners or knitters. The exceptions were the Cheynes, the school teacher and the island's only midwife; the Wilson household, headed by a woman but with no other female members above the age of five; and the Irvines of West Road, all male-dominated households, with only very young daughters and wives either dead or drawn from outside Fair Isle. Spinning and knitting was evidently an essential part of Fair Isle life – more so than on the Shetland Mainland, where a far smaller proportion of households (as low as 6 per cent in Dunrossness) gave knitting or spinning as their main profession[25] – though this could in part result from how the census data was gathered.

Their seaward connection with the world brought the Fair Islanders, and Shetlanders more generally, into contact with several possible sources of dye. Whilst woad, madder and saffron had been used for millennia, from the late sixteenth century onwards, exploration of the tropics lead to the introduction of bright and powerful dyes, including indigo, and cochineal from dried *Dactylopius coccus* beetles that live on cacti. Their bodies produce carmine so vivid that madder's rusty hues pale into insignificance.[26]

The best indigo – from the Latin for 'Indian substance' – was grown around Calicut and Malabar on the south-west coast of India. Known before the Portuguese began trading there in the sixteenth century as *anil* – from the Sanskrit *nīlī*, 'indigo plant'[27] – indigo was also grown in the Caribbean. It must be fixed with alum, which in the sixteenth century came from mines in Spain or in Tolfa, then a papal territory close to Rome. With a keener eye on their coffers than on spiritual or even political unity, the Catholic Church's treasury continued to sell Tolfan alum to England well beyond England's break with Rome in the 1530s. Only when Sir Arthur Ingram succeeded in mining alum on a commercial scale in Yorkshire early in the following century did the Papal States finally lose their English customers.[28]

As in the Hebrides, yarns could also be dyed using plants found locally in Shetland. In 1822, Samuel Hibbert recorded the use of four lichens to dye wool: *Xanthoria parietina*, for orange-yellow; *Ochrolechia tartarea* for a purple-red; *Parmelia omphalodes* for a dark blackish-purple; and *Parmelia saxatalis* for a brighter orange.[29] By 1862, Fair Islanders were selling their goods to James R. Spence of 85 Commercial Street, Lerwick, who proudly offered 'a varied assortment of curiously Knitted Goods from the Fair Isle'.[30] In 1980, Fair Isle Crafts was established, and ten years later this craftwork cooperative was able to give at least part-time employment to more than a dozen people. Now, they have a three-year waiting list for items genuinely made on the island.

At Tingwall, we start off down the runway, propeller blades whirring by our ears, and in seconds we are in the air. Up we buzz and then hang like an insect, sandwiched between clouds and land. Bressay lies beneath us, its limits edged with waves foaming white. But then the pilot shouts over his shoulder, gesturing to the horizon. We crane our necks to see the fog roll in: it is too dangerous to land in weather like this. We must turn back and try again another day. Fair Isle keeps her knitting secrets to herself.

'A dyebath is a glorified cup of tea,' says Julia Billings, a professional yarn dyer, inviting me to peer into a steaming stainless-steel cauldron. With Fair Isle frustratingly out of reach, I decide instead to learn how to dye yarn to match some of the island's traditional colours. Deep reddish-brown, Julia's brew of *Rubia tinctorum*, common madder, promises to yield reds of every shade. Madder has been used as a dye since at least Roman times – its Latin name means simply 'red dye'. Its uncultivated sister is *Rubia peregrina*, 'red that travels'. Woad, that bold blue dye favoured by the Celts, goes by the name of *Isatis tinctoria*; *Anthemis tinctoria* is dyer's camomile; *Asperula tinctoria*, dyer's woodruff. Though many plants can produce brilliant hues, from green to red, the adjunct of '*tinctorum*' or '*tinctoria*' indicates a centuries-long pedigree as an effective dye plant.

Many dyes will wash away or fade upon exposure to sunlight, unless they have been mordanted – from *mordre*, French for 'to bite'. The word took its toothy hold on English through the Anglo-Norman *mordaunt*, the tongue of a buckle that clasps two things together. To be mordant is to have a caustic tongue, a biting wit. Mordant buckles and remarks predate the dyer's term in English by some three centuries.[31]

'Substantive' dyes like turmeric need no mordanting, their hues strong and colourfast. 'Adjective' dyes, as their name suggests, require the addition of a fixative to bind their shade. Alum, urine, salt, iron, copper and soda can be used as mordants, which also strengthen a dye's base tones: alum brings out orange-yellows; iron browns and grey; copper adds a yellow-greenish tint.

Sitting beside me in the dye class is an extremely adept knitter, wrapped in a splendid hand-knit sweater in shades of palest yellow, copper-green, bright yellow and warm umber. The base tone of this jumper is a greenish yellow, the colour of a primrose petal's outer edge. When I ask its owner where the colour came from, she replies, 'Ground elder.' Sick of the prevalence of a weed dead set on blighting her garden, she decided to get creative. The addition of iron, copper, madder, soda and logwood to a dye bath of ground elder turned the yarn a kaleidoscope of browns, greens and oranges, which she then knitted into the beautiful patterns marching along her arms and chest. It is a gardener's frustration turned to art.

After a morning of dipping strands of yarn in chemical tisanes, Julia has led us through twenty-five shades of maddered yarn, from orangey cumin through to the purple-black of aubergine. Rhubarb leaves' oxalic acid gives tobacco-browns and seaside rust, the dusty spice of cinnamon and cumin. Copper turns madder to ruby, cinnabar and garnet; alum yields pinkish pomegranate and red cayenne. We debate the names of the shades: 'bloodstone' for the mid-grey yarn rippled with ruby, 'gingerbread' for the light orange of copper on untreated yarn. One of our class is a retired English teacher, and she searches for the perfect word for her bright yarn: 'a little pepper, a hint of zing – a little more cayenne'.

I leave with yarn in twenty-six shades, a clutch of strands to work into the scarf. Back at Betty Mouat's, I begin to work them into the pattern, though the colours seem to shift their hues in the fireglow of the *böd*. It is not just the peat-fuelled light: a relationship between two colours can be complex and tricky to predict. Expert colourwork knitters are often commended on their ability to blend colours to best suit their patterns – a skein of J&S's 'Shaela' yarn might appear dark grey in isolation, but it reveals a hint of blue or yellow when placed next to Jamieson's 'Burnt Ochre', 'Flax' or 'Moorgrass'.

In my notebook, I plot more Shetland patterns, turning to
my stash of yarn to pick out colours. It has been a week of vivid
sunsets, and my knitting mirrors them in shades of oyster and
salmon, peach and tangerine. This is my Shetland sampler, a scarf
of memory and history, place and people. As I work on grading
the colours, two raincoated birdwatchers arrive, intending to stay
the night. But after half an hour, the men decide that their delicate constitutions cannot withstand a night in an unheated bunk
room, and repair to a hotel. Three of us stay on, me and a Dutch
mother and daughter, not put off by chilly bedrooms. The three
of us are here specially for Wool Week. Cor and Wimpje come
from Katwijk, a coastal Netherlands town with a strong tradition
of knitting fishermen's sweaters. Each evening we return to the
böd and knit until bedtime. As I work the scarf's rounds, Cor's
fingers are busy making a gansey in the Katwijk pattern, all tight-
bound ropes and purled panels. Her daughter Wimpje finishes a
pair of dark-brown mitts and then begins a jumper.

I learn that Cor has three daughters and a son, but only she and
Wimpje knit. Each April in Katwijk, the townsfolk dress in traditional costume and celebrate its fishing history. Katwijk sailors
may well have been some of those who sailed to Shetland several
centuries ago. Listening to Cor and Wimpje's stories distracts
me from my knitting, and when I have to rip out failed row after
failed row they laugh and say, '*Praten en breien*' – 'Talking and
knitting', an apt Dutch expression for this universally distract-
ing problem.

The next day I wake to silence. The wind has dropped overnight and the sun is shining as I pull back Betty Mouat's curtains.
I am so used to the sound of howling in the chimney that the *böd*
now seems unnaturally quiet. Striking out for Sumburgh Head in
the morning light, I do not pass a single walker, and as I cut along
West Voe beach, nothing more than a soft September breeze
comes whistling from the sea. The waves break into benign foam

and the rush and suck and swirl of them catches my ear. Here in Shetland, my eyes have feasted on colour and texture, my head flooded with information and my hands busy with new skills. My ears have hardly had a listen-in.

I sit for an hour, attending to the timbre and tone of the beach. Knitting and sound are not obvious bedfellows, but one artist who has brought the two together is Felicity Ford. Known to everyone as Felix, she is a sound artist and knitter whose inspiration comes not from the past but from the here-and-now, the oft-ignored beauty of the familiar. She is the originator of the KnitSonik creative method, closely observing daily life to inspire patterns of stranded colourwork that reflect the knitter's own unique environment. In the same way as Situationists wandered through the streets of Paris, London and New York in the mid-twentieth century to unearth a new and neutral relationship with their environment, Felix prowls the streets of her home town to break it into patterns and colours, to see the familiar with fresh eyes. She uses the Victorian terraces and abandoned factories of Reading, the rolling tarmac of the A4074, the plants in her suburban street and the fruitcake made by her aunt to inspire her knitting. It is the antithesis of didactic pattern design. Instead, her method comes closer to an artistic vision, a crafting flâneurism that makes the knitter the authoring observer of their world. Like Harris Tweed, its yarn mixed to mirror the Hebridean heather and moss, bog and crotal, sea and sky, colourwork designs inspired by the KnitSonik system hold up a glass to the world of their inventors.

Many knitting patterns and textile traditions seem to come from places often viewed as remote and rural. From Harris Tweed to Shetland lace, Jersey grey-bellies to Dentdale gloves, almost all have been preserved thanks in part to their geographic isolation from the busy worlds of cities, suburbs and factories. But Felix's call to arms is that one's daily life is not something to be escaped from; the suburban should not be seen only in disdainful contrast to the pureness of the rural. She resists the siren call of the abstract idyll, and uses knitting as a way to overcome her sense of alienation within urban spaces.

As Felix talked to me at the end of her knitting class, enthusiasm warmed her voice, rich with estuary vowels and glottal stops, and spilled into her gestures. 'I hate this idea that we live for the specialness of weekends, holidays and art galleries, that we think all the rest of our time and environment is a bit crap.' Knitting can help us connect, add meaning, deepen our understanding. I realize that what I am trying to do with my sample scarf is to fix the experience of being in Shetland, creating a garment that I can use like a magic charm to take me back here with one flick of its colourful end.

Padding to the kitchen at Betty Mouat's in my socks, I feed one last pound coin into the greedy meter. It is enough for a short hot shower, then porridge made on the tiny two-ring hob. It is the last day of Wool Week, and waking up to this knowledge feels almost like relief. It has been inspiring and intense, my head full of new words and names and faces, my hands full of new movements.

Wool Week ends with a comfortable, well-catered tea at Tingwall, where those of us left standing join the islands' knitters for one last bun fight. I get a lift to the ferry with Carol Christiansen, Shetland Museum's textiles curator, who takes me back to Lerwick in her little car. The wind rattles and shakes its tin-can body as we draw into the terminal, and rain batters the windows, smearing the windscreen into a sheet of distorting water. I wait for the storm to subside and Carol shows me a website where each weather front is plotted and each change in wave height is shown in deepening bands of colour. It is really for surfers, chasing that elusive perfect wave, but where their hearts would jump with excitement at the promise of walls of water, mine quickens with nerves. On the map, pools of green and yellow swamp the seas between Lerwick and Aberdeen, waves more than 4 metres high. Carol advises me to pay for a cabin for this return trip, recommending a place to lie down as an antidote to the boat's jerking sinks and shudders. Fortunately, there are several spaces left, and I book myself a berth to make the crossing.

Joining the boarding queue, I spot Swedish Sara, companion on my nearly trip to Fair Isle, and we buddy up for the voyage. She's an experienced sailor who spent much of her childhood in small boats out in the sound between Sweden, Denmark and Germany. She advises that we eat straight away, and we wash down our final fish and chips of the trip with bottles of Shetland ale. Then it's out onto the deck at the ship's stern, eyes fixed on the horizon.

As the ship lurches from its moorings, I can feel the whole weight of myself against my legs. Like an unsteady infant, I roll helplessly from seat to seat, shrieking with giddy laughter. At the back of the ship, we are sheltered from the worst of the wind. The rain lessens as we leave Lerwick and I wave goodbye to the week as this tiny island capital slips away. Along the coast, I see all the villages I passed each day on the bus: Gulberwick, Fladdabister, Voxter, Hoswick, Toab. Then finally the narrow tongue of Scatness and Sumburgh's fat curve, punctuated by the red lights of the airport runway.

Then there is no more horizon to see as the land turns to sea and light turns to night. The white foam of the waves increases as we leave Shetland's shelter, and the deck pitches and turns beneath our feet. To keep our stomachs still, we first fixate on lighthouses – Sumburgh Head, then Fair Isle's twin glittering points – and then we look to the stars. The night has cleared and our eyes pick out Orion and the Plough.

We are not alone on deck. Beside the door is a huddle of smok-
ers, and beyond them a man with a tuft of white beard looks for
something in the pockets of his overalls. He produces a small
box, and puts it to his lips. It is a harmonica, and as night draws
in around us, he starts a reel. The notes fly out into the spray and
scatter on the deck. Having a new rhythm gives purpose to our
movement, and we stamp our feet in time to his tunes as we hold
onto the rail in the teeth of the boat's pitch and toss. Dancing is
the only way to meet this floating world's erratic rise and fall.

10

Monmouth Caps
and Funeral Stockings

Back in Fife, October continues warm and bright, and at home
I rise early to cloudless autumn skies. After a heady week in
Shetland, it is time to turn my footsteps south again and head
to Wales, a country long synonymous with sheep farming and
home to more than three million fleecy *defaid*. These numbers
are significant: in 2016, sheep outnumbered the country's human
population three to one.

With a nod to memories of tending sheep with Mr Griffiths,
I pass through his home county of Herefordshire on my way to
Monmouth, 2 miles from today's Welsh border. Since 1542, the
boundary has threaded its way from Flint Sands by the River Dee
to the Severn in the south, an invisible dividing line that pulls
Chester into England, cups Wrexham within Wales, and finally
cuts Welsh Chepstow from English Sedbury, where the Severn
and Wye meet. Until 1836, the county town of Monmouth, with
a population of 10,000, came under the auspices of the diocese
of Hereford, and legislation relating to the area was couched in
terms of 'Wales and Monmouth'; only in the Local Government
Act of 1972 was Monmouth classified as fully Welsh.

In my head are Dunja Roberts's Welsh words from the
summer: *gwlân, ffermwr, nyddu*. Sheep have long shaped this

country's identity, economy and culture; since the time of the great feudal landowners of the Middle Ages, huge estates have been dedicated solely to the raising of sheep. By the eighteenth century, sheep farming had become the main countryside occupation, though it was a precarious existence. In April 1799, Thomas Johnes, a farmer from Hafod, wrote that the hard winter had taken a great toll on mountain farmers: 'the losses among the sheep and lambs are very great indeed. I know not when to expect an end of it, for it snows and hails as fast as if it was December instead of April.'[1]

Wales is home to many sheep breeds. The oldest, with their roots in the first century CE, are Badger Face Black Mountains, both the *torddu* (black belly) and *torwen* (white belly). One the photographic negative of the other, both have stripes around their eyes, from which the English breed name is derived. Their older Welsh name was *defaid Idloes* – sheep of St Idloe, a seventh-century Celtic figure who remains uncanonized but has a lasting memorial in eponymous Llanidloes, Powys. As with the Good Shepherd and St Blaise, saints and sheep go hand in hand.

Most sheep breeds as understood and recognized today were only established from the late nineteenth to the mid-twentieth century. Welsh breeds include the rare Balwen, its name taken from the white blaze adorning their dark noses. The darkest of Wales's sheep are the sooty Black Welsh Mountains, the palest the all-white Brecknock Hill Cheviots and Llandovery White Faces. In between are grey-nosed, tan-faced Hill Radnors and sturdy spotted Kerry Hills, both from the Marches. The twentieth century saw the development of the black-legged, white-fleeced Llanwenog, first registered in 1957.

The wool from its sheep allowed Wales to develop several subsidiary industries. As in East Anglia, Flemish weavers settled here, particularly in the south and west. They exported their wares through the ports of Tenby and Carmarthen, though between the sixteenth and nineteenth centuries the Crown demanded that Shrewsbury drapers hold the monopoly of finishing and selling Welsh cloth.[2] Welsh double-weave woollen blankets, *carthenni*, have long been produced in the valleys' mills and sold all over the world, with wool for flannel becoming the chief export of Monmouthshire and Merioneth. The founder of the Calvinistic Methodist Church, Howell Harris, also set up the Breconshire Agricultural Society in 1755, and in 1758, £400 was used to build eight looms to boost the woollen industry in the district.[3] Harris also recorded that of the sixty adults resident in Trefeca in the Brecons, thirty-six women picked and spun wool and flax, and knitted stockings sold in Brecon, Hay and Hereford.

Much of the traditional Welsh costume for women, excluding its distinctive tall-crowned hat, was made from wool. Worn on the top half, the 'bed gown' was a sort of jacket that could be made in a variety of styles, either loose or close-fitting, long or short. A wardrobe staple across Europe during the seventeenth and eighteenth centuries, gowns like this continued to be worn much later in Wales and were subsequently adopted as part of the country's national dress.[4] A handkerchief would be tucked into the gown at the neck, and a woollen cape worn over it, either navy or – as became popular later – red.

Below this gown hung dark woollen *pais* (skirts), often striped with red or white, worn with a *fedog* (apron). A *siôl*, or shawl, often woven with a check and fringed, would be wrapped around the shoulders, or worn as *siôl magu* (a rearing shawl) or *siôl nyrsio* (a nursing shawl) – a plain weave of wool used to tie an infant close to its mother's body for easy feeding and comfort. In 1795, Sarah Eardley-Wilmot noted that the inhabitants of Cardigan wore this garb, which was 'Remarkable and similar to that in Pembroke. It consists of a striped flannel petticoat and a brown jacket over it, a blue handkerchief tyed over their heads & a black beaver hat upon that, a large brown, or blue flannel wrapper which goes round the waist & over the shoulders & serves the double purpose of a cloak & cradle for one or two children they generally carry at their back; and altogether gives them the appearance of the Laplanders.'[5] Woollen *siôl magu* continued to be used in some Welsh communities until at least the 1970s.

Men's clothing was generally less regionally distinctive. Their dress most often consisted of 'a quaint coat and waistcoat of homespun cloth', worn above knee-breeches 'of the same fabric or of corduroy'.[6] Gaiters, made of a brown woollen fabric known as kerseymere, kept up black stockings, knitted from undyed wool. In 1873, the Royal Land Commission of Wales found that, whilst some men wore suits made from local wool, not everyone did, though 'They are considered the best clothing and the strongest whatever for wear.'[7]

Woollen hats and caps were widely worn, denoting status and wealth. One particular type was the Monmouth cap, a plain knitted head covering worn by the mediaeval military. Felted for both warmth and strength, these unprepossessing caps had a looped top and could be worn underneath a helmet. The first written record of the Monmouth cap dates from 1576, when Lord Gilbert Talbot of Goodrich Castle sent his father, as a new year's gift, 'a Monmouth Cappe, and a rundlette of perrye, and I must require pardon to name the other homely thing, a pair of Rosse boots'.[8] These unpretentious gifts from Wales – a cap from Monmouth, a cask of perry, and a pair of boots from nearby Ross-on-Wye – were a son's gift for the ninth Earl of Shrewsbury.

In Shakespeare's *Henry V*, the Welsh captain, Fluellen, reminisces with the king about the Battle of Crecy of 1346, remarking that 'the Welshmen did good service in a garden where leeks did grow, wearing leeks in their Monmouth caps; which, your majesty know, to this hour is an honourable badge of the service'.[9] A glance at the army rolls of men who fought at Agincourt in 1415 backs up Fluellen's words: Monmouthshire Man-at-Arms Thomas

Capper is listed under the command of Humphrey of Lancaster, Duke of Gloucester, brother of Henry V.[10]

Arriving in Monmouth on the trail of this style of cap, I find myself reversing into a parking space as a redoubtable woman in her eighties waves me into place. Following the shuffle of her slippers and the tap of her stick, I enter her house through a narrow hallway, stepping into another world. This is the home of Kirstie Buckland, a skilled knitter who has spent many years researching and knitting caps to designs from the mediaeval and early modern eras.

Made in varying styles to denote status and wealth, these 'signs of some degree' were knitted in England, Wales and Scotland from at least the fifteenth century; York's 'capknytters' were first mentioned in 1422, Ripon's in 1465,[11] and the sisters Joan and Isabella Capper were recorded as working in Nottingham as 'Cappeknytters' in 1478.[12] On Kirstie's table, a deft charcoal sketch drawn by Hans Holbein the Younger in the 1520s shows John More, son of lawyer, scholar and author Sir Thomas More, wearing a fashionable flattened cap, like a brimmed beret. With a rounded brim, soft body and a short piece of thread rising from its centre, the cap is a not-quite perfect pancake. In almost all of Holbein's notable portraits – of the merchant Georg Giese, the French ambassador Jean de Dinteville, Henry VIII, the wealthy Hanseatic Wedigh family of Cologne – their subjects wear similar flat caps. In the words of the chronicler John Stow, Henry VIII's 'youthfull Citizens also took them to the new fashion of flatte caps, knit of woollen yarne blacke'.[13] A member of the court might plump for a jauntily angled cap, worn cocked over one ear and perhaps adorned with a ribbon, feather or medallion. There were also soft-smooth woven velvet caps, dyed madder-red or black, for those who could afford them.

But thick, globular Monmouth caps were practical rather than fashionable items. In 1596, Sir Francis Drake ordered thirty-six

Monmouth caps for his expedition to the West Indies, while in
the 1620s a hundred men setting out for the New World with the
Massachusetts Bay Company were equipped with reddish knitted
caps 'thick, warm, fulled by hand-and-foot beating'.[14] Monmouth
caps were still approved headwear for Britain's navy in 1663.[15]

Some 50 miles north of Monmouth on the Severn's banks,
Bewdley too became famed for its caps. In *The Worthies of
England* (1661), the historian Thomas Fuller writes that 'The best
caps were formerly made at Monmouth [. . .] But on the occasion
of a great plague happening in this town, the trade was some
years since removed hence to Bewdley in Worcestershire, yet so
that they are called "Monmouth caps" unto this day.'[16] In 1712,
Daniel Defoe noted that Monmouth caps were still being made
at Bewdley, with many being sold to Dutch sailors, the same
'Hollanders'[17] who bought knitted goods from Shetland. This
trade appears to have continued until the nineteenth century, as
the 1820 *Directory* of Worcestershire records that Bewdley's cappers manufacture 'Dutch and sailors' caps [. . .] a considerable
number of which are sent to London for exportation.'[18] And as
late as 1862, the English writer George Borrow records meeting
a Welsh farmhand who, atop his mop of unruly red hair, wore 'a
soldier's cast-off Monmouth cap, so highly varnished with grease
as to appear waterproof'.[19]

In her long barrel-vaulted living room set with heavy wooden
furniture, Kirstie brings over a woven wicker basket. Inside are
knitted woollen hats, gently bell-curved and thick-brimmed.
Reds, blacks and undyed white, these sixty-stitch round caps all
share a thick brim and are topped with a rounded button. At their
base is a knitted loop; an ordinance of 1544 required 'every man
to have a cap to be made to put his salette in',[20] a 'salette' being a
light armorial headpiece without a crest.

Kirstie's involvement with Monmouth caps started fifty
years ago, when the town's museum was finding a new home

in the 1960s. Along with other members of the Monmouthshire Antiquarian Association, Kirstie helped transport and unpack its collections. She found, squashed into a box, an unlikely bundle of brown knitting, a bowl of seamless stocking stitch with a double brim. 'Being a nosey parker, I thought, "What's this?" and took it out.' Head-hugging in its form, it was eight inches deep, knitted in thick two-ply, with two and a half stitches to the inch. Kirstie suspected it might be a Monmouth cap, and she lost no time examining it and then sending it to the Victoria and Albert Museum for further testing. They assured her that 'there is nothing opposing a sixteenth-century date' – it could be Wales's oldest knitted item. The cap is now proudly displayed in Monmouth's Nelson Museum and Local History Centre.

Kirstie then set about recreating the cap. I ask her how she came to do it. 'I always made things,' she says, giving me the look of one with seven decades of experience in her finger-tips. 'In the war you had to.' Sent away from Portsmouth to the relative safety of boarding school, Kirstie, like her peers, was encouraged to knit 'dreadful' sea-boot stockings whilst Winston Churchill boomed from the wireless. After leaving school, she swept floors for high-society fashion designer Norman Hartnell in Mayfair before trading her London life for that of a Monmouthshire farmer's wife. She became involved in the Monmouthshire Antiquarian Association, and from there with Monmouth caps. For more than forty years, Kirstie has been Monmouth's only capper, making period headgear for everyone from Gérard Depardieu and Liam Neeson to Russell Crowe to wear on screen. Ian McKellen, Diana Rigg and Simon Russell Beale have sported her creations as they strut and fret upon the National Theatre's stage, and caps from Kirstie's hands have featured in the BBC series *Sharpe*, *Lorna Doone*, and *Hornblower*.

Kirstie's research reveals that cappers served as bailiffs, burgesses and jurors in the town, and that Monmouth caps were exported and sold across England and Wales, and more widely in Europe. Wool working was an important part of the town's industry by 1449: the hundred court rolls from that year include the surnames Hosier, Dier, Glover, Lace, Cardmaker and Capper.[21] As well as the gloves and caps made in Monmouth, yarn was carded and dyed on the banks of the rivers that run through the town.

Leaving Monmouth under heavy skies, I head south-west towards the St Fagans National Museum of History outside Cardiff, with its collection of antique knitwear. After a night cocooned in a heavy duvet in a shepherd's hut deep in the Black Mountains, kept awake by the unfamiliar rumbles of cattle and the shriek of tawny owls, I arrive at the museum bright and early. The curator has put out several boxes of knitted items for me; to make sure they last another century, I don thin examination gloves to stop my hands from soiling these treasures.

The Monmouth cap is not the only knitted military headgear to be produced and exported from the west of Britain. One of Wales's earliest extant knitted garments is the 'Welsh wig' – an example from 1854 is preserved in St Fagans.[22] With a close-fitting brown crown and an unusual cluster of woollen loops at its neck, it was made in Bangor and sent to Leeds as sample headwear for British soldiers in the Crimean War of 1853–6. Welsh wigs were also included in the list of items taken by Admiral John Ross and his nephew, Captain James Clark Ross, on their expedition to find the North-West Passage between 1829 and 1833, when they became the first Europeans to reach the magnetic North Pole. In 1875, Welsh wigs were still standard issue for polar exploration, included on the kit list for Sir George Nares's expedition to the North Pole via Smith Sound,[23] together with hand-knitted balaclavas.

Two balaclavas from the Nares voyage are kept in Cambridge's Scott Polar Research Institute. Dubbed 'Balaclava helmets' in honour of the Battle of Balaclava in 1854, they were first known as 'helmet caps'. Later they became known as 'Eugenies' or 'Eugenie wigs', in honour of the exiled French Empress Eugénie, wife of Napoleon III, who presented them to the Nares expedition. Embracing the causes of her new nation, Eugénie's gift of these 'homely but most useful articles'[24] was welcomed by Nares and his second-in-command, Albert Hastings Markham, who wrote in his memoir of the expedition: 'The name of her Imperial Majesty the Empress Eugénie must always be associated with the expedition as one of its warmest friends. Her kind and considerate present, consisting of a fine woollen cap for each individual, contributed materially to our comfort whilst engaged in the onerous duties of sledging.'[25] In a further token of gratitude, Nares named the Eugénie Glacier on Ellesmere Island, in Canada's Nunavut territory, after his benefactor.

Outside the army and the world of exploration, Welsh wigs were recognizable if not fashionable. Mr Fezziwig, in Charles Dickens's *A Christmas Carol*, sports one: visited by Scrooge and the Ghost of Christmas Past, Fezziwig (whose name is a nod to his cap) is the embodiment of times past, which suggests that the wearing of a 'Welch wig' in company was out of fashion when the book was written in 1843, though Scrooge's memory dates from perhaps thirty years earlier. In *Dombey and Son* (1846–8), Dickens introduces us to Solomon Gills, 'a slow, quiet-spoken, thoughtful old fellow', who runs a shop selling nautical instruments. Like Fezziwig, he appears as an outmoded relic from an earlier age, wearing a 'Welsh wig, which was as plain and stubborn a Welsh wig as ever was worn, and in which he looked like anything but a Rover'.[26]

Beside the wig at St Fagans are two immaculate stockings, knitted in cream and cherry red. These belonged to Eliza Lewis, whose name is worked in red yarn just below the garter band. Whilst stockings were worn across Britain by everyone from clergy to carters and maids to magistrates for hundreds of years, very few survive today. As with ganseys, hand-knitted items for daily domestic use were seldom kept. Worn to the point of disintegration, any parts that survived would be unravelled and the yarn repurposed. But these stockings are something special, made for the only universal and inevitable occurrence of a person's life; a macabre relic from an older age, they are funeral stockings.

Funeral stockings like Eliza's were knitted specifically for a person's laying-out. As with wedding trousseaux, these were important garments, and, like the shroud and funeral cap, were laid aside for use only at the last. Along with coffin wood, they would be given as wedding presents, or as gifts for children, a practice that continued in some areas into the twentieth century. Reading about it reminds me of a story told at my wedding, about a Quaker marriage that took place in the same Meeting House decades earlier. An elderly attender rose to his feet during the ceremony and intoned, 'Although this is a day of joy, we must remember that all is preparation for the grave.' These stockings may well have formed part of Eliza's trousseau; they were certainly knitted many years before her death, as it was only because she became ill with dropsy in later life that she was not buried in them.

Before it became common to die in hospitals or hospices, where bodies are attended by nurses and morticians, most people would breathe their last at home, their corpse washed and dressed by family or neighbours. Attired in nightshirts or nightdresses, with stockings or socks beneath, their jaws would be tied with a handkerchief or cap band, and sometimes their faces covered. Wales was not the only place in Britain where funeral stockings were made and worn: the historian Gwen Davies has found examples in Angus, Cambridgeshire, Cumbria, Durham, Lancashire, Leicester, Lincolnshire, Northumberland, and Yorkshire.[27] Of those that survive, Davies notes that most are white and made of wool or cotton, though only a handful have been handmade. The Leicestershire stockings are the oldest extant and date from the 1820s; the most recent pair date from the early 1960s.

The travel writer and novelist Bruce Chatwin writes the knitting of funeral stockings into *On the Black Hill* (1982), the fictional history of a Welsh family told around the story of their farm, The Vision. Hannah, grandmother of the brothers at the book's heart, is old-fashioned in her actions and attitudes, particularly towards her son's new wife. In warm July, she 'spent the head of the day in the kitchen [...] knitting very slowly – a long pair of white woollen socks'.[28] As her daughter-in-law prepares for the birth of her baby, Hannah mumbles as she knits: 'It's a coffin, not a cradle, she'll be needing.'

Old Hannah has kept her wedding trousseau for more than fifty years, and as she nears the completion of the socks, she takes out 'a single white cotton nightdress to wear with the white socks when they laid her out as a corpse'.[29] Come the beginning of August, she turns the heel of her second sock; from then on, she 'knitted slower and slower, sighing between the stitches and croaking, "Not long now."' The progress of her knitting acts as a signifier for her hastening death: 'That night, Hannah rounded off the toe of her second sock and, three days later, died.'[30]

Funeral stockings formed a tiny part of the stocking industry in Wales. As in the Dales and parts of Scotland, commercial handknitting was most prominent in areas with a ready supply of wool. The earliest mention of hand-knitted Welsh stockings comes from John Aubrey's *Perambulation of the County of Surrey* of 1673, when Welsh cattle-drovers sold hand-knit stockings 'from Michaelmas to Christmas' as far east as the market town of Farnham.[31] By the 1780s and 1790s, around 190,000 pairs of stockings, with an annual value of some £18,000 – the equivalent of around £2 million in 2018 – were arriving in London to be sold in the capital and exported across the Continent.[32] Bala in Merioneth, Llanrwst in Denbighshire, and Tregaron in Cardiganshire all had thriving woollen industries centred on their markets: in 1800, Bala's stocking sales stood at 200,000 pairs a year; very fine ones could sell for as much as 5*s*., with children's socks 8*d*. a pair. But the advent of machine-made hose imported from the Midlands began to eat away at the Bala industry; by 1851, only 250 people were working in stocking manufacture in North Wales.

The stockings often combined two colours; for economy, the toe and welt were knitted in undyed yarn, lanolin-rich and more hard-wearing,[33] resistant to pokey toes and weathering above the tops of boots. The legs and feet of men's stockings would be made from dyed blue-grey yarn, a colour known as 'pot blue', the women's more commonly black or speckled lichen-brown, either dyed at home or at the mill. Such stockings weren't just worn in Wales, but exported internationally, as this poem by 'Sarnicol' (schoolmaster and poet Thomas Jacob Thomas) attests:

> *Stocking wearers of all creation,*
> *Here are found,*
> *The blue and white stockings of the Cardi,*
> *On the world's legs are found.*[34]

Ornamental patterns known as 'clocks' or 'quirks' were also knitted in, and could command a higher price. Some stockings were footless, knitted without a sole, and anchored in place with a loop of wool around the big toe. Going barefoot was common among the poor; 'the women are generally without shoes or stockings',[35] observed visiting politician Sir Christopher Sykes in the eighteenth century. Alas no original examples of these footless stockings appear to have survived.[36]

As in Yorkshire and the Channel Islands, in Wales knitting was not seen as a woman's occupation. Revd John Evans noted in his *Letters Written During a Tour Through North Wales* (1804) that in Bala knitting was 'the common employment of the neighbourhood, for both sexes of all ages, even the men frequently take up the needles and assist the female, in labour, where the chief support of the family is derived.'[37] Although the stockings did sell, once costs were covered a knitter might only be left with a shilling a week, and they had to work intensively to make even this meagre sum. Knitting could also be competitive, as Evans observed on a visit to Ceredigion: 'They frequently knit what they call *guird* for no other wager but honour; they let loose from bottoms or balls equal lengths of yarn tied together, and the first that knits up to the knots becomes the conqueror and receives the praise. This emulation tends to give them a facility and great quickness in the use of needles.'[38]

As the minister of Glenmuick noted in Scotland, it was often the women in these rural communities who worked the hardest. Walter Davies, in his 1810–15 survey of South Wales, commented:

'Such is the employment and such the only means of subsistence within reach of the poorer sort of females [...], although these are as remarkable for industry as the males are for an aversion to labour.'[39] From Wales to Yorkshire, Shetland to Cornwall, hand-knitting was for centuries the work of the poor.

At St Fagans, I paw through stockings and exquisite knitted bedspreads, twentieth-century cardigans and dresses, hand-made from wool. Taking a look in the museum shop as I leave, I spy Welsh four-ply *gwlân* from the Cambrian Mountains, the perfect weight for a pair of stockings. Perhaps I could make myself a pair? The yarn is smooth and beautiful, but as I turn it over in my hands the thought of knitting for the dead me of the future is unnerving. The idea of knitting them for someone else also repulses, but a century ago it was many people's one last act of love, a taking of responsibility in the inevitable face of death. I leave funeral stockings for another year.

I decide, instead, to replicate the Monmouth cap. For this I need some 'Lemster Ore', the wool of the Ryeland sheep. Just as lustrous Longwool 'Cotswold Lion' fleece com-manded high prices at mediaeval markets, so too did fine fleece from Leominister in Herefordshire. 'Lemster Ore' was sold at Leominster thanks to Mary I's charter, which estab-lished a wholesale market there that was unrivalled in the west of England.[40] Ryeland sheep had been developed by the Benedictine monks of Leominster in the fourteenth century, on the surrounding rye pastures that gave the breed its name, and Monmouth cappers used the wool from this rich area of land to make their caps.

Ryelands are today farmed most commonly as 'hobby sheep' in small flocks; as a result, pure Ryeland yarn is not easy to buy. On the hunt for some, I point the car north towards Ceredigion, leaving Cardiff as autumn's wet weather draws in from the Atlantic. This hunt is something of a fool's errand – modern downland breeds are mostly nineteenth-century inventions, cross-bred and fattened up, and the fleece of today's improved sheep is much thicker than that of their mediaeval forebears.

My quest for wool is a modern version of the ancient Welsh tradition, *gwlana*, 'to gather wool', a custom similar to *lloffa*, gleaning corn from the fields after harvest, and *blota*, the begging of flour by the poor. In Breconshire in the east, and in Cardiganshire, Merioneth and Carmarthenshire in the west, women combed the hedges and hills for wool to spin for their knitting. The routes they took were known as *llwybrau gwlân* – woollen paths. The women would sometimes walk for a fortnight in small groups, carrying provisions pick-a-back and pillowcases or sacks to transport their cargo home, sheltering in barns and farmhouses.

Gathering would start at daybreak and go on until sundown, and each woman might collect as much as four pounds of wool in a day. Weather had an impact on the quality of the wool: hard winters followed by a warm, wet spring were favoured, as they encouraged the growth of new fleece, which was then shed in quantity. The disdainful sense of 'wool gathering', to mean day-dreamy idle fancies, dates from the sixteenth century, used by writers from across the British Isles. Whilst gathering may have lingered longest in west Wales, it was clearly a practice widely known – and belittled. In 1742, John Torbuck, the author of *A Collection of Welch Travels, and Memoirs of Wales*, came across 'a crew of these Pickering Wool-gatherers, the very Emblems of Beggary', who wore 'Locks of Wool, tuck'd like Scuts under their girdles, as a Badge of their Profession and some cramm'd stockings bobbling at the Sides, as Trophics of their Pyracies'.[41] Gathering was still taking place in 1893, when Maric Trevelyan notes children in rural villages 'had the privilege of collecting wool from the hedges and picking up the bits that were left after the shearing', supplying the women of their families with fleece to card, spin and knit.[42]

Although some denigrated the gatherers, gathering parties were often welcomed in rural communities, their arrival eagerly anticipated in isolated mountain farmsteads. Women would often return to the same farms year on year, bringing with them news from other villages. The right to a fortnight's wool-gathering was often secured as part of a female servant's employment. Women would then spin and knit their wool into clothes, or take it to be spun and woven into blankets at the mills.

Not all wool-gathering consisted of women scouring the fields and hedges for cast-off scraps of wool. In some areas, *gwlana* was more like a self-appointed farm tithe, similar to Islam's *zakat*. As Huw Evans observed in 1922, farmer's wives would put aside two or three fleeces specifically for these itinerant labourers. The gatherers would take to the road in small groups, led by an experienced middle-aged woman who introduced them at each farm. This regular gatherer would receive a generous bundle of fleece, whilst the newly introduced received a smaller portion.[43] As historian S. Minwel Tibbot notes, *lloffa*, *blota* and *gwlana* were accepted methods by which rural society could provide for its poorest members in the days prior to the existence of the welfare state.[44]

In the 1970s, some elderly Welsh women remembered *gwlana* taking place in Montgomeryshire, and families still owned blankets made from *gwlana* wool gathered by previous generations. The tradition of *noson weu* or *cymmorth gwau* – knitting nights or assemblies – was long-standing. Just as in the Yorkshire Dales and the Channel Islands, Welsh women would gather to craft and talk. In 1747, the Welsh antiquarian and naturalist Thomas Pennant wrote of a *cymmorth gwau* in Bala: 'During the long winter nights the females, through love of society, often assemble at one another's house, to knit, sit around a fire, and listen to some old tale or [...] antient song or the sound of a harp'.[45] Lady Eleanor Butler, one half of the literary 'Ladies of Llangollen', a pair of

Irish gentlewomen who moved to Llangollen in 1780, also noted the gathering of knitters, this time at a fair:

> *White glittering frost [. . .] A fair in the village. What a picture*
> *might be drawn from our parlour window of the crowds describing*
> *the opposite mountain and passing through the field before our*
> *cottage [. . .] the women knitting as they went along.*[46]

It wasn't just knitting that was done communally in the winter: the plucking and stuffing of feathers at *noson bluo* and the peeling of rushes for rush-lights at *noson bilio* were other sociable parts of Welsh farm life.

It is a bright and blustery October day when I rattle the hired car up a rutted track in the Teifi valley in west Wales to find Garthenor farm. Meaning 'view of Garth', Garthenor has likely stood since Roman times – in nearby Llanio, the remains of a Roman bathhouse and fort are discernible. At 217 metres high, Garth is more hill than mountain, but its presence defines the places for miles around. The farm hunkered on its slopes is simply Garth; on the hill's northern side is Ochr Garth – *ochr* meaning 'side'. Before it lies Godre'rgarth, 'on Garth's edge', and on its eastern slope is Cefn-garth-uchaf, 'high on Garth's back'.

Garthenor is more than just a sheep farm. Set up in the 1990s to sell Ryeland, Shetland, Herdwick and Manx Loaghtan yarn to knitters who wanted 'real wool' on their needles, Garthenor was Britain's first organic yarn producer. When it began to trade, the certification 'Pure Organic Wool' did not exist; its owner, Sally Davies, worked closely with the Soil Association to develop the standard, and in 2003 her yarn gained the first fully organic certification in the world. Today Garthenor is run by Sally and her son Jonny, and Cornwall's Natural Fibre Company spin fleeces sent to them by Garthenor from organic flocks across

Britain. Between 2016 and 2017, the company expanded twenty-five-fold, as Jonny's eye for brand and style matched his mum's fleece expertise. You might expect sleek, glossy sheds marching over the hillside, but Garthenor is still run from the barns of this thousand-year-old farm.

Together we walk through the fields where Sally and Jonny tend their Shetland and Ryeland flocks, and we stop to admire their three prize Ryeland rams. Dark stocky Selwyn with his love of apples, pale teddy-bear Serge, and tiny boisterous Winston, this year's most promising ram lamb, all come to us without needing the enticement of the bucket. A couple of fields away, Ryeland and Shetland ewes graze, and we walk down to meet tiny Mary, a white Ryeland with the rarest of appurtenances – two horns, where most Ryelands have none. Bob the dog shakes her tail and pesters us to throw sticks, and slinky brown-black cats entreat our ankles, begging to be carried. Garthenor is a place of care as well as commerce. I leave with two skeins of Ryeland yarn, one a mottled deep grey-brown, the other white, from which to make a Monmouth cap.

Back home, I unpack these skeins and inhale their dry, sheepy smell, redolent of the farmyard. In the Middle Ages, Ryeland sheep were famed for their fleece's fineness, but unlike the Cotswold Longwool, Ryeland now has a much shorter staple, perfect for woollen spinning, which emphasizes the fibres' loft and lightness.[47] After winding the skein into a ball, I work this chunky yarn on 9 mm needles into thirty rounds of sixty stitches, decreasing evenly to a small circle of eight stitches, and finish it with a neat I-cord loop. The brim I work down from the cast-on edge, adding in three stitches across the round and doubling each stitch to make it warmly dense. Kirstie Buckland always felts her caps, thickening them in the warm agitation of a washing machine before leaving them to dry on head-shaped moulds. I have the anxious neophyte's reluctance to ruin my knitting by bunging it in the washing machine, so instead opt for the manage-able safety of the sink, where I plunge it into water hot then cold. I need not have worried. After the first hot-cold dip, the hat remains exactly as it was. I try again, and again. This yarn takes some persuading: as I repeat the hot-cold water baths, I remind myself that this is not the ancient Ryeland that Monmouth's cap-pers would have known, but a more robust modern wool.

After many agitations and heat treatments, the cap eventually shrinks a little to become a tough acorn-cup of wool. I pop the cap on and look in the mirror. This is not a stylish item: it cups my head like a bowl, and its jaunty loop stands up like an acorn's stalk. Worn under a helmet, I can see how it would have provided an essential layer of soft protection. Outside the world of film and historical re-enactment, the market for Monmouth caps can only support a manufactory of one.

I think back to the last tale of caps I heard in Monmouth. In May 1927, one of Kirstie's friends watched the funeral of Mrs Lucia Rosher, aged ninety-six, of Trewyn in the Black Mountains. She had requested that her Monmouth cap should go to the grave with her. It was brought to Oldcastle Church in the horse-drawn hearse, and lies within her weed-covered grave in a spot gloomy and isolated even on the brightest day.[48] I don't think I will request to be buried with mine.

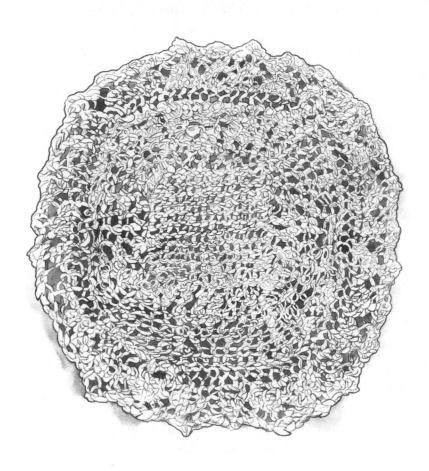

11

Haps, Shawls and New Arrivals

October closes with heavy frosts, turning the grass to glitter and filming the car in rime. Autumn draws towards winter and, as the leaves brown and fall, we turn back clocks, turn up the heating, and settle into the season's rhythm. We return home after the sun is set, and there are a few more weeks of bright mornings before the beckoning solstice pulls the curtain down. Soups and stews sustain us as the last salad leaves wilt in the garden and this year's remaining blackberries turn to mush in the hedge.

Many knitters thrill at the change in weather, a chance to dig out favourite jumpers, hats and scarves. The organized shake out the heady scent of cedar from their neatly folded woollens; the rest of us give our winter wardrobe a quick once-over with our fingers crossed. We pick up needles too, lengthening nights driving us inside early. Cold hands long for new gloves; chilly foreheads for new hats.

As the days shorten, I feel a familiar pull on my solar plexus – a yearning to be among the tall buildings and crowded streets of a city. Towns draw us to them in the darkening days, their shop lights like beacons that promise companionship, luxury and warmth. Every winter, I head to London to catch up with friends, cementing friendships with tea and beer and conversation. This year I will also be picking up other threads, following the knitters' trail.

Arriving almost fresh from the night train on a clear November day, I head west towards Kensington, bound for the archives of London's Victoria and Albert Museum. Among the V&A's large collection of historic patterns and knitted garments in the archives near Olympia is one of Britain's oldest surviving pieces of infant knitwear. Dating from the mid-seventeenth century, this white baby jacket is believed to have adorned the infant Charles II. Knitted with cotton, in stocking stitch decorated with textured geometric patterns, the open-fronted T-shaped coat has a square moss stitch neck and is believed to have been knitted in the round and steeked (cut open).

At the archives desk, the first slender box of knitting patterns is weighed carefully like a newborn before being handed over. Untying the broad cream string, I prise open the brown packet with gentle fingers. This is one of a multitude of boxes containing handwritten Victorian patterns, often little more than paper scraps folded into minute envelopes. Trapped safely between acid-free archive sheets, the patterns date from a time before the ubiquity of knitting shorthand, and show how patterns travelled directly woman-to-woman, the twice-daily penny post connecting them like a hand-inked Ravelry. Knitting patterns record friendships and connections, knitting people together through their craft.

At 22 Connaught Terrace, Hyde Park, Mrs Barton received a letter containing a pattern for a 'Raised Knitting Sock of Bell or Foxglove Stitch'. In nearby Kensington, Mrs King opened an envelope embossed with the initials 'R.M.' to find a pattern for 'Shell Mittens'. Several patterns were sent to Mrs Manclark of High Street, Rochester, who appears to have been something of a pattern collector. One of her friends, a Mrs Benifold, wrote: 'I have written these directions from memory and I think you will find them correct. I called today hoping to be able to explain to you by word of mouth, how the thumb was cast.' A pattern for a 'Newly Arranged Knit Polka Jacket' arrived from Sittingbourne in Kent by penny post, signed 'Catherine Dodd', followed by a polka jacket pattern delivered 'with Mrs Drage's Compliments'. I catch a glimpse of private friendships and familial relations from over a century ago, demonstrated through the medium of knitting patterns.

Knitting for babies exerts one of the strongest pulls between a knitter and her needles. Most knitters have made hats, bootees, mittens and blankets for imminent arrivals. Knitting welcomes new life, the stitches in these garments trapping tiny pockets of air to warm, comfort, and protect. Friends and relatives pick up their needles as soon as a pregnancy is announced, and in hospitals babies are welcomed with minute hats made by hands they'll never know. Each inch of yarn passes through the knitter's hands, and the final raiment will later lie against the skin of a brand-new person, warming their small body. It's as close as you can get to touch. For those of us who show affection through our making, knitting is an act of love.

At home, stuffed into an overflowing suitcase, are three skeins of yarn, waiting for me to begin my next piece of knitting. One is a sandy shade of fawn, one creamy white, one dun-coloured. Feather-light and fine, these lace-weight yarns were given to me at a farm in Orkney as September came to a close. On my way to Shetland Wool Week, I had visited the home of Jane Cooper and her flock of Borerays at Burnside Farm on Mainland, Orkney. Boreray is the UK's rarest sheep breed: in 2017, the Rare Breeds Survival Trust listed them as 'vulnerable', with fewer than nine hundred breeding ewes. Borerays are named for the island in the St Kilda archipelago, west of the Outer Hebrides, where the largest population of them still live, in splendid isolation from regular human contact. A small, compact sheep with fleeces both dark and light, some Borerays are not horned, but 'scurred' – sporting small pseudo-horns attached not to the skull but to the skin.

Living on this most inaccessible island in the St Kilda archipelago, the Boreray breed is the result of isolation combined with judicious husbandry. Boreray, with its steep cliffs and huge seabird population, offered good grazing on its smooth top, though it was difficult to transfer sheep to and from the island. Until 1930, St Kilda's men visited Boreray once a year to shear their sheep, taking a few back to their homes on Hirta for meat. Other than this, the sheep were left to themselves, although there is archaeological evidence from the Iron Age of more permanent human habitation on the island. At times throughout their history, St Kildans were known to row to Harris, 41 miles due east, to bring back fresh-blood sheep to improve their flock. In the 1870s, four Blackface rams from Lewis reached St Kilda this way. Also known as Hebridean Blackface, this breed was itself a hybrid, mixing Scottish Blackface with the dark, multi-horned Hebridean. When the islanders were evacuated from St Kilda, at their request, in August 1930, their sheep were either taken with them to the mainland or destroyed – save for a clutch that remained on Boreray. For over forty years, the world's entire population of Borerays weathered Atlantic storms alone on their eponymous island.

In 1971, the modern world intervened. Three ewes and three rams were brought from Boreray to the mainland by the Brathay Exploration Group, to become part of the breeding research flock at Roslin, near Edinburgh. It was discovered that the breed combines elements of the Scottish Tan Face, the Old Scottish Shortwool, and the Hebridean Blackface with the wild Soay. In 1981, the Rare Breeds Survival Trust recognized the Borerays as a distinct breed, and three groups went to farms across Britain.

One of only a handful of Boreray flocks in the UK, Jane Cooper's is descended from the Roslin flock. A hand-spinner who for many years lived in Newcastle, she is a relative newcomer to island living, drawn to Orkney by the possibilities of the good farming life. Her flock now numbers around fifty sheep and, like many farmers, she knows each beast and its pedigree on sight. Hearing of my quest for knitting yarns and stories, she invited me to meet her on her farm. Orkney was on my route to Shetland, so I decided to pay Jane and her Borerays a visit.

As light rain turned the hills to mist, Jane kitted me out in wellies and full-body waterproofs, and together we headed out into the soft mizzle. Burnside is a hill farm, its fields steep and boggy, often running with water. Ewes and lambs thronged the lower field and one of this year's new arrivals, tiny Ferdinand, ran to feed from us and let me hold him in my arms. Jane keeps the rams at the top of the farm, and we plodged further up the hill to meet them, our wellies sinking knee-deep in soft moss. Chief among these rams is the aptly named Bollocks, who ran towards the bucket we rattled, and munched close to our feet, almost oblivious to our presence. I enquired about the origins of his unusual moniker. 'This is what happens when you let your adult children choose your sheep's names,' Jane remarked, giving her prize ram a companionable scratch on his hard poll.

When I left Burnside Farm, Jane pressed into my hands a rich bundle of yarn. Three skeins in colours like sand, they mirror the muted silver-cream and stony brown of Orcadian beaches. Soft and lightly haloed, this yarn twists together strands of ancient ovine DNA. Spun by the Natural Fibre Company in Cornwall for Blacker Yarns, the yarn combines Jane's Boreray fleece with both Soay and Shetland wool. Only tiny batches are available each year – the Boreray clip numbers around thirty good fleeces. Dubbed 'St Kilda Laceweight', it is among the rarest yarn in Britain. In giving me her unused skeins from the first-ever batch of St Kildan yarn, Jane handed me a rare and special gift. I left Orkney with my heart full and a commitment to make something special from this yarn.

These skeins were not the only thing that travelled with me to Orkney. Though I did not then know it, a baby was already taking shape inside me. I escaped seasickness on the ferry, but now, seven weeks into my pregnancy, it comes to catch me. Nausea ambushes me throughout the day, striking hardest when I am on my feet or concentrating on a task. I have to retreat to bed or the sofa at odd times, incapable of concentration. With my world skewed by strange sensations, I am forced to put down my knitting needles.

My eyelids and yawning mouth betray me as I struggle to make it through conversations, books, even television programmes. Where once I stayed up past eleven, now my body demands to sleep at nine each night, pinning me horizontal with exhaustion. A stranger has worked its way into my body, resetting my clocks and tuning me to a different time. At four in the morning, I wake, too sick to sleep. My insides suck and swirl like sea eddies, pulled by a new current. This pre-dawn era is a weird and soundless time, when no cars whine past the window and even the street lights slumber.

All is quiet, but not lonely. Inside me, a tiny life flickers, too small to feel the beat of itself. The doctor tells me my body began to form this baby seven weeks ago, but it is too soon to feel or see a tell-tale bump. I have to divine its continuing presence using other witchcraft. I must read my body anew, to distinguish between the discomfort of pregnancy and the war-drummings of illness. This is a sickness I do not need to starve or purge. It is to be anticipated, tholed, treated with caution, fed like a cold. More than this, I learn that this nausea is to be welcomed. It is a harbinger of good things, a message from my baby to my body that all is well within. In this liminal time before a reassuring scan or a visible bump, it is my sensory divining rod.

This baby will be the recipient of something knitted from my St Kilda Laceweight yarn. I ponder what to knit for my firstborn, dazzled by a wealth of patterns, contemporary and historic. When friends have had children, I have supplied a steady stream of hats, cardigans, mittens and bootees; baby knits are quick and often easy. I have a stash of baby knitting patterns for everything from bonnets to all-in-one rompers, and I tend to work these in acrylic or cotton yarns, attuned to a new parent's need for easy washing. But for my own baby, sensible garments seem less important. What I knit for it must be beautiful, special, a work of art – a fitting herald for this particular new person.

Trawling through the V&A's later patterns, I find a 1950s booklet published by the yarn giants Patons & Baldwins: 'For the New Baby – 8 Woollies for the First Six Months'. It contains patterns for matinee jackets – scaled-down versions of the once-fashionable coats worn to matinee performances[2] – as well as knitted dresses, vests, and 'pilch knickers'. I've never heard this term before, but a sepia illustration shows a pair of loose-fitting drawers, with elasticated legs and waist, designed to be put over a baby's nappy. The word 'pilch' dates to 1674, in the sense of a woollen or flannel cloth wrapped around an infant's bottom. By 1799, Michael Underwood, a male midwife, wrote in *A Treatise on the Diseases of Children* that the practice 'of wearing a pilch (as it is called;) [is] an old fashion still too much in use'. This disdain appears not to have been widely felt, for, in 1869, Mrs Beeton recommends that new mothers will need 'four pilches' and 'two water-proof pilches' in addition to four dozen nappies for their baby. Wrappers remain an essential component of today's reusable-nappy kit – a pilch by another name, though no longer knitted.

I wonder about knitting a shawl in which to wrap my baby. 'Mrs Hunter's Shawl', also known as the 'Cloud Drift Baby

Shawl', was one of the most popular patterns of the twentieth century, knitted from Shetland to Australia, Canada to London. Its roots are in North Shetland, but its name is not traditional: it was chosen by Patons & Baldwins' chief designer, James Norbury. Kate Davies has traced its probable origins to Agnes Hunter (nee Smith) of Muness, Mainland, who was bedridden and in her eighties when Norbury visited Shetland in the 1950s.

Patons & Baldwins had begun life as two separate companies. Baldwins was set up in Halifax in 1785 by James Baldwin as a wool-washing and fulling business. In 1814, 200 miles away in Alloa, Clackmannanshire, John Paton began to spin and dye wool, buying machinery from England and importing machine-spinners to teach local workers how to use them.[3] Throughout the nineteenth century, the family-run firms of John Paton & Son and J. & J. Baldwin and Partners continued to operate in parallel – and in competition. The year after Baldwins' Beehive trademark was registered in 1876, Patons patented their 'Rose and Hand' motif, its clasped fist flanked by the motto *Virtue Viget* – 'it thrives by its goodness'. Both companies were in a period of empire-building and expansion, buying vast quantities of wool from abroad, with Baldwins swallowing up the smaller yarn companies of R. H. Barker and Isaac Briggs from West Yorkshire and John Whitemore of Leicestershire.

As knitting became a hobby among the expanding middle classes of the nineteenth century, it became clear that hand-knitters were keen for instructions as well as yarn. In 1896, Patons produced their *Knitting and Crochet Book*, designed, of course, to encourage their customers to buy more of their yarn, priced at 1*s.* and containing over a hundred patterns. In 1899, they published *The Universal Knitting Book*, priced at 1*d.*, which ran to three editions before being combined with Baldwins' *Woolcraft*.

In April 1920, the two old rivals joined to form Patons & Baldwins, though the Halifax and Alloa factories continued to operate separately. In a spirit of ostentatious compromise, it was decided to hold the new firm's board meeting precisely halfway between the two workshops. The company chartered a private carriage on a Midland Railways train to bring the southern directors north, and the Scottish board travelled south from Stirling on the London train, tucking into lunch as they sped through the Borders. At four o'clock, the two trains converged on Carlisle, where fourteen directors and all their attendant staff finally began their meeting after their respective 110-mile journeys.

In 1946, James Norbury was working as Patons & Baldwins' chief designer. A heavy-set, balding man with definite opinions on what was and wasn't 'proper' knitting, Norbury wrote *The Penguin Knitting Book* (1957), as well as presenting television programmes extolling knitting's virtues and imparting technique. Didactic and self-centred, Norbury nevertheless did much to popularize the craft of knitting, though some of his research and pattern 'designs' may be considered sketchy and at times even plagiaristic.

A case in point is 'Mrs Hunter's Shawl'. 'Designed in Shetland' proclaims the cover of the Patons & Baldwins' printed pattern, and the original garment from which the stitch patterns are copied has been kept in the Knitting & Crochet Guild archives near Holmfirth in West Yorkshire. 'Brand-iron' edges give way to borders of trees and geometric shapes, dissolving into a central 'cat's-paw' panel. But 'Mrs Hunter's Shawl' is not a true Shetland pattern: its construction – it is put together by knitting separate sections and then grafting them into a single piece – is rarely if ever found on the islands.[4]

Shetland haps, knitted shawls made for everyday use and worn by women and girls as they went about their daily life since at least the early nineteenth century, are most commonly knitted from the outside in, known as 'borders-in'. The hap's edge is peaked or scalloped, bordered with 'old shell' lace, and some measure as much as 2 metres in diameter. Once worked, the edge stitches are picked up and grafted together, weaving the shawl's central body within this frame. This method of construction means that a shawl or hap's composite sections can be knitted together as you go, without the need for lots of seaming at the end.

As I look through patterns, I am reminded of last winter in Grasmere, where I sat in the Wordsworth Museum examining boxes of knitting patterns. Some were in the hand of Wordsworth's daughter Dora, who, with the words 'cast on nine loops', flickered to life. Beside Dora's pattern was a little red volume with a cover scratched and worn; it belonged to Sara Hutchinson, Dora's cousin, and contained a mixture of notes, recipes and knitting patterns, signed 'L. Dew', 'J. Lethert' and many more. A domestic scrapbook or 'commonplace book', there were also tiny knitted samples pinned to its pages. An egg cosy, Johnny's sock, Dora's night cap: the minutiae of lives through the lens of their knitwear. Opening it, I found a ghost inside: a thin paper pattern of an infant's sock, pinned to the inside cover. On the final page, Dora had written out a pattern for a baby shawl: 'I think my shawl has two coloured rows to one of white. Two half-pound skeins of coloured and one half-pound of white are required for my shawls.'

While in Shetland, the first week of my baby's internal existence then unknown to me, I drove through heavy rain to the north Mainland village of Ollaberry, on the hunt for shawls. On that wild autumn afternoon, Ollaberry Hall was hung with haps, which, at first glance, look like lace – filigreed froth made with bobbins. But they are knitted open-work, shaped with two needles.

Where 'shawl' is Kashmiri in origin, its long drawling vowel invoking Victorian drawing rooms, 'hap' is a hiccup, a small ordinary word. The two are sisters, one that decorates and one that works. In the words of the designer and writer Kate Davies, whose book on haps traces the history of these workaday shawls, a hap is 'a thing of doing and using, and the shawl [...] a thing of being'.[5] 'Hap' is a riddle in a syllable: happiness, mishap, hapless – 'hap' connotes good luck, its absence the reverse. But these knitted haps have their roots not in the abstraction of Anglo-Saxon good fortune, but in practical physical comfort. 'To hap' means to wrap or cover; this usage was common across the British Isles in the Middle Ages, but today is largely restricted to a few communities in northern England and Scotland.

Ollaberry Hall was busy with knitters, plying their pins and spinning wheels, or serving tea and homemade cakes. Truly, this was a 'hap-pening': a celebration of haps. I sat down beside Betsy and Linda Williamson, sisters whose knitting wins prizes among the high standards of north Shetland. They learned to knit as children, Betsy from a visiting grand-uncle when she was four years old, and were trained up gradually, graduating from plain knitting to lace and colourwork. They were desperate to use a knitting belt like their mother's, and were also taught to use a *raepin* string, a length of twine that runs through the knitting and is tied to the knitter's clothing to maintain tension.

Unlike Wales's densely woven *siôl magu*, Shetland's baby shawls seemed spider-spun. I picked my way through a lacy cathedral of knitting hung from the hall's wooden walls, the haps' delicate tracery echoing Gothic windows. They were exquisite, catching the eye like glistening cobwebs at sunset. Some were pinned against dark boards, the better to show the fineness of their stitches, others had been draped over dummies or boxes, their filigree fanning out like the tails of exotic birds. Some were worked in coloured yarn – warm chocolates and light fawns; others gleamed white as frost, their rounds of perfect loops like frozen ripples on a pond.

Most of Ollaberry's haps have been knitted from the finest grades of Shetland wool, some spun by hand. Carol Christiansen, curator of Shetland Museum's textile collections, notes that there is a perceptible change in yarn quality between the nineteenth century and today, and that fleece selection and breed has in turn been shaped by fashion. Hand-spun garments that date from the second half of the nineteenth century often contain coarse, long fibres which give the yarn a worsted quality, whereas machine-spun yarns from the 1920s are much softer, more like Merino but with a lustre all their own. Yarns knitted up in the 1960s were generally woollen-spun and therefore fluffier and thicker than earlier yarns.[6]

North Shetland is famous for its lace knitting – the best is said to come from Unst. Just 12 by 5 miles, tiny Unst is Shetland's – and Britain's – most northerly inhabited island. Like many of Scotland's islands, its population has long been in decline, decreasing from 2,780 in 1871 to 1,127 in 1971, and hovering around 700 in 2017. In

1851, more than two hundred knitters of either stockings or shawls were listed in Unst's census, along with almost fifty knitters of other items, and more than a hundred spinners. This was not unusual for the Shetland Isles: in 1856, it was estimated that three quarters of Shetland's income, excluding that from urban Lerwick, was from the sale of knitted items. Throughout the nineteenth century, Unst's knitters grew in number, with almost four hundred islanders earning their keep by their pins in 1891.

As with Fair Isle and its vibrant colourwork, Unst carved out its own knitting niche. Lace yarn is the lightest, finest of all yarn weights. Sold as either one- or two-ply, it is almost always smoothly worsted-spun. Unst became known for its breathtaking 'wedding-ring' shawls – lacy wraps that can measure six feet square but remain light and fine enough to pass through a wedding band. The Unst Heritage Trust has estimated that a 5-foot shawl contains more than 7 miles of hand-spun two-ply yarn and more than one million stitches, yet weighs barely 70 grams.

It is not known exactly when Unst became famous for its fine lace-knitting. In 1845, a visiting minister from the Free Church of Scotland was shown some shawls and remarked: 'The fibres were so slender and the texture so fine, that one would mistake them for Brussels lace. Knitting is the grand employment of all the females.'[7] In 1856, Eliza Edmonston, author of *Sketches and Tales of the Shetland Islands*, noted that open-work knitting 'is an invention for which the Shetland females themselves deserve all the credit' and that its popularity had been achieved 'without the aid either of pattern-book or of other instruction, than the diligence and taste of the natives themselves',[8] though she also remarked that stockings, gloves and other colourwork items were also knitted on the island.

Bleached with sulphur in a barrel or smoke-box, yarn was hand-spun and plied from two spools set in a 'sweerie box'. Uyeasound, on Unst's southern coast, became a byword for fine spinning, and even in the 1920s a young spinner, grandmother-taught, was able to earn 7*d.* for a 36-inch hank of a hundred hand-spun threads. In 1882, Unst's lace knitting was included in the definitive six-volume encyclopaedia *The Dictionary of Needlework*.[9]

Many lace knitters were women – but there were some notable exceptions. The scholar Roslyn Chapman has explored the stories of some of Shetland's male knitters, including James Moar of West Shore, Uyeasound, who knitted shawls 'for titled ladies' and won first prize for his 'Fine White Shetland Shawl' in the Highland Industries Knitting Competition of July 1894.[10] Born on

Yell in 1856, the youngest of seven, James Moar was listed as an 'invalid' in the census. In 1881, he wrote to a 'Lady', whose identity is unknown, to offer his services as a knitter,[11] explaining that he has taken up the task of 'female work' so that he could contribute to the household income. Moar also sold the hosiery he knitted to the shop in Uyeasound, and in the 1901 census he is listed as a 'lace knitter, of wool, silk and cotton'.[12] His death certificate from November 1919 gives his occupation as a 'knitter of lace hosiery'.

Chapman also tells the story of Gilbert Williamson, an Unst-born Shetlander who worked as a butcher and knitted more than six hundred items in both silk and wool. A local newspaper marvelled at the fineness of his work: 'with the same hand he cleaves a meat bone and delicately builds up shimmering fabrics'.[13] David Sutherland, born at Colvadale on Unst in 1850, worked as a watchmaker, and also designed lace knitting patterns. A shawl made to a pattern of his invention was sent to the Duke and Duchess of Kent upon their wedding in 1935, though Sutherland himself had died in September 1928.

Looking through my collection of patterns as a twenty-first-century mother-to-be, I realize that not much has changed in babywear design. Baby bonnets have been a staple of an infant's layette from at least the eighteenth century; often they were knitted in cotton and featured a central star or circle that would sit atop the baby's head, with ornate lacy borders and edges worked out from this.[14] As the knitwear historian Sandy Black points out, 'This consistency in production has not always ensured popularity with those who had to wear the clothes. An association of knitting with subsistence living and poverty [...] persisted in popular perception';[15] she cites examples from the 1960s of women sewing labels from shop-bought clothes into their children's handmade garments. No doubt I am already embarrassing this proto-child with my knitting.

Most of my knits for babies have been small, simple pieces, knitted in front of the television or on a long journey. Looking back over my year of exploration, I see how knitting traditions developed and survived longest in communities that needed diverse sources of income, where existence could be marginal. In island and rural communities, dependent on the vagaries of the weather, sea and harvest, knitting was a flexible occupation, part of life that could be picked up and put down, fitted in around whatever needed doing most. With its repetitive and memorable patterns, knitting still slots in around our modern lives. Many of us knit less in summer and more in winter, susceptible to the seasons. We knit to the television and the radio, to audiobooks, to the background chatter on the bus and whilst we talk with friends. Only for more complex designs do I find myself shutting out the rest of the world, concentrating fiercely over pins and pattern.

I decide to knit a hap: not a fine christening shawl but a serviceable hap, beautiful and useful. My child, as yet only as a smudge of moving limbs and the flutter of a heartbeat on an ultrasound scan, will need a wool wrap for the cold winters of Scotland's east coast. Lying in bed at night with my hands over my stomach's tiny swell, I will this foetus on, to keep growing and living so that in six months I may hold it in my arms, outside my body. I want to hap it in the warm embrace of wool.

I learned to knit my first hap during Shetland Wool Week with Donna Smith, a Shetland knitter with an impeccable pedigree. Donna learned the craft from her great-aunt, Emma Isbister, who has been knitting for nigh on a century and can turn out a hap in a week. She can knit perfect hap after perfect hap as soon as pins and yarn are in her hands, but struggles to talk someone through a pattern in the abstract. Like Karie Westermann, unconsciously casting on after years without knitting, Emma's body remembers what her mind can forget. 'Nothing written doon,' Donna says in her rolling Shetland burr, 'she'll just turn dem ooot.'

At her Wool Week workshop, Donna handed me a ball of J&S's 'Ultra', a creamy two-ply lace-weight yarn. It is the closest available today to 'hap weight', an airy yarn spun commercially during the first part of the twentieth century, specifically for knitting haps. Lace, hap, spencer, jumper and three-ply were the five old yarn weights spun for both Jamieson's and J&S, used respectively for shawls, haps, knitted bodices, and jumpers. *Swarra* was the name for heavier, homespun yarn, used for everyday non-commercial knitwear.

In our class, talking was, by a wordless consensus, restricted to necessary cries for help. Each alternate row of this mini-hap was different, a mix of slipping and knitting stitches to create waves and leaves and shells. Unlike standard knitting, with its easy pattern repetitions that can be worked without counting, knitting lace requires constant concentration – though Great-Aunt Emma, almost blind, only halted when she dropped a stitch and could not see to pick it up. As we worked on our tiny haps, no bigger than doilies, Donna reminded us that until the 1980s, it was widely frowned upon to knit on Sundays, or do anything that could be regarded as work. This included knitting and even watching television. Her great-aunt is of the generation that did not regard their extremely skilful knitting as remarkable – it had to be done to earn money, and some knitters could churn out as many as six pairs of mittens a week throughout the winter.

After three hours' knitting, my would-be hap was a mess of yarn, moulded in sweat-damp hands and tugged by fingers unused to the light touch lace requires. Yet this latest collection of holes tied together with string had come together, my fingers performing the enigmatic shorthand of ssk, yo, k2tog with something close to skill. Twenty-eight waves made up the border, surrounded by eight scalloped shells. It needed only to be 'dressed' – washed and then pinned out to dry – to glory in its pattern.

That evening, back at Betty Mouat's, I pinned out my tiny hap, fresh from soaking in the sink, above the peat stove, using tacks gleaned from a noticeboard. This was not the proper way to dress a hap, but I had nothing else with me and, truly, necessity has always been closer to the heart of knitting than adherence to any 'right' way. I pinned the point of each wave at the hap's edge and the pattern bloomed in between. This mini-hap – a *Hapchen*, in the German neologism of my hap-knitting classmates – was the first unwitting connection between me and my baby.

In the V&A, I found many lace patterns from the nineteenth century, though none was for a complete shawl. There were numerous hand-written nineteenth-century notes for decorative edging and lace-work: an ornate Grecian lace pattern penned on pink paper; another with the legend 'Venetian pattern' printed in a precise hand. Spanish Lace, Gothic Lace, Scotch Stripe – all jostled for space beside tiny, time-faded, ink-stained samples. In an age when most people owned far fewer clothes than we do today, knitting whole outfits would have been impractical and expensive. Instead, scraps of patterns sent between friends showed how a knitted cuff or edge could reinvigorate a favourite or faded outfit. Comparing them to the haps I had seen at Ollaberry, I picked my favourite: a series of swagged stitches dubbed 'Old Shale'. Taking its name from the pattern the waves make on a shale shoreline, 'Old Shale' will form my hap's border. Combined with the simple edging pattern I learned from Donna, it will create the impression of a wave-washed shore around the shawl's edge.

The Boreray yarn in my suitcase is undyed, its palette named for the sea stacks of St Kilda, ranging from white through fawn-coloured 'Isle of Dùn' to darker brown 'Stac Lee'. To these I have added three balls of Jamieson & Smith's two-ply lace-weight, choosing shades of pale blue and azure to echo the sea's

swell. My baby will be wrapped in the colours of its first unconscious journey.

Wedged into the night train's wide seats on my way north from
Euston station, I unpack the palest lace-weight yarn and a metre-
long 4 mm circular needle. Casting on eleven stitches, I form the
first edge of my hap, its waves worked back and forth to create a
long edge of loops. I work sixteen rows of knit stitches, alternating yarn-overs and knit-togethers in every row to create a narrow
skim of knitted peaks and troughs. The pattern repeats fifteen
times along each of the four edges of the hap.

Knitting on public transport draws people like moths round a
flame. On the ferry to Guernsey, a couple saw me working the
gansey's navy rounds; curiosity piqued, they came over to tell
me about a collection of ganseys held in the National Trust of
Guernsey's Folk & Costume Museum in Saumarez Park. Before
long, I had a bus number and stop description to get me there,
along with the curator's name and a host of other places on the
island that might be of interest. Waiting at the train station on my
way to Edinburgh Yarn Festival, an old man sat beside me and
chatted to me about his late wife's knitting – he hadn't realized it
is popular with 'young folk' again. People smile at me as I ply my
pins on boats and buses, emboldened by knitting's comfortable
conversational gateway. 'What are you making?' they ask, before
telling me about their own knitting, or that of a friend or relative.
Knitting is a safe postern between the oft-shuttered worlds of
strangers.

Being pregnant also makes people keen to talk, displaying concern and interest that takes me by surprise. On the train home,
sweaty and exhausted, I impart my body's secret – though it is
before the magic three-month date – to the conductor, begging
her to turn down the heating in the carriage. She smiles con-
spiratorially, asks excitedly about the baby, and disappears. Before
long, cool air is blowing from the vents, a breezy benediction. My

body, hot with the effort of growing person and placenta, drifts off to sleep, lulled by the train's jink and sway.

The following week, we return to the hospital to see our baby again, in a grainy black and white sonogram that shows the blurry outline of its waving limbs and rounded head. As the sonographer moves her jellied probe across my stomach, we chat about my work, and she remarks that knitting and midwifery have long been intertwined. In 1996, the obstetrician and natural-birth advocate Michel Odent first highlighted the importance of midwives knitting in the birthing room – he observed that the presence of a knitting midwife, her hands occupied and her mind partially engaged with her needles, encouraged women to labour free of critical observation.[16] In 2004, Odent went on to suggest that the presence of a midwife could even help women to give birth without pain relief.[17] Odent is himself a knitter, taught to knit socks for soldiers during his wartime childhood in the 1940s,[18] and many of those he interviewed agree that 'knitting helps keep midwives' adrenaline levels low, ensuring a sense of security all round.'[19]

Back home, I continue the hap's narrow edge. Shetlanders famously distrust purl stitches, dubbing them 'the wrang stitch'; my whole hap will be worked in knit stitches only. Unlike the gansey's dense stitches, with hardly a gap between them, lace knitting centres on the space created between stitches. As with sculpting a block of stone, lace knitting is as much about what is left out as what is made. Architecture and fabric, sculpture and stitching – their arching beauty in tension is the same.

Once the edge is complete, I begin the broader borders in Old Shale's scallops. Picking up 120 stitches along my first waving edge, I knit four rows of knit stitches with pale blue yarn. Then I switch to dusty 'Isle of Dùn' and work four more, creating a strip of sand-coloured loops to sit against the lapping sea, followed by one row in wave-tip white, creating the curves of 'Old Shale' in a pattern of yarn-overs and knit-togethers. Then it's back to blue for five rows. I will repeat this forty-six times for each side – but not just yet. As December's days get closer, I am reminded that a new month's challenge presses on: knitting gifts for Christmas.

12

A Time of Gifts

If a knitter wishes to give handmade gifts at Christmas, by December they had better begin to craft in earnest. Some industrious knitters have, like assiduous squirrels, a stash of presents made earlier in the year. But others, like singing crickets, laid down their needles in the warmer months, and now must pick them up again with haste. Laying aside the hap, I concentrate on knitting for other family and friends.

Making presents, whether knitted or not, is more complicated than buying gifts. When there is a straight exchange of presents with a known material value – say a book with its price declared above the barcode – the receiver of an unwanted gift may feel only a frisson of guilt when driven to repurpose it. With handmade items, there is an implicit double rejection. Whilst we reassure ourselves that discarding shop-bought gifts allows us to keep only that which brings us joy, getting rid of a handmade hat, scarf or jumper throws up more problems. It is not just the thing itself we cast aside, but the time and effort – and by extension, love – that was offered to us with it.

Many knitters only rarely knit for themselves. I am one of these: in the last decade before beginning this year of knitted challenges, I made only two hats and a single pair of gloves for myself. During that time, I have churned out a nursery's worth of baby goods, as well as jumpers, hats, gloves, socks and scarves – even the odd balaclava – for family and friends.

I knitted my first scarf too long ago to remember its exact failings. The second, given away as a gift, stays with me, cocooned in the mortifying flush of teenage memory. New at high school and, for the first time, with more than one friend to furnish with a Christmas present, I had a problem. Not yet old enough for a Saturday job and too old for pocket money, I had only the proceeds of a Thursday-evening paper round to fund gifts for a gaggle of pubescent friends.

When asked for money, Mum dug in the loft for boxes of yarn from her college days, emerging with a ball of bright blue acrylic and a handful of rainbow twists of odds and ends. I decided to knit a scarf for my friend Pip, who wore a brightly coloured fleece over her uniform, and ducked out of classes early for her oboe lessons.

I cast on, weeks passed, and suddenly the last day of term dawned. The scarf had grown, inching down from my needles – but not enough. Time had defeated me. Too late to make anything else, I stared at the sad square of knitting. Not long enough for a scarf – but maybe it could be rebranded? Not one to let a lack of imagination stand in my way, I decided this was, in fact, an oboe warmer. Pip received it with gracious equanimity, draping its motley stripes carefully over the small box containing her instrument. We laugh about it still, this peculiar and imperfect present.

As two decades have since passed, I decide it is time to make another, more successful, scarf to give as a gift. This one will be a present for my father-in-law, Jeff: a bar-striped football scarf. Jeff is crazy for the beautiful game; more specifically, he's mad about Middlesbrough, and keeps me up to date on the progress of the mighty 'Boro', whether I want to know or not. He's occasionally threatened to take me to a game, but I've heard too many stories of violence, ventricle pies, and games played with an orange ball on snow-whitened pitches to be very enthusiastic about the prospect.

Jeff isn't the only member of my married-in family who adores football. His father-in-law, Ken, was a customs officer in Liverpool, and a lifelong Everton supporter. Ken grew up in the 1920s and 1930s in an inner-city district defined by poverty. Football was the lifeblood that drew the city's communities together, but it also threatened to tear them apart – not just through inter-club conflict, but through the have/have-not divide of those who did or did not have cash for tickets. The Pilgrim Trust, studying long-term unemployment in Liverpool in the first half of the twentieth century, wrote that on match days there was 'the wretched spectacle of men on the dole silently lining the streets and watching those in work make their way to the game'.[1]

As small boys, Ken and his friends hung around outside Everton's Goodison Park, waiting for the gates to be opened at half-time so that they could creep in for free to watch the end of the match. Such was his hatred of Liverpool FC that Ken would never wear red, the colour of his team's arch-rivals. Offering to lend him a scarf or hat in that colour, even on the coldest days, met with polite but definite scorn. In the teeth of a gale on the prom at Southport, at ninety-two Ken would rather freeze to death than wear his rival's colours in the form of Jeff's Boro scarf.

Although football's knock-about origins go back hundreds of years, the modern game dates from the mid-nineteenth century. The world's oldest football club, Sheffield FC, was founded in 1857, and by 1863 the Football Association existed in embryonic form. At first, players wore no specific club colours or strips:

Sheffield's founding set of rules includes instructions for players to bring red and navy flannel caps to matches, 'one colour to be worn by each side'. By 1870, club colours began to be introduced, and by the time of the first English FA Cup final in 1872, the Wanderers, clad in pink, black and cerise, beat the red-and-navy Royal Engineers 1–0. Striped, or 'hooped', shirts in different colourways were popular, as were plain white ones, both less expensive than a bespoke colourful kit.

When did team colours translate into scarves for the fans? Peter Holme, curator at the National Football Museum in Manchester, says that no one is quite sure when the first football scarves were made and worn. By the time professional football took off in the 1880s and teams began to wear shirts in fixed hues, fans wanted to show their support visibly, as well as vocally – to show their 'true colours'. At first, they would decorate themselves with colourful 'favours' – ribbons pinned to coats and shirts – but by the turn of the twentieth century, rosettes, painted rattles and coloured hats were displayed with pride. Scarves, as well as being a tribal banner, are also practical for keeping fans warm on the terraces; the football season mostly runs through autumn, winter and spring, and stands are open to the elements on at least one side.

Peter reckons that football scarves were probably first knitted in team colours by the fans and their families between the First and Second World Wars. By the 1950s, two-colour bar scarves were being sold commercially, but handmade scarves were also common in the post-war period. The oldest scarf in the National Football Museum dates from the 1930s, but Peter's favourite is one from the 1950s, captured in a photograph that shows a group of supporters heading to see Preston North End play in the FA Cup semi-final of 1954.

Striding towards the camera, wreathed in smiles, rosettes and scarves, are five young women. Three of them wave rattles blurred in noisy support, their mouths frozen open in jolly smiles. They wear neat dark shoes below tidy ankles and long, thick winter coats, and their hair has been waved and parted. All sport scarves, most with names and initials overstitched onto them. One of the scarves has since been donated to the museum and, peering at the tipsy capitals embroidered on it, I can make out the names A. Kelly, J. Barton, G. Ross, B. Patrick – a once-sacred litany of players. On closer inspection, I can see the names are interspersed with nicknames and achievements: 'Eire Int', 'Eng Int', 'Black Prince', 'Captain of Eng Youth'.

More than simply a statement of support, this scarf plots history. Decorated in celebration, it registers sixteen names in all, headed by Captain H. Kendall. The stitching is uneven, off-centre and wobbles away towards the right-hand edge. Someone perhaps not familiar with a needle was inspired enough to render this important match in tapestry. It is their blue-and-white miniature Bayeux.

I have never been to a football match, professional, local or amateur. My own family couldn't care less about the game, and the county I grew up in had only one team of even minor note: Ipswich Town, the Tractor Boys. But to understand the importance of a football scarf, I need to understand the game. I ask Jeff to take me to one so that I can stand in the noise of a stadium and soak up its roar.

Jeff decides we should see Raith Rovers versus Queen of the South at Stark's Park in Kirkcaldy. The Rovers and Queens both play in blue – Raith in navy, their opponents in a brighter shade – so I decide to knit Jeff's scarf in blue and white. I opt for the navy of the Rovers: we'll be watching a match at their ground, so it seems a safer shade to sport. Scanning Ravelry for patterns, I decide on a simple knit two, purl two band, thirty-two stitches wide, to be worked in chunky wool that knits up quickly.

Jeff lives in Grasmere, in the heart of the Lake District, so I decide to make the scarf using a yarn local to him. Town End Yarns fits the bill exactly: for more than thirty years, Jeff has lived in part of Grasmere called Town End. Arriving in the autumn of 1981, my father-in-law began his working life as an apprentice at the Wordsworth Museum. There he met and married his wife, brought up three sons, and is now the museum's curator. With a life lived and worked in the same 100 square metres, he is a Town Ender through and through.

Town End is also where I first met Jeff. One wintery December morning with snow on the ground, he interviewed me for an apprenticeship, the modern version of the scheme that drew him there. Most people meet their in-laws long after their partners: mine came first, vetting me for a job, and later as a daughter-in-law. My husband, Tom, spent his childhood in Town End; we met each other yards from his first home. When we married five years later, the house from which we wed and to which we returned as husband and wife was the same he lived in as a little boy. Town End binds this family together.

Town End Yarns do not come from the same Town End. It is a common place name in Cumbria, simply denoting the area at the end of a town – or, more often, village. Town End Yarns hail from Crosthwaite, 15 miles south of Grasmere on the edge of Whitbarrow Scar. Still, it is close enough, the name creating a serendipitous connection. They spin alpaca fibre for its softness, combining it with silk to make a yarn that feels luxurious against the skin; I buy four skeins, two each of blue and cream.

The scarf grows quickly and I finish it in four evenings. Knit two, purl two on thick wooden needles, this is light years away from the tight-knit stitches of the gansey worked on steel pins, or the minute stitches of the Dentdale gloves. I am aware of the tension in my fingers shifting as I work, loosening up to let this scarf take shape. I finish it the day before the game, tying off the last few tassels just before we leave and presenting to Jeff. He winds it round his neck and pronounces it perfect for the day ahead.

The following morning, we head to Kirkcaldy, the sun bright above us and the air crisp. After queuing at the turnstiles, we pay our dues and slip between the rotating bars, climbing the concrete steps to the South Stand. 'Here comes the good bit,' Jeff says, turning to me with a smile, and together we emerge into the middle of a thousand Rovers fans. The noise of the crowd rushes around me, and my heart lifts. The proximity of so many people, gathered together for a common purpose, is electrifying. Looking at the other end of the pitch, the away stand is almost empty. 'One hundred and twenty-four Queen of the South fans' crackles the announcer – from across the pitch it doesn't even look that many.

After a minute's silence in memory of victims of far-away atrocities, the whistle is blown and the game is on. The bubble of chatter grows to a roar ten minutes in, when Rovers' forward Ryan

Hardie scores a goal, and a few repetitions of 'He scores when he wants' goes round the home crowd. It's looking good for Raith, but, before we know it, Queens have equalized, a controversial kick that seems to bounce off the bottom of the goalpost before careering back onto the pitch. The Rovers fans are incensed, on their feet and shouting, but the goal is awarded.

Suddenly it's half-time and everyone streams from their seats to the makeshift cafe under the stand. Jeff and I split a Scotch pie, washed down with Bovril. It's my first cup of this savoury drink, watery gravy for a greasy grey pie. Back in place for the second half, the mood at the home end is one of resignation. Stark's Park is bordered on the east side by a road and on the west by a train line. In the course of the final forty-five minutes, the road and the tracks see more action than either goal, with three balls soaring out of the ground. This proximity to the railway is an added bonus for my father-in-law: an afternoon of trains, pies and football is going to be difficult to beat, whichever way the game goes.

Behind us, fans are losing patience with their team. 'Come on, Rovers!' they exhort, the voices ratcheting up despair with every cry. Another asks, 'Which team deserves to lose the most?' the question hanging unanswered in the air. Someone near the front starts up a chant: the words are lost to me, but I don't think they flatter either side. Ninety minutes comes and the score is still one apiece when the whistle goes.

The stands empty quickly. Jeff and I divert to the club shop, pawing over placemats, hats and shirts. Jeff inspects a coaster, printed only slightly off-centre. 'Reduced from two pound, no, two-fifty,' the salesman half-heartedly patters. Jeff hands over a pound and we head out into the sunshine. Back at the car, we toy with hanging the scarf out of the window as we drive home, but decide against it. Scarves, singing, Bovril, pies – the match has only been a sliver of the day's action. Being part of the crowd and spending time together is what we really came for. The buzz reminds me of the jolly atmosphere of Edinburgh Yarn Festival or Shetland Wool Week. Like a Bousta Beanie, Phrygian Cap or Pussyhat, a football scarf is a symbol of belonging.

This year is the first time I have been able to knit without looking at my fingers. Eleven months of almost daily practice has sped up my hands to the point where I can make a chunky hat in a day, a pair of fingerless mitts in an afternoon. I test my speed on a hat for my brother, using a skein of deep blue 'Godrevy' yarn from Cornwall's Pipps & Co. After two hours watching nature documentaries, it's done: a simple ribbed beanie with a gently curving crown.

I want to knit for everyone this year – hats, mittens, scarves and socks. But waiting for me is the gansey – Dad's seventieth birthday falls not long after Christmas, so the Yuletide deadline stands for this too. The gansey has grown little over the autumn. I managed several patterned bands across its front on the ferries to and from the Channel Islands at the end of the summer, using a Cornish knitting stick from Polperro to build up speed. But now the evenings are darker, I'm struggling to see the shiny navy stitches without the sun's illuminating glare.

At least with family the 'sweater curse' cannot apply. A phrase bandied about by knitters on both sides of the Atlantic, it refers to the inevitability of a relationship breakdown when one partner embarks on knitting a sweater for their lover. I can see the practical pitfalls of knitting something as large and time-consuming as a jumper: they take so long to complete that all but the most hardwearing relationship might founder before it can be finished. Guilting me from the bottom of my knitting basket, the gansey is still many hours off completion.

I was mercifully unaware of the sweater curse when I began a jumper for my then-boyfriend Tom almost a decade ago. We had been together for a few months when he announced that he would spend the spring and summer of the following year in Greenland. Studying for his doctorate in glaciology, his task was to measure the melting of a glacier during the warmer summer months. From April to September, he would be living and working by the Greenland ice sheet – in a tent. To undertake fieldwork in the Arctic is to become personally acquainted with an inhospitable environment.

Stocking up on ball after ball of pale-grey DK yarn, I knitted my way furiously through the winter. Although working to a pattern, I had to adapt it for Greenlandic conditions. Longer sleeves needed to end in anchoring thumb-holes to warm hands battered by the ice sheet's katabatic winds. To minimize the gap twixt trouser and top, I added extra rows for warmth. With its 100,000 loops in steely grey, the finished garment looked more like a chainmail tunic than a cosy jumper.

I am utterly unable to finish any sort of work without the most unbreakable deadline – my knitting is no different. For this Greenland-bound gift, I was still stitching sleeve to armscye minutes before the research party left for the airport. But, save for a few stray threads, it survived five months of wicked sun, constant wind and endless abrasion of dust ground from the bedrock beneath the glacier. It outlasted T-shirts, trousers, even tents, all ripped to ribbons by the hardship of camp life. So did we – for, reader, I married him.

As this December hurtles towards Christmas, the temperature plunges and Britain is buried under snow and ice. We wake to a world entombed in heavy frost, everything coated in a sparkling rime that does not melt under the sun's weak winter gaze. As I approach the end of my first trimester, the nausea lessens, and I can sign whole days over to knitting. The gansey is long enough for me to wear as a dress, though it still lacks a full complement of sleeves.

I follow the pattern for the Manx gansey to create the top of the sleeve, but the first one I knit turns out too bulky. Its broad wale of raised purl stitches at the top of the arm gives it the dense appearance of navy armour. Dissatisfied, I begin knitting its sister plain, seventeen rows of stocking stitch in place of the raised purls. This second sleeve is smoother and, pleased with its appearance, I continue to the wrist. But then I must go back, rip out the other sleeve top and replace it with a plainer piece. To avoid having to reknit the entire sleeve, I slice into the purled piece and unpick it, reknitting yarn and re-joining using the three-needle cast-off that renders seams invisible.

As I carefully pull away the snipped row of stitches, Barbara Kingsolver's words from the soundtrack to the 2016 film *Yarn* run through my head: 'Wool is a stalwart crone who remembers everything, while empty-headed white-haired cotton forgets.' Like a creased or folded sheet of paper unable to forget how it was handled, woollen yarn retains the bouclé twist and purled curl last put into it. But it is adaptable, too: one dip in water and the old memory can be washed away.

It is perfect wintertime as I head south towards my family for Christmas. A long cold spell has held the country in its thrall for much of December, and the Border hills are a symphony in black and white below the bright blue of the afternoon sky. These modest mounds look alpine in their glittering mantle of snow, and small rivers wear a crust of rippled ice, thick as window glass, that catches the sun's last rays as we head into the night.

The gansey doubles as a welcome blanket now, its bulky body covering my lap and legs as I work my way from shoulder to wrist, first once, then a second time. It warms my lap as I work each sleeve, knitting round and round. Outside is freezing darkness as the train speeds over slick black rails etched deep into frozen earth. Under the gansey's warm embrace my three-month foetus swims and turns in its internal goldfish bowl. The train pulls into

Oxenholme with the sun's last light still staining the sky above the hills, and everything is silhouette, reflected in the skim of ice on frozen puddles.

My year's pilgrimage draws to a close where it began – in Cumbria, that daydream county where I met and married my husband. My in-laws welcome us with rituals long-practised: cautious checking of the weather, a house overfull of brothers. Here knitting becomes a way to absent myself from family debates. Churning out the gansey's sleeves in stocking stitch is repetitive, and I soon memorize the pattern for their decrease, knitting two stitches together at the start and end of rounds. When the rest of the family becomes mired in debate, I pull the jumper onto my lap and busy myself with its stitches, making rapid progress in these dark days short and heavy with rain and snow.

My Dad's birthday comes a little after Christmas, and I am bursting with excitement as I work the last stitches of his gansey. It has taken me the best part of a year to make, fitted in around the rest of life. In its omnipresence, it has come to feel like a silent member of our family, but I must let it go: its new and useful life starts now. At last it is done: over a kilo of tightly spun blue yarn turned into a jumper that I hope will exactly fit my father's body.

As Dad lives several hundred miles away, I wrap up the gansey and post it off in an enormous envelope. The following morning, my phone pings with a flurry of pictures: Dad standing outside his front door in a rare patch of winter sunshine, blue eyes crinkled with smiling, the light picking out each raised stitch on his proud chest. Dad sat by the living-room window, still grinning, showing off his gansey. He is pleased as punch – and I am too. For me, it is delight mixed with relief: the gansey fits him perfectly.

As the old year becomes the new and the gansey is finally free from my needles, it is time to take stock of my knitted journey. An adventure in handmade clothes, this year has seen me craft a pair of gloves, two jumpers, Highland stockings, a bikini, a nålebound sock, two scarves, three hats, and begin a baby's hap. It has also been a year of collecting stories: of women, knitters, farmers, spinners. Tales of fisher lassies and cap makers, designers and artists, nuns and mechanics. Knitting's history is everywhere, in mountain landscapes and industrial estates, sprawling cities and tiny villages. It is an old craft – and a new one, its banner raised by legions of knitters and designers for whom it is more that 'just a hobby'. For many knitters, this craft has self-defining, life-affirming power.

Whilst knitting undoubtedly has many traditions, 'tradition' itself is a fraught word that divides opinion. Many of us feel comfortable about, and comforted by, the idea of a preordained way of crafting, as if by reaching back into the past we can authenticate ourselves and what we make. We seek origins and earlier inspiration, drawing on archives and memories and ideas handed down to us from sources specific, shadowy and singular. The idea of one truth, a single and all-encompassing method or technique that dictates how things must be done, beguiles. Like the tablet handed down to Moses from on high, it is a patriarchal model. It is also elitist in its unassailability, potentially stifling individual voices with a universal 'truth'.

Looking to the world of folk music, where the concept of 'tradition bearers' is strong and relevant, I find a useful parallel. Singers not only transmit older songs learned – often by ear – from other singers, but are also free to amend lyrics, tempo, tune and style. Authenticity can be difficult and complex to define, but, providing their original source is openly acknowledged, usually in the form of a spoken introduction or track note, a singer's role is to enliven as well as preserve, to breathe new breath into the old songs. Unless they are sung, the old songs die, and though folk-music diehards may bemoan new styles of performance, they grudgingly acknowledge the need for newness. In this way, folk memories, melodies and lyrics do not die but grow on, like a vined plant twisting itself across the body of an old tree. To me, tradition is important not just because of its attempt to preserve the ever-changing, but because of its ultimate function – to draw humanity together, to help communities coalesce.

In twelve months, I have slowly crossed the knitter's Hellespont, changing from casual acquaintance to passionate enthusiast, occasional crafter to eager postulant. After a year of knitting everywhere – in libraries and farmyards, on buses and swaying ferries – I find I am unable to sit without my hands working yarn and needles. In a faint modern echo of Shetland's women knitting with *kishies* full of peat on their back, or fisher lassies knitting as they walked, any spare scraps of time I have I now give over to knitting. My speed and productivity have increased apace: in addition to the pieces knitted for this book, I have also made baby jumpers, hats and mitts, unable to resist the call of births and birthdays.

Looking back, the correlation between bad climate and good knitwear is striking: communities for whom existence could be precarious, particularly those at Britain's mountainous or sea-washed margins, are often those with a strong knitting heritage – Shetland, Wales, the Channel Islands. The Viking influence, from the sea-faring sheep of the Hebrides to Fair Isle's colourful patterns and York's Coppergate Sock, is strong; so too is that of the mediaeval Huguenot refugees and their skill with woollen yarn. Observed through the lens of its knitted history, Britain is a country defined by its coast, by immigration, by farming – and by economics. The pressures and opportunities of trading with the Continent have, since Roman times, been a driving force for Britain's wool trade, harnessed by everyone from kings to Fair Isle's knitters.

Now it is New Year, and my focus shifts. There is someone else to knit for now: my baby's arrival is scheduled for the summer.

As the old year fades, I dig out the hap's unfinished borders and take up my needles. From its edge, I pick up seven stitches, for this new person. This is an act of faith, of hope, of love – my first of parenthood.

Notes

Prologue

1   Igor Kopytoff, 'The Cultural Biography of Things: Commoditization as Process', in *The Social Life of Things*, ed. Arjun Appadurai (Cambridge University Press, 1986), p. 67

1 Dentdale Gloves

1   *Holinshed's Chronicles*, in William Youatt, *Sheep: Their Breeds, Management and Diseases* (London: Baldwin and Cradock, 1837), p. 194
2   Rob Harvey Long, in conversation, 5 June 2018
3   13 Eliz., c. 19, 'Hattes and Cappes', 1571, *The Statutes of the Realm: Printed by Command of his Majesty King George the Third*, ed. Alexander Luders et al. (Dawsons of Pall Mall, 1810–28), p. 555
4   National Archives Currency Converter, https://www.nationalarchives.gov.uk/currency-converter/#currency-result, last accessed 7 May 2018
5   'An Act for Burying in Woollen', Charles II, 1677 & 1678, in A. Amos, *The English Constitution in the Reign of King Charles II* (London: Stevens and Norton, 1857)
6   Francis T. Buckland, *Curiosities in Natural History*, 4th series (London: Richard Bextley, 1888), p. 354
7   Alexander Pope, '*Moral Essays*, Epistle I: Of the Knowledge and Character of Men' (1733), in *The Poetical Works of Alexander Pope* (London: Macmillan, 1869)
8   'Township', an Anglo-Saxon portmanteau, is roughly cognate with 'parish'. More familiar in the words *worship* and *hardship*, the suffix denotes a state of being; a township was a self-sustaining unit.
9   Grosgain, or grogram, is a coarse textile made from silk, wool and mohair;

parramatta is a light fabric woven with a woollen weft and a warp of silk or cotton; princetta is a worsted of silk warp and worsted woollen weft.

10   Westermann, Karie, *This Thing of Paper* (Karie Westermann, 2017), p. 19
11   Robert Southey, 'A True Story of the Terrible Knitters e' Dent', reprinted as Interchapter XXIV in *The Doctor* (Longman, 1847), p. 78
12   Sue Leighton-White, 'The Needles' Music: Handknitters of the Dales', *Knitting Traditions* (Winter, 2011) p. 13
13   Peter Brears, 'The Knitting Sheath', *Folk Life*, 20 (1982), pp. 16–40
14   Richard J. P. Allen, 'Scottish Island Sheep', *The Ark: The Monthly Journal of the Rare Breeds Survival Trust* (June 1984)
15   Geoffrey Chaucer, 'The Knight's Tale', *Canterbury Tales*, in *The Hengwrt Chaucer Digital Facsimile*, ed. Estelle Stubbs (2003), line 270
16   Opinion on the root of this word is divided: it seems the Old Dutch word *ostades* may have been used for a worsted-type of cloth before Norfolk's manufacturers' rise to prominence. Yet the association persists and the etymology remains unresolved.
17   Penelope Lister Hemingway, 'Playing with a Piece of String: The Story of a Dentdale Knitter in The Retreat Asylum, York', *Knit Edge*, 3 (May 2013)
18   Ibid.
19   Ibid.
20   Marie Hartley and Joan Ingilby, *The Old Hand-Knitters of the Dales* (Clapham, Lancs., 1951)
21   Ibid.
22   John Willis Clark and Thomas McKenny Hughes, *The Life and Letters of the Reverend Adam Sedgwick*, vol. 1 (Cambridge University Press, 1890), p. 25
23   William Howitt, *The Rural Life of England*, vol. 2 (London, 1838), p. 309
24   Hartley and Ingilby, *The Old Hand-Knitters*

2 Proper Ganseys

1   David Taylor, *The Wild Black Region: 1750–18* (Edinburgh: Birlinn, 2016), p. 263
2   Neil MacGillivray, 'Dr John Mackenzie', *Journal of Scottish Historical Studies*, 33:1 (Edinburgh University Press, 2013), pp. 81–100
3   J. A. Scott Watson, 'The Rise and Development of the Sheep Industry in the Highlands and North of Scotland', *Transactions of the Highland and Agricultural Society of Scotland*, 5th series, 44 (Blackwood and Sons, 1932), p. 5
4   Alexander Fenton, *Country Life in Scotland: Our Rural Past* (Edinburgh: Birlinn 2008), p. 14
5   Ibid. pp. 15–16
6   W. J. Carlyle, 'The Changing Distribution of Breeds of Sheep in

Scotland, 1795–1965', *The Agricultural History Review*, 27:1 (British Agricultural History Society, 1979), pp. 19–29

7 Scott Watson, 'Rise and Development of the Sheep Industry', p. 5

8 Neil M. Gunn, *The Silver Darlings* (1941; London: Faber, 1969), p. 12

9 Report quoted by Mary Miers, *Highland Retreats: The Architecture and Interiors of Scotland's Romantic North* (New York: Rizzoli International Publications, 2017), p. 18

10 Ewan MacColl used the saying in the song 'Fisherman's Wife' (1959)

11 Belle Patrick, *Recollections of East Fife Fisher Folk* (Edinburgh: Birlinn, 2003), p. 70

12 Rae Compton, *The Complete Book of Traditional Jersey and Guernsey Knitting* (London: Batsford, 1984)

13 Gladys Thompson, *Patterns for Guernseys, Jerseys and Arans* (London: Batsford, 1955), p. 140

14 Michael Pearson, *Traditional Knitting* (London: Collins, 1984)

3 Revolutionary Knitting

1 Invented by artist Betsy Greer in 2001; cf Jacqueline Witkowski, 'Knit for Defense, Purl to Control', *InVisible Culture*, 15 April 2015, https://ivc.lib.rochester.edu/knit-for-defense-purl-to-control/#fn-3529-26; last assessed 26 February 2019

2 'Dickens's twelfth novel has done more to shape popular impressions of the French Revolution than any other book in the English language': Irene Collins, 'Charles Dickens and the French Revolution', *Literature and History*, 2:1 (Spring 1990), p. 40

3 Charles Dickens, *A Tale of Two Cities* (1859; London: T. Lacy, 1860), Book I, Chapter V

4 Dickens, *A Tale of Two Cities*, Book II, Chapter VII

5 Dickens, *A Tale of Two Cities*, Book II, Chapter XV

6 Dickens, *A Tale of Two Cities*, Book II, Chapter XVI

7 Ibid.

8 Ibid.; although Joseph-Ignace Guilllotin had mooted the idea of the guillotine in 1789, it wasn't until 1792 that it was first used for executions in Paris.

9 Virginia Stephen to Leonard Woolf, letter, Tuesday 5 March 1912, *Collected Letters of Virginia Woolf*, vol. 2, ed. Nigel Nicholson and Joanna Trautmann (New York: Houghton Brace Jovanovich, 1976), p. 491

10 For further discussion see E. I. Blanche, 'The Expression of Creativity through Occupation', *Journal of Occupational Science*, 14:1 (2007), pp. 21–9; and B. Hosegood, 'Whip Your Hobby into Shape: Knitting, Feminism, and Construction of Gender', *Textile: The Journal of Cloth and Culture*, 7:2 (2009), pp. 148–63

11 E. Holmes et al., 'Trauma, Films, Information Processing and Intrusive Memory Development', *Journal of Experimental Psychology*, 133:1 (2004), pp. 3–22

12 Herbert Benson, 'Mind-Body Pioneer', *Psychology Today*, 34 (2001), pp. 56–60

13 Virginia Stephen to Leonard Woolf, letter, Tuesday 5 March 1912, *Collected Letters*, p. 491

14 Sayaka Okumura, 'Women Knitting: Domestic Activity, Writing, and Distance in Virginia Woolf's Fiction', *English Studies*, 89:2 (2008), pp. 166–81

15 Edith Sitwell to Geoffrey Singleton, letter, 11 July 1955; reprinted in Susan Ratcliffe, *Oxford Dictionary of Quotations by Subject* (Oxford University Press, 2010)

16 Lytton Strachey to John Maynard Keynes, letter, 24 September 1914, *The Letters of Lytton Strachey* (London: Viking, 2005)

17 Lytton Strachey to Clive Bell, letter, *The Letters of Lytton Strachey* (London: Viking, 2005)

18 Virginia Woolf, *To the Lighthouse* (London: Hogarth Press, 1927), p. 8

19 Hermione Lee, *Virginia Woolf* (London: Vintage, 1997)

20 Woolf, *To the Lighthouse*, p. 62

21 Ibid., p. 7

22 Earl G. Ingersoll, *Screening Woolf: Virginia Woolf on/and/in Film* (Maryland: Fairleigh Dickinson University Press, 2017), p. 31

23 Woolf, *To the Lighthouse*, p. 59

24 Okumura, 'Women Knitting', pp. 166–81

25 Dominique Godineau, *The Women of Paris and Their French Revolution*, trans. Katherine Striep (Berkeley: University of California Press, 1998), p. 4

26 Godineau, *The Women of Paris*

27 Witness LXXIX in *Procédure du Châtelet*, quoted in N. H. Webster, *The French Revolution: A Study in Democracy* (London: Constable, 1919), p. 137

28 Godineau, *The Women of Paris*, p. 54; in eighteenth-century Paris, sewing 'was women's primary work'

29 Ibid., p. 12

30 Ibid., p. 212

31 A. Aulard, *Paris Pendant la Réaction Thermidorienne* (1898), vol. 1, p. 485

32 The original inscription reads, '*Les Tricoteues Jacobines, ou de Robespierre. Elles étoient un grand nombre à qui l'on donnoit 40 sols par jour pour aller dans la tribune des Jacobins applaudir les motions révolutionnaires.*'

33 Godineau, *The Women of Paris*, p. xviii

34 Paul Friedland, *Seeing Justice Done: The Age of Spectacular Capital Punishment in France* (Oxford University Press, 2012), p. 255

35 Fleury, alias Abraham Bénard, *Mémoires de Fleury de la Comédie Française* (Paris: J. B. P. Lafitte, 1836)

36 Collins, 'Charles Dickens', pp. 40–57

37   Thomas Carlyle, *The French Revolution: A History* (London: Miles, 1837), Book 1, Chapter 3.2.VI

38   Ibid.

39   Godineau, *The Women of Paris*, p. xviii

40   Paul Curzon, 'Dickens Knitting in Code', *CS4FN*, Queen Mary University of London, http://www.cs4fn.org/ada/dickensknitting.php, last accessed 16 February 2018

41   Dickens, *A Tale of Two Cities*, Book II, Chapter XV

42   Jenna Fear, 'The Knitting War Spies of History', *Interweave*, 21 July 2017, https://www.interweave.com/article/weaving/knitting-war-spies-history/, last accessed January 2018

43   Kathryn J. Atwood, *Women Heroes of World War I: 16 Remarkable Resisters, Soldiers, Spies, and Medics* (Chicago Review Press, 2014), p. 74

44   Robert Mendick, 'Wartime Spy Finally Accepts She is a French Heroine', *Daily Telegraph*, 22 November 2014, http://www.telegraph. co.uk/history/world-war-two/11248032/Wartime-spy-finally-accepts-sh e-is-a-French-heroine.html, last accessed 30 January 2018

45   Natalie Zarrelli, 'The Wartime Knitters Who Used Knitting as an Espionage Tool', *Atlas Obscura*, 1 June 2017, https://www.atlasobscura. com/articles/knitting-spies-wwi-wwii, last accessed 15 February 2018

46   'MI6: A Century in the Shadows', *BBC Radio 4*, 27 July 2009, http://www. bbc.co.uk/programmes/b00lrsnk, last accessed 3 April 2014

47   Fear, 'The Knitting War Spies'

4: Highland Kilts and Stockings

1   National Museums of Scotland, cloth fragment, NMS X.FR 483 http:// nms.scran.ac.uk/database/record.php?usi=000-100-036-743-C

2   No one knows when checked woven cloth was first worn in the Highlands, but the eleventh-century Norse Saga of Magnus Barelegs is often cited as the first written reference to Highland kilts. The Viking king Magnus Olafsson raided the Hebrides in 1098 and 1099, and though Magnus returned home to Norway, many of his men settled in the Western Isles. Those that went back to their homeland took Hebridean customs with them, and Magnus popularized the wearing of Highland dress abroad: 'when King Magnus came home from his Viking cruise to the Western countries, he and many of his people brought with them a great deal of the habits and fashion of clothing of those western parts. They went about on the streets with bare legs, and had short kirtles and over-cloaks; and therefore his men called him Magnus Barefoot or Bareleg': Snorri Sturluson, *The Heimskringla: Or, Chronicle of the Kings of Norway*, vol. 3, trans. Samuel Laing (London: Longman, 1844), p. 139

3   Hugh Cheape, '*Gheibhte Breacain Chàrnaid* – Scarlet Tartans Would Be Got', in *From Tartan to Tartanry*, ed. Ian Brown (Edinburgh University Press, 2010), pp. 13–31

4   See Edward Dwelly, *The Illustrated Gaelic Dictionary* (Fleet, Hants: Dwelly, 1918)

5   George Buchanan (1581), in Hugh Cheape, *Tartan: The Highland Habit* (Edinburgh: National Museums of Scotland, 1991)

6   Act of Proscription, 1746, Act 34 in the Reign of George II, *The Statutes at Large*, vol. 7 (London: Mark Basket, 1764)

7   Cheape, *Tartan*, p. 7

8   Ibid.

9   Viccy Coltman, 'Party Coloured Plaid? Portraits of Eighteenth-Century Scots in Tartan', *Textile History*, 41:2 (2010), p. 184

10 Cheape, *Tartan*, p. 21

11 Phillip Stubbes, *The Anatomie of Abuses* (London: R. Iones, 1583)

12 Ibid.

13 *Oxford English Dictionary*, http://www.oed.com/view/Entry/10682, last accessed 13 February 2018

14 With thanks to Bert Innes, research volunteer, Gordon Highlanders Museum, Aberdeen

15 Isabel F. Grant, 'An Old Scottish Handicraft Industry', *Scottish Historical Review*, XVIII (1921), p. 279

16 James Rae, *A Compleat History of the Rebellion from its First Rise in 1745* (London: Robert Brown, 1749), in ibid., p. 280

17 *The New Statistical Account of Scotland* (1845), vol. XII, 'Aberdeen', in Alexander Ross, *Scottish Home Industries* (1895; Glasgow: Molendinar Press, 1974)

18 Referenced in Grant, 'An Old Scottish Handicraft Industry'

19 Ibid., p. 280

20 J. H. Dixon, *A Guide to Gairloch and Loch Maree* (Edinburgh: Cooperative Printing Company, 1886), p. 11

21 'Gairloch Knitting Pattern' (Gairloch and District Heritage Society, 1981); from the archives of the Highland Folk Museum, retrieved 14 November 2017

22 Andy Wightman, *Who Owns Scotland* (Edinburgh: Canongate, 1996)

23 Jeremy Fenton, *The Story of Gairloch: A Brief History of Gairloch and District*, p. 16, http://www.jeremyfenton.scot/Booklet%20Gairloch%20History%20lo.pdf

24 Ibid., p. 33

25 J. Mackenzie, letter to Lord John Russell on Sir John McNeill's *Report on the State of the West Highlands and Islands of Scotland* (Edinburgh and London, 1851), p. 3

26 Lady Mackenzie, quoted in Dixon, *Guide to Gairloch*

27 Ibid.
28 Letter to the Destitution Board in Edinburgh, 1847, 'Gairloch Pattern Stockings' (Gairloch Heritage Museum, 2015)
29 Dixon, *Guide to Gairloch*
30 *Land Magazine* (Gairloch Heritage Museum, 2017)
31 *Transactions of the Highland and Agricultural Society of Scotland* (1895); winners from Gairloch included Ann MacDonald of 18 Sand, Gairloch
32 Harris Tweed Act (1993), c. xi, http://www.legislation.gov.uk/ukla/1993/11/contents/enacted, last accessed 8 May 2018
33 Ross, *Scottish Home Industries*, p. 62
34 Ibid., p. 63
35 House of Commons Sessional Papers, *Inventory Control Record 1*, vol. 46 (1910)
36 Scott Watson, 'Rise and Development of the Sheep Industry', p. 5
37 Finlay J. Macdonald, *Crowdie and Cream* (1982; Little, Brown, 1996)
38 Macdonald's three volumes of autobiography – *Crowdie and Cream* (1982), *Crotal and White* (1983) and *The Corncrake and the Lysander* (1985) – chronicle his childhood and adolescence in the 1920s and 1930s on Harris
39 Vikingeskibsmuseet, Roskilde, Denmark, https://www.vikingeskibsmuseet.dk/en/professions/boatyard/experimental-archaeological-research/maritime-crafts/maritime-technology/woollen-sailcloth/, last accessed 4 June 2018
40 Quoted in Nancy Bazilchuk, 'The Sheep That Launched 1000 Ships', *New Scientist*, 24 July 2004, https://www.newscientist.com/article/mg18324575-900-the-sheep-that-launched-1000-ships/, last accessed 4 June 2018
41 Vikingeskibsmuseet
42 Bazilchuk, 'The Sheep That Launched 1000 Ships'

5: A Not-So-Itsy-Bitsy Bikini

1 Scott Watson, 'Rise and Development of the Sheep Industry', p. 6
2 Edward Harrison, 'Scottish Woollens', (National Association of the Scottish Woollen Manufacturers, 1939)
3 Edward Harrison, 'History of the Scottish Woollen Trade' (National Association of the Scottish Woollen Manufacturers, 1935)
4 Clifford Gulvin, *The Scottish Hosiery and Knitwear Industry 1680–1980* (Edinburgh: John Donald, 1984)
5 The term 'stockinger' was first recorded around 1741, and seems to have dropped from common usage by the end of the nineteenth century.
6 Geoffrey Bowles and Siobhan Kirrane, *Knitting Together: Memories of Leicestershire's Hosiery Industry* (Leicestershire Museums, Arts and Records Service, 1990) p. 3

7   Shima Seiki Company History, http://www.shimaseiki.com/company/history/, last accessed 13 October 2018
8   Doreen Taylor, 'Days of Change in Hawick', *Scots Magazine*, August 1971
9   Ibid.
10 Olivia B. Waxman and Liz Ronk, 'Swimsuit Evolution', *Time*, 5 July 2016 http://time.com/4383860/swimsuit-evolution-bikini-origins-history/, last accessed 5 June 2018
11 Kate Davies, 'Nautical!', *TextIsles*, 3 (2012)
12 Sandy Black, *Knitting: Fashion, Industry, Craft* (V&A, 2012), p. 84
13 *Science in the News*, http://www.scienceinthenews.org.uk/contents/?article=8, last accessed 9 May 2018
14 Black, *Knitting*, p. 83
15 '8 Facts About Clothes Rationing in Britain During the Second World War', Imperial War Museum, http://www.iwm.org.uk/history/8-facts-about-clothes-rationing-in-britain-during-the-second-world-war, last accessed 30 May 2017
16 Margaret Murray and Jane Koster, *Practical Knitting Illustrated* (London: Odhams, 1949)
17 Brian Hyland, 'Itsy Bitsy Teenie Weenie Yellow Polkadot Bikini', written 1958, released 1960, Kapp Records

6: Carding, Combing and Cricket

1   Patricia Baines, *Spinning Wheels, Spinners and Spinning* (New York: Scribner, 1977), p. 38
2   Ibid., p. 17
3   Namaste Farms, *Fibre Fineness Table*, http://namastefarms.com/sandbox/fiber-fineness-by-micron-and-spinning-count/, last accessed 24 May 2018
4   Nigel Heard, *Wool: East Anglia's Golden Fleece* (Lavenham, 1970), p. 30
5   Kevin Stroud, 'Dyed in the Wool', *The History of English Podcast*, Episode 110, http://historyofenglishpodcast.com/2018/04/07/episode-110-dyed-in-the-wool/, last accessed 4 June 18
6   *Oxford English Dictionary*, http://www.oed.com/view/Entry/189069?rskey=OCtji9&result=2&isAdvanced=false#eid, last accessed 24 May 2018
7   Heard, *Wool*, p. 44
8   *Ciba Review*, 14, in Baines, *Spinning Wheels*, p. 30
9   Deborah Robson, 'When is a Down really a Down?', *PLY: The Magazine for Handspinners*, 16 (Spring 2017), pp. 10–17
10 Baines, *Spinning Wheels*, p. 35
11 *Oxford English Dictionary*, http://www.oed.com/view/Entry/27829#eid 10178845, last accessed 14 May 2018
12 *Oxford English Dictionary*, http://www.oed.com/view/Entry/193711?redirectedFrom=suint#eid, last accessed 14 May 2018

13 Baines, *Spinning Wheels*, p. 28

14 *Universal Magazine of Knowledge and Pleasure*, 5 (John Hinton, August 1749), p. 85

15 First recorded written usage dates from the sixteenth century, and it was used in this context until the nineteenth century.

16 John Lydgate (c. 1450), in Derek Hurst, *Sheep in the Cotswolds: The Medieval Wool Trade* (Stroud: History Press, 2005), p. 15

17 *Oxford English Dictionary*, http://www.oed.com/view/Entry/42451?redirectedFrom=cotswold#eid, last accessed 9 May 2018

18 Jane Bingham, *The Cotswolds: A Cultural History* (Oxford University Press, 2009), p. 34

19 Ibid., p. 33

20 Rob Harvey Long, in conversation, 5 June 2018

21 W. Cunningham, *The Growth of English Industry and Commerce*, 5th edn (Cambridge, 1922), quoted in R. A. Donkin, 'Cistercian Sheep-Farming and Wool-Sales in the Thirteenth Century', *Agricultural History Review*, 6 (1958), p. 2, http://www.bahs.org.uk/AGHR/ARTICLES/06n1a1.pdf, last accessed 16 May 2017

22 Richard Martin, 'The Golden Fleece of the Cotswold Sheep' (2012), http://www.cotswoldwoollenweavers.co.uk/Cotswold sheep.pdf, last accessed 18 May 2018

23 Richard Goddard, *Lordship and Medieval Urbanisation: Coventry, 1043–1355* (Royal Historical Society, 2004), p. 88

24 First written as 'Leyn de Coteswold', *Rolls of Parliament* (*Rotuli Parliamentorum*, 1327)

25 Heard, *Wool*, p. 43

26 Dan Jones, *Magna Carta: The Making and the Legacy of the Great Charter* (London: Head of Zeus, 2014)

27 Information board, St Peter & St Paul's, Northleach, October 2017

28 Ibid.

29 Baines, *Spinning Wheels*, p. 30

30 *Book of Trades* (1815), quoted in Baines, *Spinning Wheels*, p. 32

31 Joseph Plymley, *General View of the Agriculture of Shropshire* (London: Richard Phillips, 1803), p. 246

32 Chris Mason, 'Cricket "was invented in Belgium"', *BBC News*, 2 March 2009, http://news.bbc.co.uk/1/hi/world/europe/7919429.stm, last accessed 28 May 2018

33 *Oxford English Dictionary*, http://www.oed.com/view/Entry/44388, last accessed 28 May 2018

34 Peter Frawley, CEO of International Cricket Group, in an interview with Cerys Matthews, *BBC 6 Music*, 20 May 2018

35 *Guild Merchant Book* (1598), in *Oxford English Dictionary*, http://www.oed.com/view/Entry/44388, last accessed 28 May 2018

36 William Gilbert Grace, 'How to Score', in A. G. Steel and R. H. Lyttelton, *Cricket*, Badminton Library of Sports and Pastimes (London: Longmans, 1890), p. 51

37 Ibid., p. 51

38 Ibid., p. 52

39 Rutt, Richard, *A History of Hand Knitting* (London: Batsford, 1987), p. 194

40 Ibid.

7: Vikings, Socks and the Great Yorkshire Llama

1 Interpretation panel, Vindolanda Museum, visited July 2017

2 For more information, see Beth Williamson, *The Madonnas of Humility: Development, Dissemination & Reception, c.1340–1400* (Woodbridge: Boydell Press, 2009)

3 John, 19:23, King James Bible

4 Mateusz Kapustka and Warren T. Woodfin (eds), 'Clothing the Sacred: Medieval Textiles as Fabric, Form and Metaphor', *Textile Studies*, 8 (Berlin, 2015)

5 Carol Lee Anderson, *A History of the Belknap Mill: The Pride of Laconia's Industrial Heritage* (Stroud: History Press, 2014)

6 National Archives Currency Converter, https://www.nationalarchives.gov.uk/currency-converter/index.php#currency-result, last accessed 11 May 2018

7 Charles Dickens, *Household Words* (London: Bradbury and Evans), 27 November 1852

8 United Nations Educational, Scientific and Cultural Organization website: https://whc.unesco.org/en/list/1028, last accessed 20 October 2018

8: Knit-frocks, Guernseys and Jerseys

1 Mary Wright, *Cornish Guernseys and Knit-Frocks* (Polperro Heritage Press, 1978), pp. 6–7

2 Ibid., p. 3

3 S. Winifred Paynter, *Old St Ives: The Reminiscences of William Paynter* (St Ives, 1927)

4 Wright, *Cornish Guernseys*, p. 14

5 Ibid., p. 15

6 Ibid., p. 13

7 Joan Thirsk, *Rural Economy of England* (London: Bloomsbury, 2003) p. 240

8 Quoted in G. R. Balleine, *A History of the Isle of Jersey*, 3rd edn, (Chichester: Phillimore, 1998)

9 Samuel William Beck, *The Draper's Dictionary: A Manual of Textile*

Fabrics, Their History and Applications (London: The Warehousemen and Drapers' Journal Office, 1882)

10 *The Golden Fleece* (1657), http://www.oed.com/view/Entry/101112?rskey=Y 5KUot&result=1#eid, last accessed 27 February 2019

11 William Camden, *Britannia: Or a Chorographical Description of Great Britain and Ireland, Together with the Adjacent Islands* (London: Mary Matthews, 1586)

12 Quoted in Balleine, *History of the Isle of Jersey*

13 Quoted in 'The Jersey Pullover, Summerland of Jersey', Jersey Archives, L/A/10/J2/1

14 Jean Poingdestre, *Cæsarea: Or a Discourse of the Island of Jersey* (Jersey, 1662)

15 Philip Falle, *Cæsarea: Or, An Account of Jersey: The Greatest of the Islands Remaining to the Crown of England of the Ancient Dutchy of Normandy* (London: T. Wotton, 1734)

16 J. Stead, *A Picture of Jersey: Or, A Stranger's Companion Through That Island* (Jersey: J. Stead, 1809)

17 Richard Valpy, quoted in ibid.

18 Ibid.

19 Alan S. Raistrick, 'Spinning Wheels of the Channel Islands', *Journal for Weavers, Spinners and Dyers*, 208 (December 2003), p. 14

20 Valpy, quoted in Stead, *Picture of Jersey*

21 Audrey M. Journeaux, *Jersey Old and New* (1970)

22 Colin Ireson of L'Office du Jèrriais, in conversation, October 2018

23 Philip Falle and Edward Durell, *Cæsarea: Or, An Account of Jersey, to Which Are Added, Notes and Illustrations by the Rev Edward Durell* (Richard Giffard, 1837), p. 385

24 Ibid.

25 *A Guide to the Island of Jersey, Describing its History, Government, Commerce, Productions, Public Buildings, Inhabitants, etc.* (London: T. Baker, 1842), p. 72

26 Ibid.

27 *Jersey Times*, 28 February 1851

28 Ibid.

29 J. Hawkes and T. D. Kendrick, *Channel Islands: The Archaeology of the Channel Islands* (London: Methuen, 1928)

30 Poingdestre, *Cæsarea*

31 Philip Falle, *An Account of the Isle of Jersey, the Greatest of Those Islands That are Now the Only Reminder of the English Dominions in France* (London: John Newton, 1694)

32 Poingdestre, *Cæsarea*

33 Michael Drayton, *Poly-Olbion* (1612), Song I, ll. 49–50; http://poly-olbion.exeter.ac.uk

34 Poingdestre, *Cæsarea*

35 Frank Le Maistre, *English-Jersey Language Vocabulary*, with Albert Lucien Carré and Philip M. De Veulle (Gorey: Don Balleine Trust, 1972)

36 Falle and Durell, *Cæsarea*, p. 385

37 *Report of the Jersey Society*

38 T. F. Priaulx, 'Guernsey's Knitting Trade', *Quarterly Review of the Guernsey Society* (Autumn 1959)

39 Spencers were a style of fitted, knitted bodice common in the nineteenth century, named after the short jackets worn and popularized by George John Spencer, second Earl Spencer (1758–1834).

40 Mrs Bury Palliser, *History of Lace*, ed. Alice Dryden and Margaret Jourdain (Scribner, 1911)

41 Priaulx, 'Guernsey's Knitting Trade'

42 *Oxford English Dictionary*, http://www.oed.com/view/Entry/67722, last accessed 10 October 2018

43 *Acts of the Privy Council*, Sept 1627–June 1628 (London, 1940), p. 309

44 Guernsey Archive, 15 August 1629, University of London Library, MS 190, f. 52r.

45 Edgar MacCulloch (1876), in Priaulx, 'Guernsey's Knitting Trade'

46 Priaulx, 'Guernsey's Knitting Trade'

47 Committee Minute Books of the Directors of the Town Hospital, 1801–22, *Hopital De St Pierre Port – Deliberations B*, ed. Gillian Lefensey, Guernsey Archive

48 Channel Islands Knitwear Company, Jersey Archive, L/A/10/J1/6

49 Sister Peter, Sacré Cocur Orphanage, December 1994, Jersey Archive, L/A/10/J1/2

50 States of Jersey Textile Department Committee Meeting Minutes, Jersey Archive, L/A/10/F1/1–3

51 *Jersey Evening Post*, 10 March 1995

52 Channel Islands Knitwear Company, Jersey Archive, L/A/10/J1/5

53 'The Jersey Pullover, Summerland of Jersey', Jersey Archive, L/A/10/J2/1

54 National Archives Currency Converter: http://www.nationalarchives.gov.uk/currency-converter/#currency-result, last accessed 9 October 2018

55 Channel Islands Knitwear Company, Jersey Archive, L/A/10/J1/9

9: Shetland Stitches

1 'An Exact and Authentic Account of the Greatest White Herring Fishery in Scotland' (1750), in Rutt, *History of Hand Knitting*, p. 170

2 Brian Smith, 'Stockings and Mittens, 1580–1851', *Shetland Textiles*, p. 53

3 Ibid., p. 57

4 Carol Christiansen, 'Shetland Sheep and Wool', *Shetland Textiles: 800 BC*

to the Present, ed. Sarah Laurenson (Shetland Amenity Trust, 2013), p. 20

5   John Shirreff, in Oliver Henry, *Jamieson & Smith: A Shetland Story* (Shetland: Jamieson & Smith, 2017), p. 18

6   R. Sibbald, 'Description of the Islands of Orkney and Zetland' (1711), in Brian Smith, 'Wadmal', *Shetland Textiles*, p. 44

7   Samuel Hibbert, 'A Description of the Shetland Isles' (1822), in Rutt, *History of Hand Knitting*, p. 176

8   J. G. Lockhart, *Life of Sir Walter Scott*, in Smith, 'Stockings and Mittens', p. 56

9   Carol Christiansen, *A Shetlander's Fair Isle Graph Book* (Shetland Guild of Spinners, Knitters, Weavers and Dyers, 2016), p. 10

10 Ibid., p. 10

11 Shetland Archives, SA 3.1.115, in ibid.

12 Carol Christiansen, 'From Selbu to Scalloway, via Whalsay and Lerwick: Tracing the So-Called "Churchill" Pattern', *Shetland Wool Week Annual*, 3 (Shetland Amenities Trust, 2017), p. 76

13 Oliver Henry, *Jamieson & Smith: A Shetland Story* (Jamieson & Smith, 2017), p. 9

14 Ibid., p. 22

15 Valerie M. Thom, *Fair Isle: An Island Saga* (John Donald, Edinburgh, 1989), pp. 15–16

16 Ibid., p. 86

17 *Oxford English Dictionary*, http://www.oed.com/view/Entry/67722?redirectedFrom=fair+isle#eid, last accessed 4 June 2018

18 Official Guide to the 1886 Exhibition, in Thom, *Fair Isle*, p. 85

19 Thom, *Fair Isle*, p. 6

20 Ibid., p. 80

21 Sir Walter Scott, letter, 10 August 1814, in Rutt, *History of Hand Knitting*, p. 177

22 Thom, *Fair Isle*, p. 34

23 Ibid., p. 53

24 Ibid., p. 84

25 1851 census, Shetland Archives

26 G. D. Ramsay, *The English Woollen Industry, 1500–1750* (London: Macmillan, 1982), p. 11

27 *Oxford English Dictionary*, http://www.oed.com/view/Entry/7726#eid 3295081, last accessed October 2017

28 Ramsay, *English Woollen Industry*, p. 12

29 Hibbert, *Description of the Shetland Isles*, p. 179

30 *Shetland Advertiser*, January 1862, in Thom, *Fair Isle*, p. 84

31 *Oxford English Dictionary*: http://www.oed.com/view/Entry/122152#eid 36048284, last accessed October 2017

10: Monmouth Caps and Funeral Stockings

1   Thomas Johnes of Hafod, letter, 15 April 1799, in Ken Etheridge, *Welsh Costume in the Eighteenth and Nineteenth Century* (Llandybie: Dinefwr Press, 1977), pp. 15–16

2   Pat Hudson, 'The Welsh Textile Industry: A Brief Survey', in *History After Hobsbawm: Writing the Past for the Twenty-First Century*, ed. John H. Arnold et al. (Oxford University Press, 2018), p. 167

3   Etheridge, *Welsh Costume*, p. 15

4   Michael Freeman, 'Components of Welsh Costume', *Welsh Costume*, https://welshhat.wordpress.com/elements-of-welsh-costumes/, last accessed 21 May 2018

5   Sarah Eardley-Wilmot, National Museum of Wales, MS179554, in Freeman, 'Components of Welsh Costume'

6   Marie Trevelyan, *Glimpses of Welsh Life and Character* (London: J. Hogg, 1893), p. 47

7   Etheridge, *Welsh Costume*, p. 87

8   Ibid., p. 16

9   William Shakespeare, *Henry V*, Act 4, Scene VII

10 *The Soldier in Later Medieval England*, https://research.reading.ac.uk/medievalsoldier/, last accessed 27 February 2019

11 *Ripon Chapter Acts, 1452–1506*, Surtees Society, vol. 64 (1875), p. 120, in Kirstie Buckland, 'The Monmouth Cap', *Costume*, 13 (1979)

12 *Records of the Borough of Nottingham (1399–1485)*, vol. II, in Buckland, 'The Monmouth Cap'

13 John Stow, *A Summarie of Englyshe Chronicles* (1565)

14 Anne L. Macdonald, *No Idle Hands: The Social History of American Knitting* (New York, 1983), p. 3

15 Hudson, 'The Welsh Textile Industry', p. 174

16 Thomas Fuller, *The History of the Worthies of England* (1657), ed. P. Austin Nuttall (London: Nuttall and Hodgson, 1840), p. 6

17 Daniel Defoe, *A Tour Through the Whole Island of Great Britain* (1712), quoted in Buckland, 'The Monmouth Cap', p. 8

18 Buckland, 'The Monmouth Cap', p. 12

19 George Borrow, *Wild Wales: Its People, Language and Scenery* (London: John Murray, 1862), p. 289

20 Buckland, 'The Monmouth Cap', p. 8

21 Ibid., p. 1

22 St Fagans National Museum of History, accession number F69.353

23 Hudson, 'The Welsh Textile Industry', p. 174

24 George S. Nares, *The Official Report of the Recent Arctic Expedition* (London: John Murray, 1876), p. 84

25 Albert Hastings Markham, *The Great Frozen Sea: A Personal Narrative*

of the Voyage of the 'Alert' During the Artic Expedition of 1875–6 (London: K. Paul, 1878; reprinted Cambridge University Press, 2012), p. 7

26 Charles Dickens, *Dombey and Son* (London: Bradbury and Evans, 1846–48), Chapter 4

27 Gwen Davies, 'Stockings Prepared for Laying Out and Burial Held by Museums in the United Kingdom', *Textile History*, 23 (1992), p. 103

28 Bruce Chatwin, *On the Black Hill* (London: Vintage, 1998), p. 35

29 Ibid., p. 36

30 Ibid., p. 37

31 Rutt, *History of Hand Knitting*, p. 162

32 Hudson, 'The Welsh Textile Industry', p. 165

33 S. Minwel Tibbot, 'Knitting Stockings in Wales', *Folk Life*, 16 (1978), pp. 61–73

34 Thomas Jacob Thomas (1873–45) wrote the original in Welsh: '*Gwisgwyr sane'r greadigaeth, A ddaw yna 'nghyd, Sane glas a gwyn y Cardi, Geir ar goesau'r byd*'; translation provided by Michael Freeman of Ceredigion Museum

35 Sir Christopher Sykes, in Etheridge, *Welsh Costume*, p. 20

36 Etheridge, *Welsh Costume*, p. 29

37 Revd John Evans, *Letters Written During a Tour Through North Wales* (London: C. & R. Baldwin, 1804), pp. 67–68

38 Revd John Evans, *Letters Written During a Tour Through South Wales* (London, C.&R. Baldwin, 1804) p. 374

39 Walter Davies, *General View of the Agriculture & Domestic Economy of South Wales*, vol. 2 (London, 1815), in Minwel Tibbott, 'Knitting Stockings in Wales', p. 65

40 John Goodridge, *Rural Life in Eighteenth-Century English Poetry* (Cambridge University Press, 2005), pp. 100–101

41 John Torbuck, *A Collection of Welch Travels, and Memoirs of Wales* (Dublin, 1742), pp. 25–6

42 Trevelyan, *Glimpses of Welsh Life*, in Etheridge, *Welsh Costume*, p. 51

43 Huw Evans, *Cwm Eithin* (Liverpool: Gwasg y Brython, 1922), translated in Minwel Tibbott, 'Knitting Stockings in Wales', p. 62

44 Minwel Tibbott, 'Knitting Stockings in Wales', p. 62

45 Thomas Pennant, *Tours in Wales* (1810), in Minwel Tibbott, 'Knitting Stockings in Wales', p. 65

46 Eleanor Butler, *Journal*, 22 November 1781, in Rutt, *History of Hand Knitting*, pp. 162–3

47 Deborah Robson and Carol Ekarius, *The Fleece and Fiber Source Book* (North Adams, MA: Storey, 2011), p. 304

48 Buckland, 'The Monmouth Cap', p. 13

11: Haps and New Arrivals

1   V&A, T.30–1932, in Black, *Knitting*, p. 31
2   First used in Iowa, USA, in 1882, *Oxford English Dictionary*, http:// www.oed.com/view/Entry/114996?redirectedFrom=matinee+jacket #eid37821620
3   Michael Harvey, *Patons: A Story of Handknitting* (Ascot, Berks: Patons, 1985), p. 52
4   Kate Davies, *The Book of Haps* (Kate Davies Designs, 2016), pp. 37–41
5   Ibid., p. 33
6   Christiansen, 'Shetland Sheep and Wool', p. 24
7   Revd James Ingram, *Statistical Account, Unst* (1841), in *A Stitch in Time: Unst's Fine Lace Knitting* (Unst Heritage Trust, 1995), p. 2
8   Eliza Edmonston, *Sketches and Tales of the Shetland Islands* (1856), in *A Stitch in Time*, p. 3
9   Sophia Frances Anne Caulfeild and Blanche C. Saward, *The Dictionary of Needlework: An Encyclopaedia of Artistic, Plain, and Fancy Needlework* (London: L. Upcott Gill, 1882)
10 *The Dundee Courier and Argus*, 25 July 1894, in Roslyn Chapman, 'Knitting for Men', *Shetland Wool Week Annual* (2017), p. 81
11 James Moar, letter, 17 May 1881, Unst Heritage Centre, U134, in Chapman, 'Knitting for Men', p. 82
12 1901 census, in Chapman, 'Knitting for Men', p. 82
13 Chapman, 'Knitting for Men', p. 83
14 V&A, T.89–1928, T.97–1929, T.71–1912, T.31–1922, in Black, *Knitting*, pp. 42–3
15 Black, *Knitting*, pp. 114–15
16 Michel Odent, 'Knitting Needles, Cameras and Electronic Fetal Monitors', *Midwifery Today* 37 (Spring 1996), p. 14–15
17 Michel Odent, 'Knitting Midwives for a Drugless Childbirth?', *Midwifery Today* (October 2004)
18 *Essentially MIDIRS*, 4:9 (October 2013), p. 42
19 Ibid., p. 43

12: A Time of Gifts

1   Richard Holt, *Sport and the British: A Modern History* (Oxford University Press, 1990), p. 160

Select Bibliography

A Guide to the Island of Jersey, Describing its History, Government, Commerce, Productions, Public Buildings, Inhabitants, etc. (London: T. Baker, 1842)

A Stitch in Time: Unst's Fine Lace Knitting (Unst Heritage Trust, 1995)

Acts of the Privy Council, Sept 1627–June 1628 (London, 1940)

Allen, Richard J. P., 'Scottish Island Sheep', *ARK Magazine*, June 1984

Allison, K. J., 'The Norfolk Worsted Industry in the Sixteenth and Seventeenth Centuries', *Yorkshire Bulletin of Economic and Social Research*, XII: 27 (1960)

Amos, Andrew, *The English Constitution in the Reign of King Charles II* (London: Stevens & Norton, 1857)

Anderson, Carol Lee, *A History of the Belknap Mill: The Pride of Laconia's Industrial Heritage* (Stroud: History Press, 2014)

Anson, George, *A Voyage Around the World* (1748)

Appadurai, Arjun (ed.), *The Social Life of Things: Commodities in a Cultural Perspective*, (Cambridge University Press, 1986)

Arnold, John H., et al., *History After Hobsbawm: Writing the Past for the Twenty-First Century* (Oxford University Press, 2018)

Atwood, Kathryn J., *Women Heroes of World War I: 16 Remarkable Resisters, Soldiers, Spies, and Medics* (Chicago Review Press, 2014)

Baines, Patricia, *Spinning Wheels, Spinners and Spinning* (New York: Scribner, 1977)

Balleine, G. R., *A History of the Isle of Jersey*, 3rd edn (Chichester: Phillimore, 1998)

Barty-King, Hugh, *Pringle of Scotland and the Hawick Knitwear Story* (2006)

Bazilchuk, Nancy, 'The Sheep That Launched 1000 Ships', *New Scientist*, 24 July 2004, https://www.newscientist.com/article/mg18324575-900-the-sheep-that-launched–1000-ships/

Beck, Samuel William, *The Draper's Dictionary: A Manual of Textile Fabrics, Their History and Applications* (London: The Warehousemen and Drapers' Journal Office, 1882)

Bennett, Helen, 'The Scottish Hand-knitting Industry', PhD thesis (1981), http://knittinghistory.co.uk/publications/scottish-handknitting-industry-thesis/

Benson, Herbert, 'Mind-Body Pioneer', *Psychology Today*, 34 (2001)

Bingham, Jane, *The Cotswolds: A Cultural History* (Oxford University Press, 2009)

Bischoff, James, *A Comprehensive History of the Woollen and Worsted Manufactures* (London: Smith, Elder & Co., 1842)

Black, Sandy, *Knitting: Fashion, Industry, Craft* (London: V&A Publishing, 2012)

Blacker, Sue, *Pure Wool* (London: Bloomsbury, 2012)

Blanche, E. I. 'The Expression of Creativity through Occupation', *Journal of Occupational Science*, 14:1 (2007)

Borrow, George, *Wild Wales: Its People, Language and Scenery* (London: John Murray, 1862)

Bowles, Geoffrey, and Kirrane, Siobhan, *Knitting Together: Memories of Leicestershire's Hosiery Industry* (Leicestershire Museums, Arts and Records Service, 1990)

Brears, Peter C., 'The Knitting Sheath', *Folk Life*, 20 (1982)

British Wool Marketing Board, *British Sheep Breeds: Their Wool and Its Uses* (date unknown)

Brown, Ian (ed.), *From Tartan to Tartanry* (Edinburgh University Press, 2010)

Buckland, Francis T., *Curiosities in Natural History*, 4th series (London: Richard Bextley, 1888)

Buckland, Kirstie, 'The Monmouth Cap', *Costume*, 13 (1979)

Bury Palliser, Mrs, *History of Lace*, ed. Alice Dryden and Margaret Jourdain (Scribner, 1911)

Camden, William, *Britannia: Or a Chorographical Description of Great Britain and Ireland, Together with the Adjacent Islands* (London: Mary Matthews, 1586)

Carlyle, Thomas, *The French Revolution: A History* (London: Miles, 1837)

Carlyle, W. J., 'The Changing Distribution of Breeds of Sheep in Scotland, 1795–1965', *The Agricultural History Review*, 27:1 (British Agricultural History Society, 1979)

Catterall, Douglas, and Campbell, Jodie (eds), *Women in Port: Gendering Communities, Economies, and Social Networks in Atlantic Port Cities, 1500–1800* (Leiden: Brill, 2012)

Caulfeild, Sophia Frances Anne, and Saward, Blanche C., *The Dictionary of Needlework: An Encyclopaedia of Artistic, Plain, and Fancy Needlework* (London: L. Upcott Gill, 1882)

Chatwin, Bruce, *On the Black Hill* (London: Vintage, 1998)

Chaucer, Geoffrey, 'The Knight's Tale', *Canterbury Tales*, in *The Hengwrt Chaucer Digital Facsimile*, ed. Estelle Stubbs (2003)

Cheape, Hugh, *Tartan: The Highland Habit* (Edinburgh: National Museums of Scotland, 1991)

Christiansen, Carol, *A Shetlander's Fair Isle Graph Book* (Shetland Guild of Spinners, Knitters, Weavers and Dyers, 2016)

Clark, John Willis, and Hughes, Thomas McKenny, *The Life and Letters of the Reverend Adam Sedgwick*, vol. 1 (Cambridge University Press, 1890)

Collins, Irene, 'Charles Dickens and the French Revolution', *Literature and History*, 2:1 (Spring 1990)

Coltman, Viccy, 'Party Coloured Plaid? Portraits of Eighteenth-Century Scots in Tartan', *Textile History*, 41:2 (2010)

Compton, Rae, *The Complete Book of Traditional Jersey and Guernsey Knitting* (London: Batsford, 1984)

Cunningham, W., *The Growth of English Industry and Commerce*, 5th edn (Cambridge, 1922)

Curzon, Paul, 'Dickens Knitting in Code', *CS4FN*, Queen Mary University of London, http://www.cs4fn.org/ada/dickensknitting.php

Davies, Gwen, 'Stockings Prepared for Laying Out and Burial Held by Museums in the United Kingdom', *Textile History*, 23 (1992)

Davies, Kate, 'Nautical!', *TextIsles*, 3 (2012)

Davies, Kate, *The Book of Haps* (Kate Davies Designs, 2016)

Davies, Walter, *General View of the Agriculture & Domestic Economy of South Wales*, vol. 2 (London, 1815)

Defoe, Daniel, *A Tour Through the Whole Island of Great Britain* (1712), 6th edn. (London: J. Osbourne, 1742)

Devine, T. M., *Clanship to Crofters' War: The Social Transformation of the Scottish Highlands* (Manchester University Press, 1994)

Dickens, Charles, *A Tale of Two Cities* (1859; London: T. Lacy, 1860)

Dickens, Charles, *Dombey and Son* (London: Bradbury and Evans, 1846–48)

Dickens, Charles, *Household Words*, 27 November 1852 (London: Bradbury and Evans, 1852)

Dixon, John H., *A Guide to Gairloch and Loch Maree* (Edinburgh: Cooperative Printing Company, 1886)

Donkin, R. A., 'Cistercian Sheep-Farming and Wool-Sales in the Thirteenth Century', *Agricultural History Review*, 6 (1958)

Drayton, Michael, *Poly-Olbion* (1612, reprinted London: John Russell Smith, 1876); http://poly-olbion.exeter.ac.uk

Dwelly, Edward, *The Illustrated Gaelic Dictionary* (Fleet, Hants: Dwelly, 1918)

Essentially MIDIRS, 4:9, (October 2013)

Etheridge, Ken, *Welsh Costume in the Eighteenth and Nineteenth Century* (Llandybie: Dinefwr Press, 1977)

Evans, Huw, *Cwm Eithin* (Liverpool: Gwasg y Brython, 1922)

Evans, John, *Letters Written During a Tour Through North Wales* (London: C. & R. Baldwin, 1804)

Falle, Philip, *An Account of the Isle of Jersey, the Greatest of Those Islands That are Now the Only Reminder of the English Dominions in France* (London: John Newton, 1694)

Falle, Philip, *Cæsarea: Or, An Account of Jersey: The Greatest of the Islands Remaining to the Crown of England of the Ancient Dutchy of Normandy* (London: T. Wotton, 1734)

Falle, Philip, and Durell, Edward, *Cæsarea: Or, An Account of Jersey, to Which Are Added, Notes and Illustrations by the Rev Edward Durell* (Richard Giffard, 1837)

Fear, Jenna, 'The Knitting War Spies of History', *Interweave*, 21 July 2017, https://www.interweave.com/article/weaving/knitting-war-spies-history/

Fenton, Alexander, *Country Life in Scotland: Our Rural Past* (Edinburgh: Birlinn, 2008)

Fenton, Alexander, *The Northern Isles: Orkney and Shetland* (Edinburgh: John Donald, 1978, revised D. A. Quine, 1982)

Fenton, Jeremy, *The Story of Gairloch: A Brief History of Gairloch and District* (2017), http://www.jeremyfenton.scot/Booklet%20Gairloch%20History%20lo.pdf

Fleury, alias Joseph Abraham Bénard, *Mémoires de Fleury de la Comédie Française* (Paris: J. B. P. Lafitte, 1836)

Ford, Felicity, *KnitSonik Stranded Colourwork Sourcebook* (Felicity Ford, 2014)

Freeman, Michael, 'Components of Welsh Costume', *Welsh Costume*, https://welshhat.wordpress.com/elements-of-welsh-costumes/

Friedland, Paul, *Seeing Justice Done: The Age of Spectacular Capital Punishment in France* (Oxford University Press, 2012)

Gilbert, Ruth, 'The King's Vest and the Seaman's Gansey: Continuity and Diversity of Construction in Hand Knitted Body Garments in North Western Europe Since 1550, With Special Reference to Armhole Shaping', unpublished MPhil thesis, Textile Conservation Centre, University of Southampton (2009)

Goddard, Richard, *Lordship and Medieval Urbanisation: Coventry, 1043–1355* (Royal Historical Society: The Boydell Press, 2004)

Godineau, Dominique, *The Women of Paris and Their French Revolution*, trans. Katherine Striep (Berkeley: University of California Press, 1998)

Goodridge, John, *Rural Life in Eighteenth-Century English Poetry* (Cambridge University Press, 2005)

Grant, Isabel F., 'An Old Scottish Handicraft Industry', *Scottish Historical Review*, XVIII (1921)

Griffin Lewis, George, *The Practical Book of Oriental Rugs* (Philadelphia: Lippincott, 1911)

Gulvin, Clifford, *The Scottish Hosiery and Knitwear Industry 1680–1980* (Edinburgh: John Donald, 1984)

Gulvin, Clifford, *The Tweedmakers: A History of the Scottish Fancy Woollen Industry 1600–1914* (Devon: David & Charles, 1973)

Gunn, Neil M., *The Silver Darlings* (1941; London: Faber, 1969)

Harris Tweed Act (1993), c. xi, http://www.legislation.gov.uk/ukla/1993/11/contents/enacted

Harrison, E. P., *Scottish Estate Tweeds* (Elgin: Johnstons of Elgin, 1995)

Harrison, Edward, 'History of the Scottish Woollen Trade', National Association of the Scottish Woollen Manufacturers (1935)

Harrison, Edward, 'Scottish Woollens', National Association of the Scottish Woollen Manufacturers (1939)

Hartley, Marie, and Ingilby, Joan, *The Old Hand-Knitters of the Dales, with an Introduction to the Early History of Knitting* (Clapham, Lancs: Dalesman 1951)

Harvey, Michael, *Patons: A Story of Handknitting* (Ascot, Berks: Patons, 1985)

Hawkes, J., and Kendrick, T. D., *Channel Islands: The Archaeology of the Channel Islands* (London: Methuen, 1928)

Henry, Oliver, *Jamieson & Smith: A Shetland Story* (Shetland: Jamieson & Smith, 2017)

Hesketh, Christian, *Tartans* (London: Weidenfeld & Nicolson, 1961)

Historic Scotland, *Hawick and Its Place Among the Border Mill Towns* (Edinburgh: Historic Scotland, 2009)

Holme, Randle, *The Academy of Armory: Or, a Storehouse of Armory and Blazon* (Chester: Randle Holme, 1688)

Holmes, E., et al., 'Trauma, Films, Information Processing and Intrusive Memory Development', *Journal of Experimental Psychology*, 133:1 (2004)

Holroyd, Michael, *Lytton Strachey: The New Biography* (London: Chatto and Windus, 1994)

Holt, Richard, *Sport and the British: A Modern History* (Oxford University Press, 1990)

Hosegood, B., 'Whip Your Hobby into Shape: Knitting, Feminism, and Construction of Gender', *Textile: The Journal of Cloth and Culture*, 7:2 (2009)

House of Commons Sessional Papers, *Inventory Control Record 1*, vol. 46 (1910)

Howitt, William, *The Rural Life of England*, vol. 2 (London: Longman, 1838)

Hurst, Derek, *Sheep in the Cotswolds: The Medieval Wool Trade* (Stroud: History Press, 2005)

Huxley Barkham, Selma, 'The Basque Coast of Newfoundland' (Great Northern Peninsula Development Corporation, 1989)

Ingersoll, Earl G., *Screening Woolf: Virginia Woolf on/and/in Film* (Maryland: Fairleigh Dickinson University Press, 2017)

Jersey Evening Post, 10 March 1995

Jersey Times, 28 February 1851

Jewell, P. A., et al. (eds), *Island Survivors: The Ecology of the Soay Sheep of St Kilda* (London: Athlone Press, 1974)

Jones, Dan, *Magna Carta: The Making and the Legacy of the Great Charter* (London: Head of Zeus, 2014)

Kapustka, Mateusz, and Woodfin, Warren T. (eds), 'Clothing the Sacred: Medieval Textiles as Fabric, Form and Metaphor', *Textile Studies*, 8 (2015)

Knox, W. W., *Industrial Nation: Work, Culture and Society in Scotland, 1800–Present* (Edinburgh University Press, 1999)

Laurenson, Sarah (ed.), *Shetland Textiles: 800 BC to the Present* (Shetland Amenity Trust, 2013)

Lee, Hermione, *Virginia Woolf* (London: Vintage, 1997)

Leighton-White, Sue, 'The Needles' Music: Handknitters of the Dales', *Knitting Traditions* (2011)

Lister Hemingway, Penelope, 'Playing with a Piece of String: The Story of a Dentdale Knitter in The Retreat Asylum, York', *Knit Edge*, 3 (May 2013)

Macdonald, Anne L., *No Idle Hands: The Social History of American Knitting* (New York, 1983)

Macdonald, Finlay J., *Crowdie and Cream* (1982; Little, Brown, 1996)

MacGillivray, Neil, 'Dr John Mackenzie', *Journal of Scottish Historical Studies*, 33:1 (Edinburgh University Press, 2013)

Maistre, Frank Le, *English-Jersey Language Vocabulary*, with Albert Lucien Carré and Philip M. De Veulle (Gorey: Don Balleine Trust, 1972)

Markham, Albert Hastings, *The Great Frozen Sea: A Personal Narrative of the Voyage of the 'Alert' During the Artic Expedition of 1875–6* (London: K. Paul, 1878; reprinted Cambridge University Press, 2012)

Martin, Richard, 'The Golden Fleece of the Cotswold Sheep' (2012), http://www.cotswoldwoollenweavers.co.uk/Cotswold sheep.pdf

Mason, Chris, 'Cricket "was invented in Belgium"', *BBC News*, 2 March 2009, http://news.bbc.co.uk/1/hi/world/europe/7919429.stm

Mendick, Robert, 'Wartime Spy Finally Accepts She is a French Heroine', *Daily Telegraph*, 22 November 2014

Miers, Mary, *Highland Retreats: The Architecture and Interiors of Scotland's Romantic North* (New York: Rizzoli International Publications, 2017)

Minwel Tibbot, S., 'Knitting Stockings in Wales', *Folk Life*, 16 (1978)

Mousset, Sophie, *Women's Rights and the French Revolution: A Biography of Olympe de Gouges*, trans. Joy Poirel (New Brunswick: Transaction Publishers, 2007)

Murray, Margaret, and Koster, Jane, *Practical Knitting Illustrated* (London: Odhams, 1949)

Nares, George S., *The Official Report of the Recent Arctic Expedition* (London: John Murray, 1876)

Philiatros, *Natura Exenterata: Or Nature Unbowelled* (1655)

Nenadic, Stana, *Lairds and Luxury: The Highland Gentry in Eighteenth-Century Scotland* (Edinburgh: John Donald Ltd, 2007)

New Statistical Account of Scotland (1845)

NicGuaire, Anna, 'Crotal: Lichen', *Uiseag: Gaelic Heritage, Landscape, Handcrafts, Place*, https://uiseag.com/2013/08/20/crotal-lichen/

Nicholson, Nigel, and Trautmann, Joanna (eds), *Collected Letters of Virginia Woolf*, vol. 2 (New York: Houghton Brace Jovanovich, 1976)

Nigel Heard, *Wool: East Anglia's Golden Fleece* (Lavenham, 1970)

Odent, Michel, 'Knitting Midwives for a Drugless Childbirth?', *Midwifery Today* (October 2004)

Odent, Michel, 'Knitting Needles, Cameras and Electronic Fetal Monitors', *Midwifery Today* 37 (Spring 1996)

Okumura, Sayaka, 'Women Knitting: Domestic Activity, Writing, and Distance in Virginia Woolf's Fiction', *English Studies*, 89:2 (2008)

Omand, Donald (ed.), *The Borders Book* (Edinburgh: Birlinn, 1995)

Page, William, and Round, J. H. (eds), *The Victoria History of the County of Essex*, vol. 2 (London: Archibald Constable, 1907)

Patrick, Belle, *Recollections of East Fife Fisher Folk* (Edinburgh: Birlinn, 2003)

Paynter, S. Winifred, *Old St. Ives: The Reminiscences of William Paynter* (St Ives, 1927)

Peacock, William T., 'The Early Stockingmakers and Their Industry', *Transactions of the Hawick Archaeological Society*, 1961

Pearson, Michael, *Traditional Knitting* (London: Collins, 1984)

Plymley, Joseph, *General View of the Agriculture of Shropshire* (London: Richard Phillips, 1803)

Poingdestre, Jean, *Cæsarea: Or a Discourse of the Island of Jersey* (Jersey, 1662)

Pope, Alexander, '*Moral Essays*, Epistle I: Of the Knowledge and Character of Men' (1733), in *The Poetical Works of Alexander Pope* (London: Macmillan, 1869)

Priaulx, T. F., 'Guernsey's Knitting Trade', *Quarterly Review of the Guernsey Society* (Autumn 1959)

Rae, James, *A Compleat History of the Rebellion from its First Rise in 1745* (London: Robert Brown, 1749)

Raistrick, Alan S., 'Spinning Wheels of the Channel Islands', *Journal for Weavers, Spinners and Dyers*, 208 (2003)

Ramsay, G. D., *The English Woollen Industry, 1500–1750* (London: Macmillan, 1982)

Ratcliffe, Susan, *Oxford Dictionary of Quotations by Subject* (Oxford University Press, 2010)

Robson, Deborah, 'When is a Down really a Down?', *PLY: The Magazine for Handspinners*, 16 (Spring 2017)

Robson, Deborah, and Ekarius, Carol, *The Fleece and Fiber Source Book* (North Adams, MA: Storey, 2011)

Rolls of Parliament (Rotuli Parliamentorum) 1278–1503 (1767–77)

Ross, Alexander, *Scottish Home Industries* (1895; Glasgow: Molendinar Press, 1974)

Rutt, Richard, *A History of Hand Knitting* (London: Batsford, 1987)

Ryder, M. L., *Sheep and Man* (London: Duckworth, 1983)

Schaus, Margaret (ed.), *Women and Gender in Medieval Europe: An Encyclopedia* (New York: Routledge, 2006)

Scott Watson, J. A., 'The Rise and Development of the Sheep Industry in the Highlands and North of Scotland', *Transactions of the Highland and Agricultural Society of Scotland*, 5:44 (Edinburgh: Blackwood and Sons, 1932)

Shetland Wool Week Annual, 3 (Shetland Amenities Trust, 2017)

Slater, Michael, *Dickens and Women* (London: J. M. Dent, 1983)

Southey, Robert, 'A True Story of the Terrible Knitters e' Dent', Inter-chapter XXIV in *The Doctor* (London: Longman, 1847)

Speed, John, *Historie of Great Britaine* (1611; London: George Humble, 1623)

Stead, J., *A Picture of Jersey: Or, A Stranger's Companion Through That Island* (Jersey: J. Stead, 1809)

Steel, A. G., and Lyttelton, R. H., *Cricket*, Badminton Library of Sports and Pastimes (London: Longmans, 1890)

Stroud, Kevin, 'Dyed in the Wool', *The History of English Podcast*, Episode 110, http://historyofenglishpodcast.com/2018/04/07/episode–110-dyed-in-the-wool/

Stubbes, Phillip, *The Anatomie of Abuses* (London: R. Iones, 1583)

Sturluson, Snorri, *The Heimskringla: Or, Chronicle of the Kings of Norway*, vol. 3, trans. Samuel Laing (London: Longman, 1844)

Taddeo, Julie Anne, *Lytton Strachey and the Search for Modern Sexual Identity: The Last Eminent Victorian* (New York: Routledge, 2011)

Taylor, David, *The Wild Black Region: 1750–18* (Edinburgh: Birlinn, 2016)

Taylor, Doreen, 'Days of Change in Hawick', *Scots Magazine*, August 1971

Thirsk, Joan, *Rural Economy of England* (London: Bloomsbury, 2003)

Thom, Valerie M., *Fair Isle: An Island Saga* (Edinburgh: John Donald, 1989)

Thompson, Gladys, *Patterns for Guernseys, Jerseys and Arans* (London: Batsford, 1955)

Torbuck, John, *A Collection of Welch Travels, and Memoirs of Wales* (Dublin, 1742)

Transactions of the Highland and Agricultural Society of Scotland (1895)

Trevelyan, Marie, *Glimpses of Welsh Life and Character* (London: J. Hogg, 1893)

Trow-Smith, Robert, *A History of British Livestock Husbandry: 1700–1900* (London: Routledge and Kegan Paul, 1959)

Turley, Joanne, *The Culture of Knitting* (Oxford: Berg, 2009)

Universal Magazine of Knowledge and Pleasure, 5 (John Hinton, 1749)

Waxman, Olivia B., and Ronk, Liz, 'Swimsuit Evolution', *Time*, 5 July 2016 http://time.com/4383860/swimsuit-evolution-bikini-origins-history/

Webster, N. H., *The French Revolution: A Study in Democracy* (London: Constable, 1919)

Westermann, Karie, *This Thing of Paper* (Glasgow: Karie Westermann, 2017)

Whittington, G., and Whyte, I. D. (eds), *An Historical Geography of Scotland* (Academic Press, 1983)

Wightman, Andy, *Who Owns Scotland* (Edinburgh: Canongate, 1996)

Williamson, Beth, *The Madonnas of Humility: Development, Dissemination & Reception, c.1340–1400* (Woodbridge: Boydell Press, 2009)

Witkowski, Jacqueline, 'Knit for Defense, Purl to Control', *InVisible Culture*, 15 April 2015

Woolf, Virginia, *To the Lighthouse* (Hogarth Press, 1927; Oxford University Press, 2006)

Wright, Mary, *Cornish Guernseys and Knit-Frocks* (Polperro Heritage Press, 1978)

Youatt, William, *Sheep: Their Breeds, Management and Diseases* (London: Baldwin & Cradock, 1837)

Zarrelli, Natalie, 'The Wartime Knitters Who Used Knitting as an Espionage Tool', *Atlas Obscura*, 1 June 2017, https://www.atlasobscura.com/articles/knitting-spies-wwi-wwii

Archives and Websites

Highland Folk Museum Archives
Gordon Highlanders Museum, Aberdeen
Imperial War Museum, http://www.iwm.org.uk/
Jersey Archives

Namaste Farms, *Fibre Fineness Table*, http://namastefarms.com/sandbox/
    fiber-fineness-by-micron-and-spinning-count/
National Archives Currency Converter, https://www.nationalarchives.gov.
    uk/currency-converter/
National Archives of Scotland, with online catalogue, www.nas.co.uk
National Library of Scotland map collections, www.nls.uk/maps
National Monuments Record, with online catalogue, www.rcahms.gov.uk
National Muscums of Scotland
Oxford Dictionary of National Biography, http://www.oxforddnb.com/
Oxford English Dictionary online, http://www.oed.com/
Science in the News, http://www.scienceinthenews.org.uk/contents/
    ?article=8
Shetland Archives
St Fagans National Museum of History
The Knitting Genie, https://theknittinggenie.com/
The Soldier in Later Medieval England, https://research.reading.ac.uk/
    medievalsoldier/
University of Exeter, *Poly-Olbion Project* online, http://poly-olbion.exeter.ac.uk/
Vikingeskibsmuseet, Roskilde, Denmark, https://www.vikingeskibsmuseet.
    dk/en/professions/boatyard/experimental-archaeological-research/
    maritime-crafts/maritime-technology/woollen-sailcloth/
World Health Organization, http://www.searo.who.int/

Acknowledgements

First and foremost, thank you to my wonderful agent, Jenny Brown, who picked up this book when it was little more than a tweet and saw it through to publication. Thanks are also due to XpoNorth, without whose 'Tweet your Pitch' competition I wouldn't have been on Twitter in the first place, and to Max Porter, who first recognized that *This Golden Fleece* could be a Granta book.

I owe a huge debt of gratitude to my editor at Granta, Bella Lacey, a most excellent literary midwife whose comments and suggestions are always thoughtful, timely and precise. Thanks are also due to Louise Scollay of KnitBritish, who met with me in the early stages of my research and suggested many useful collaborators, including expert proofreader Amelia Hodsdon. I am also extremely grateful to Creative Scotland and the Society of Authors, for awarding me a research grant and the Roger Deakin Award respectively to enable me to research this book. Further thanks are due to the diligent and knowledgeable Daphne Tagg, for her thorough and thoughtful copy-editing.

Thank you to the University of St Andrews, in particular the School of Geography and Sustainable Development, who welcomed me into their fold as Writer in Residence and provided me with access to invaluable materials and also a lovely quiet office in which to write – the view of the sea was a bonus. Special thanks are due to Professor Nina Laurie, who first nominated me for the post of Writer in Residence, and to Professor Bill Austin, for his enthusiastic support.

Tremendous thanks are due to Suzanne Murrell, who first taught me to knit and who generously allowed me to share her story. I am grateful to Sue Leighton-White and Penelope Lister Hemingway for their research into knitting in the Yorkshire Dales, and to Deb Gillanders of Whitby, who generously shared tea, time and expertise with me. Thank you to Elizabeth and Margaret Johnston of Shetland Handspun, to Marsha Willey from Arizona, and to Gordon Macdonald and Irene Scott from Hawick, for sharing your expertise and experience, and to Jo and Mica for running the excellent Edinburgh Yarn Festival, which provided me with a perfect gateway into the world of contemporary knit-wear design.

Staff in museums, libraries and archives across Britain have given unstintingly of their time and expertise, and thanks are due to Curator Jeff Cowton and Assistant Curator Melissa Mitchell at the Wordsworth Trust in Grasmere; Jen Gordon and Linda Fitzpatrick at the Scottish Fisheries Museum in Anstruther; and to the staff of the Highland Folk Museum, specifically Rachel Chisholm, Curator, and Matthew Withey, Curatorial Manager, and to Maureen Hammond, PhD researcher at UHI Centre for History and the Highland Folk Museum, who gave me access to Am Fasgadh's wonderful collections and provided invaluable feedback on draft manuscript material. Thank you to Curator Karen Buchanan at Gairloch Museum for allowing me to spend time with the stocking collections, and to the museum's volun-teers for assisting with my research. Thank you to the staff and volunteers of South Uist's Kildonan Museum and Aberdeen Art Gallery, to the staff at Hawick's Townhouse Textile Museum and Heritage Hub, in particular Hannah Bell and Kathy Hobkirk; and to Emily Carrig, who showed me how to use hand-powered knitting machines.

The Framework Knitters Museum in Ruddington: thank you to your staff and volunteers, in particular Holly Batley for showing me how the older frames work. To Anne Drew of Cymbal Knits: thank you for an excellent day at Sock School; and thanks to Annie Fern for letting me see your knitting treasure trove – and for tea and biscuits!

Thanks are also due to Dr Darryl Ogier, Archivist, and Michèle Bisson, Archives Assistant, at the Island Archives, States of Guernsey, for your assistance in researching and editing the Guernsey chapter, and to Janne White and team at Jersey Archives. Thank you to the staff and volunteers at Hamptonne Country Park and to Neil Sexton and the knitters of Le Tricoteur for sharing your stories with me. Many thanks to Colin Ireson and his colleagues in L'Office du Jèrriais for their advice and expertise regarding the Jèrriais language.

Huge thanks to Dr Carol Christiansen, Textile Curator at Shetland Museum, for all her assistance and expertise. Gratitude is also due to Dr Brian Smith and Blair Bruce in Shetland Archives, and to all the staff and volunteers involved in running the inspiring extravaganza that is Shetland Wool Week. Thank you in particular to Julia Billings, Kate Davies, Donna Smith, Betsy and Linda Williamson, and all the knitters who provided tea and exquisite haps in Ollaberry. Heartfelt thanks are also due to Felicity Ford for your infectious enthusiasm and considered expertise, and to Roslyn Chapman for your diligent research and support. Thanks too to Professor Lynn Abrams and Dr Marina Moskowitz for your research suggestions.

Kirstie Buckland: thank you for tea, lunch and stories in Monmouth. Thank you to Michael Freeman, historian and former Curator of Ceredigion Museum; to Elen Phillips and her team at St Fagans National Museum of History; and to Peter Holme, Curator at Manchester's National Football Museum.

A number of yarn producers also gave this book their support: Jan and Russ of Frangipani in Cornwall; John and Juliet Miller and the team at The Border Mill; Dana MacPhee, Neil and the team at Uist Wool; Meg and Andy Rodger of The Birlinn Yarn Company on Berneray; Rob Harvey Long and his 'Pickwick' Cotswold flock, and Town End Yarns in Cumbria.

Sincere gratitude is due to Jane Cooper of Orkney, who not only shared her encyclopaedic knowledge of all things Boreray but also allowed me to cuddle her sheep and take away some rare and beautiful wool. Likewise to Dunja and Brian Roberts of Cwndu, who shared their lives and fleece; to Richard and Peter Longbottom of West Yorkshire Spinners, who welcomed a very wet writer to their business; to Verity Britton of Baa Ram Ewe in Leeds; and to Amy Twigger Holroyd. Thank you to Oliver Henry and the team at Jamieson & Smith, who provided yarn for my Dentdale gloves and Shetland scarf, and to Sue Blacker and her team at Blacker Yarns and The Natural Fibre Company. Thanks to Sally Davies and Jonny King for the skeins of Ryeland yarn and for a memorable visit to Garthenor.

Thanks are also due to friends and relatives up and down the country, who provided me with insight, information, companionship and accommodation as I worked on the book. In particular, thank you to my mother, Gabrielle Rutter, who first introduced me to spinning wool, and to my father, Michael Rutter, who inspired the creation of the gansey. Gratitude is also due to my parents-in-law, Jeff and Gill Cowton, whose home in Grasmere provided the genius loci for the book; particular thanks to Jeff for accompanying me to my first football match, and to his brother, Steve Cowton, for taking me to my first county cricket game. Thanks are also due to Audrey Cowton for supplying me with her cricket jumper knitting pattern.

Thank you to my dear friends Jane and Rob Sparkes and Stephen and Sophie Miller, who gave me bed and board for my Yorkshire research trips, and to Naomi Garnett and Alex Heap for the same in Nottinghamshire. Much gratitude is also due to Thea Goodsell and Hannah and George Bulmer, who always look after me excellently when I come to stay in London. Thank you too to Simon Thomas and Sally Gall, who both put me up and kept me right.

To Alice Loudon, for allowing me to scrutinize your knitting; and to the Lilies for enthusiastically supporting my efforts to swim in a knitted bikini. To Elly Murrell – thank you for letting me wash the wool all those years ago and for joining me on this journey. To Emma Mathers and Pip Parmenter, for friendship and adventures; to Wimpje and Cor Rovers for your company at Betty Mouat's, and to Sara for accompanying me on our (failed) adventure to Fair Isle. Thanks are also due to Clare Rickerby and Richard Streeter for the loan and gift of several useful books.

Finally, huge thanks are due to my husband, Tom, who not only made sure that the mortgage got paid whilst I wrote this book, but also supplied me with Icelandic yarn, a handmade needle, and a model for many of my knits. Your faith in my ability to write this has been steadfast and unstinting; for being my first reader, I thank you for your judicious feedback, and for every day of your love and support. And to Rose – for your most considerately timed arrival.

Illustration Notes and Credits

Plate section

Fisher lassies knitting whilst resting against a large pile of 'Yarmouth swills'. Yarmouth, *c.* 1900. Reproduced courtesy of the Scottish Fisheries Museum, Anstruther.

Virginia Woolf by Vanessa Bell. Oil on board, 1912. 400 mm × 340 mm. National Portrait Gallery 5933. Courtesy of the National Portrait Gallery

Temperature and knitting yarn chart, Marsha Willey.

All other photographs in the plate section belong to the author.

Illustrations in text

The hand-drawn illustrations on pages 2, 8, 36, 60, 84, 104, 128, 154, 176, 204, 234, 254 and 276 are copyright © Eleanor Crow, 2019.

p. 15   Gloves knitted by Mary Allen for Mrs H. Inglis. The Wordsworth Museum, Grasmere. Courtesy of the Wordsworth Trust.

p. 41   Robertson family, photographed outside their home at Mid Shore, Buckhaven, around 1900. Whilst this image is almost certainly posed, line baiting was often done outside as the light

was better. Courtsey of the Scottish Fisheries
Museum, Anstruther.

p. 49   Cellardyke Fishermen, *c.*1910. Back row (l–r):
Robert Murray, Jim Murray, unknown. Front
row: unknown, Alex Murray, unknown. Courtesy
of the Scottish Fisheries Museum, Anstruther.

p. 75   *Les Tricoteuses Jacobines.* Gouache on cut card,
1793; by Pierre-Etienne Lesueur. In the public
domain via Wikimedia Commons.

p. 95   View across Loch Gairloch, Wester Ross,
Scotland, 2018. Photograph by the author.

p. 104   Ruins of Jedburgh Abbey, 2017. Photograph by
the author.

p. 122   Pattern from *Practical Knitting Illustrated* (1949)
for an Easy to Wear Beach Suit. Photograph by
the author.

p. 135   Carders, niddy-noddy, raw fleece, bobbins, 2017.
Photograph by the author.

p. 139   Evening at 'the Cathedral of the Cotswolds',
Northleach Church, Northleach, Gloucestershire,
2017. Photograph by the author.

p. 147   Scarborough Cricket Club, Scarborough, North
Yorkshire, 2017. Photograph by the author.

p. 148   Cricket jumper pattern printed by *Wendy c.*1980,
belonging to Audrey Cowton. Photograph by the author.

p. 158   Hand-whittled nålebinding needle and Icelandic
Léttlopi yarn by Álafoss, 2017. Photograph by
the author.

p. 166   Latched needles on Imperia knitting machine at
Anne Drew's Sock School, 2017. Photograph by
the author.

p. 179   Polperro harbour, Polperro, Cornwall, 2017.
Photograph by the author.

p. 184   *The Docker (La Travailleux D'Cauchie),* bronze
statue of a fisherman wearing a jersey, designed

by Colin Miller, St Helier, Jersey, 2017.
Photograph by the author.

p. 196 Detail of an undyed Guernsey, 2017. Photograph
by the author.

p. 206 Hay's Dock, facing Bressay Sound, Lerwick,
Shetland, 2017. Photograph by the author.

p. 210 Advertisement for hosiers Anderson & Co.,
printed in *Mansons' Shetland Almanac and
Directory*, 1892. Photograph by the author.

p. 216 Oliver Henry and Shetland fleeces at Jamieson
& Smith, 90 North Road, Lerwick, Shetland,
2017. Photograph by the author.

p. 245 Male Welsh stocking knitter, Bala. Reproduced
courtesy of Gwynedd Archives Service.

p. 263 Chrissie Cheyne, Brig o' Wass, Shetland
Museum; reproduced courtesy of Shetland
Museum and Archives Trust.

p. 265 Lace shawl knitted by Betsy Williamson and
displayed at A Happening, Ollaberry, Shetland
Wool Week 2017. Photograph by the author.

p. 279 Five Preston North End fans at Preston bus
station about to travel to the FA Cup semi-final
at Maine Road Manchester, March 1954. A crowd
of 75,000 saw Preston beat Sheffield Wednesday
2–0 to get to the FA Cup final at Wembley,
where they lost 3–2 to West Bromwich Albion.
Courtesy of the National Football Museum.

Index

Numbers in *italics* refer to illustrations; 'pl' refers to the plates.

acrylic yarn, 65
adderback pattern, *17*, 29, *pl 1*
Aelfric, abbot of Eynsham, 25
Agincourt, battle of (1415), 238–9
Agricolaus, 180
Aiken, Walter and Jonas, 166
Aileach (birlinn), 99
Álafoss *see* Léttlopi yarn
Alexander III, king of Scotland, 90
Allen, Mary, 18–19, 27, 33; gloves
    made by, *17*
Alloa, 215, 262–3
Alpaca Tweed Silk yarn, 124
alpaca yarn, 172
alum, 225, 226, 227
Am Fasgadh, 85–90
American Revolution (1775–83),
    80
Andelle, Anne Marguerite, 75
Anderson & Co., 211–13, *212*, 217
Anne, Princess, The Princess
    Royal, 196
Anstruther, 51
Aran knitting, 151–2
Argyle pattern, *84*, 88
Argyll, 40
Ariadne (mythical character), 14
Assynt, 40
Aubrey, John, 245
Ayrshire, 40

Baa Ram Ewe, 174–5, *pl 15*
babywear, 256–7, 261, 263, 264,
    269, *pl 26*
Bakewell, Robert, 107
Bala, 245–6, 246–7, *247*
balaclavas, 242–3
Baldwin, James, 262
Baldwins yarn company, 262, *pl 23*
Banks, Sir Joseph, 210
Bardi family, 139
Barrie, Walter, 116
Barrie Mill, 116
Batley, Holly, 111–12
Beck, Samuel William, 184
Beeton, Mrs, 261
Bell, Vanessa (née Stephen), 71;
    paintings by, *pl 4*
Bénard, Abraham-Joseph *see*
    Fleury
Benedetto di Bindo, 164
Bernardini, Micheline, 122
Berneray, 98–100
bersugget, 24
Bertram of Minden, Master, 164
Bewdley, 240
bielset, 24
bikinis, *104*, 122–7, *pl 12*
Billings, Julia, 226, 227; yarns dyed
    at workshop, *pl 20*
bird's eye pattern, 49

The Birlinn Yarn Company, 98–100
birlinns, 98–100
Bishop, Justin, 'Cousy' (cricketer), 148
Black, Sandy, 269
Blacker Yarns, 259, *pl 26*
Blaise, St, 180, 193–4
blankets, 237, 250
Bleibtrey, Ethelda, 122
Bliss, Debbie, 74
blocking, 271–2
bobbins, *137*
böds (booths; bothies), 219–22
Bonington, Chris, 201
Book of Kells, 152
Border Mill, 124
the Borders, 40, 89–90, 105–11, 113–21
Borders Textile Towerhouse, 111
Boreray island, 257–8
Borrow, George, 240
Boston Museum of Fine Arts, 79–80
Bourton-on-the-Water, 139
Boxgrove, 180
Boyle, Charlotte, 122
Bradford, 13, 171, 172
Bradley, Annie 'Nan', 168–9
Brathay Exploration Group, 258
breeding *see* sheep: line-breeding; sheep breeds and types
British Wool Marketing Board (BWMB), 215–16
British Wool Society, 107
Brora, 215
Brown, Jessie, 120–1
Brown, Jock, 120–1
Brunel, Marc Isambard, 166
Buckhaven, *43*
Buckland, Kirstie, 239–42, 252
bump, 32
Burford, 140
Burnt Njal Saga, 223
Butler, Lady Eleanor, 250–1
Buxtehude Altar, 164
BWMB *see* British Wool Marketing Board

cabling, 45, 151–2, 177, *pl 27*
Cairngorms, 85, 103
Cambridge University, MRC Cognition and Brain Sciences Unit, 70–1
Camden, William, 185
camomile, 226
canals, 172
Capper, Joan and Isabella, 239
Capper, Thomas, 238–9
carding, 13, 135, 137
Carlyle, Thomas, 78
Carrington, Dora, 72
casting on, 20–1
Cellardyke, *51*
Chamberlain, Sir Leonard, 194–5
Chanel, 116, 118
Channel Islands, 183–202
Channel Islands Knitwear Co., 185–6, 198–201
Chapman, Roslyn, 268–9
Charles II, king of England, Scotland and Ireland, 12, 256
Charles, Prince of Wales, 196
Chatwin, Bruce, 245
Chaucer, Geoffrey, 25
Cheyne, Chrissie, *265*
Chipping Camden, 140
Christiansen, Carol, 230–1, 266
Churchill pattern, 213–14
cinema *see* films
Cirencester, 140
clews, 25
climate, and knitwear, 290
Cloud Drift Baby Shawl, 261–2, 263
Clun Forest yarn, 145, *pl 13*
Cochrane, Adam L., 114
code, knitted, 80–2
Coffin, Sir Edward Pine, 41
colourwork *see* stranded colourwork
Columbine (boat), 221
combinations, 117
combing, 142–4, 180, 193–4, 195
Compton, Rae, 46, 47–8, 58
Cooper, Jane, 257, 259–60
copper, 226, 227

Coppergate Sock, 157, 159, 161, 175
Cornwall, 177–83, 251, 259, 285
Cotswolds, 66, 138–42
Cotton, William, 113
Cowton, Audrey, 150
Cowton, Jeff, 278–85
Cowton, Steve, 148–50
Cowton, Tom, 102–3, 159, 160, 282–3, 285–6
Coyle, Kat, 67
craftivism, 68
creativity, and knitting, 73
cricket, 145–53
cricket whites and pullovers, 146–8, 150–3, *150*, *pl 13*
Crimlisk brothers, 51
crimp, 134, 144
crofting, 39–40, 92, 95
Crosthwaite, 283
crotal, 97
Crowe, Russell, 241
Crusoe, Robinson, 223
Culley, George and Matthew, 108
Cumbria, 4, 16–19, 264, 282–3
Cuthbert's Sock yarn, 66

Dales knitting, *8*, *17*, 16–22, *17*, 26–34, *pl 1*
Davies, Gwen, 244–5
Davies, Kate, 214, 262, 264–5
Davies, Sally, 251–2
Davies, Walter, 247–8
De Beauvoir, Peter, 195–6
death and funerals, 12, 243–5, *pl 24*
deer, 101
Defarge, Madame (Dickens character), 68–70, 74, 78–9, 80
Defoe, Daniel, 240
Delaney, Ken, 279
Dentdale knitting, *8*, 16–22, *17*, 26–34, *pl 1*
Depardieu, Gérard, 241
Derby, 109
Dickens, Charles, 68–70, 74, 78–9, 80, 171, 243
Diocletian, Roman emperor, 11
Dinsdale, Martha, 32

Dinteville, Jean de, 239
Dionysius Alexandrinus, St, 10
distaffs, 136
Dixon, J. H., 93
dizes, 143
dog hair, 133
Drake, Sir Francis, 239–40
Drayton, Michael, 191
Dress Act (1746), 87
dressing, 271–2
Drew, Anne, 167–70
drop spindling, 135–6
Dryburgh, 104
Dubied knitting machines, 114–15, *pl 10*
Dunbartonshire, 40
Dunmore, Catherine Murray, Countess of, 93–4
Duns, 124
Durell, Edward, 190, 193
dyeing, 11, 97, 224–5, 226–7, *pl 19–20*

Eardley-Wilmot, Sarah, 237–8
East Anglia, 9–10, 131–2, 143
Edinburgh, Prince Philip, Duke of, 196
Edinburgh Yarn Festival, 62–7
Edmonston, Eliza, 268
Edward I, king of England, 132
Edward III, king of England, 11, 132
Edward VIII, king of Great Britain and Ireland, 211
Egypt, 155
Eildon, 105
Elizabeth I, queen of England and Ireland, 12, 185–6, 195
Elizabeth II, queen of Great Britain and Northern Ireland, 196
Embleton Bay, 127, *pl 12*
Emily (knitwear design student), 114–16
espionage, and knitting, 80–2
Eugénie, empress of France, 243
Evans, Huw, 250

Evans, Revd John, 246–7
Everlast, 117
Evesham Abbey, 139

Fair Isle, 210, 222–6, *pl 21*
Fair Isle Crafts, 225
Fassett, Kaffe, 214
Fates, the three, 14
fell wool, 156–7
felting, 252–3
festivals and shows, 62–7, 205–32,
    264–6, 270–2, *pl 19–20*, *pl 25*
Filey, 49–50
films, and knitwear, 241
Finland, 173
First World War (1914–18), 80–1
fisherman's rib (fancy rib), 125
Fisherrow, 50
fishing, 38–43, *43*, 52–4, 178;
    herring women, 52–4, 217, *pl
    2*; *see also* ganseys; guernseys;
    jerseys; knit-frocks
Fitzgerald, Colin, 90
Flamborough, 50
flannel, 237
fleece: in mythology, 13–14;
    preparation, 134; raw, *2*, *137*,
    pl 14; weighing, 142; weight of
    typical, 23
Flemish textile workers, 11, 132,
    139, 236–7
Fleury (Abraham-Joseph Bénard),
    78
Florentine Wool Guild, 139
football, 278–85, *281*
Ford, Felicity (Felix), 229–30
Fortey, John, 141–2
Fowler, Lady, 93
Framework Knitters Museum,
    111–12, 169, *pl 11*
framework knitting, 108–13, *pl 11*
Framlingham, 63
France, 196
Frangipani yarns, 47
French Revolution, 68–70, 74–80,
    77
Frescobaldi family, 139

Friedland, Paul, 77–8
Fuller, Thomas, 240
funerals *see* death and funerals

Gairloch estate, 90–3, *91*, 95, 101
Gairloch Museum, 101, *pl 6*
Gairloch stockings, *84*, 90–3,
    95–103, *pl 6*
gaiters, 238
Galashiels, 108, 113–16, 215, *pl 10*
ganseys: author's project, *36*, 44–9,
    58–9, 61, 105, 177, 273, 285,
    286–8, *pl 27–8*; etymology, 38;
    in general, 37–59; needles, 36,
    47; and owner identification,
    49, 56; patterns and designs,
    43–5, 47–54, 56–8, 228;
    Shetland Dandy, 114; time
    taken to knit, 45; traditional
    shape, 47; yarns and colours,
    43, 47, 50, 54, 55; *see also*
    guernseys; jerseys; knit-frocks
Garthenor farm and yarn, 66, *234*,
    251–2
gathering (*gwlana*), 249–50
Gattonside, 105
gender issues: the blood taboo,
    41–2; men knitting, 31, 71–2,
    192, 246–7, *247*, 265–6, 268–9;
    women and fishing industry,
    41–2, 52–4, 217, *pl 2*; women
    and political protest, 67–8,
    74–9; working women and
    marriage, 120
Genoa, 163
George III, king of Great Britain
    and Ireland, 210
George Woodcock and Sons, 119
Gernreich, Rudi, 122–3
Giese, Georg, 239
gift knitting, 277–8
Gillanders, Deb, 54–7
Glain, Madeleine, 75
Gloucester Abbey, 139, 140
gloves, *8*, 15–22, 26–9, 33–4, 195,
    pl 1
Godineau, Dominique, 76, 79

golfwear, 118, 211
Golomb, Joseph, 117
Gordon, Colonel John, 97
Gordon Cathcart, Lady, 97
Gordon Highlanders, 88–9
Grace, W. G., 146–7
Graham, Jessie, 120–1
Grant, Dr Isabel, 85–6, 90, 95
Grasmere, 16–19, 264, 282–3
Griffiths, Walford Arnold, 9, 10
Griswold, Henry, 166
grosgrain (grogram), 13, 293–4
ground elder, 227, *pl 19*
Guernsey, 38, 184, 194–8, 273;
    language, 195
guernseys, 184, 196–7, *197*
guillotines, 68–70, 295
Gunn, Neil, 40–1
Gylfe, Ernest, 173–4

Haccombe, 180
Haddington, 110
Hald, Margarethe, 161
Halifax, 13, 171, 193–4, 262–3
Hamptonne Country Life
    Museum, 189, *pl 16–17*
Hansen, Egon, 161
haps, *254*, 263–75, *267*, *pl 26*;
    etymology, 264–5; yarn, 271,
    272–3
Hardie, John, 110
Hardie, Ryan, 283–4
Harding, Lewis, 179
Harris, 258
Harris, Howell, 237
Harris Tweed, 93–4
Harrison, Edward, 107
Harrogate College, 131
Hartley, Marie, 29–33
Hartnell, Norman, 241
Harvard Medical School, 71
hats and headwear: baby bonnets,
    269; balaclavas, 242–3;
    historical legal obligation to
    wear, 12; Monmouth caps, 238–
    42, 248, 251–3, *pl 22*; Phrygian
    caps, 79–80; Pussyhats, *60*,

67–8, 73–4, 82, *pl 3*; Shetland
    caps, 206–7, 209–10, *pl 21*;
    Welsh wigs, 242–3
Hawick, 108–11, 116
Hawker, Robert Stephen, 178
Heald Brow wood, 4
health: and wool, 147; *see also*
    mental health
Hebrides, 96–100
Hemingway, Penelope Lister, 27–8
Henderson Technical College, 119
Henry VI, Holy Roman Emperor,
    140
Henry VIII, king of England, 239
Henry, Bill, 211–12, 213
Henry, Oliver, 215, 217, *218*
Heriot-Watt University School of
    Textiles and Design, 114–16,
    pl 10
herring trade, 52–4, 217, *pl 2*
Hertfordshire, 143
Heselton, Doug, 56
Hibbert, Samuel, 210, 225
High Ickenthwaite, 4
Highland Clearances, 39, 40–1
Highland Folk Museum, 85–90,
    pl 6
Hildred, 'Hippy' Alf, 55
hit and miss pattern, 49–50
Hitra Coastal Museum, 99
La Hogue Bie, 189
Holbein, Hans, the Younger, 239
Holme, Peter, 280
hose, 88, 195; *see also* stockings
Howitt, William, 32
Huguenots, 132, 193, 290
Hunter, Agnes, 262
Hunters of Brora, 215, 216
Hutchinson, Sara, 264

Iceland, 159–60
Imperia sock knitting machines,
    167, *168*
India, 225
indigo, 225
Ingilby, Joan, 29–33
Ingram, Sir Arthur, 225

Iona, 65, 66, 85–6
Ipswich, 132
Isaac Briggs yarn company, 262
Isbister, Emma, 270, 271
Isle of Man, 57–8
Italy, 139, 163, 225

Jaeger, 147
James I and VI, king of England, Scotland and Ireland, 195
James IV, king of Scotland, 40, 107
James Hutton Institute, 98
Jamieson, James (sailor), 221
Jamieson, James (wool buyer), 215
Jamieson & Smith, 4–5, 214–17, *218*, 271, 272–3
Jamieson's of Shetland, 216–18, 271
Jane (crafter), 63
Jantzen, Carl, 122
Jarlshof, 209
Jarmson, Jeannie, 213
Jason and the Argonauts, 13–14
Jeandeau, Pierre, 166
Jedburgh, 105, *106*
jennies, 143, 171
Jèrriais language, 188
Jersey, 183–94, 198–202, *pl 16–17*; language, 188
jerseys, 185, *186*, 192, 200–1, *pl 17*; etymology, 184
Jesus Christ, 162–4
John Whitemore yarn company, 262
Johnes, Thomas, 236
Johnston, Elizabeth, 64
Johnston, Gilbert, 216
Johnston, Gudrun, 206
Johnston's of Elgin, 107
Jolliff, Charles, 182
Jolliff, Jane, 182
Jorvik socks, *154*, 158–62, 164–5, 170, 175

Katwijk pattern, 228
Keighley, 171, 173–5
Kellerman, Annette, 121–2

Kelso, 105, 106
kemps, 134
Kersel, Robert, 116
kerseymere, 238
Keynes, John Maynard, 71
Kiewe, Heinz, 152
Kildonan Museum, 97, 99
kilt pleat pattern, 44
kilts, 86–7
King, Jonny, 251–2
King's Lynn, 132
Kingsolver, Barbara, 287
Kirkbride, Mary ('Molly i' t' Wynd'), 30–1
Kirkby, Stephen, 19
Kirkcaldy, 283–4
Kissling, Werner, 96
knit-frocks, 178–83
knit nights and gatherings, 32, 189–90, 250–1
knit stitch, 25
KnitSonik, 229–30
knitting: author's abilities, 15, 126–7, 290; flexibility in everyday life, 270; history of, 162–4; learning, 5–6; making to measure, 45–7; popular attitude to handknit items, 269; progress of typical projects, 61–2; in public, 53, 183, 188–9, 190, 273; in the round, 162–4; speeds, 110, 182; vocabulary, 24–5
Knitting & Crochet Guild, 263
knitting belts, 266
knitting frames *see* framework knitting
knitting guards, 182
knitting sticks, 285
knitwear industry: Channel Islands, 196–201; machine-knitting, 108–21, 166–70, 196–201; mediaeval history, 132, 139; Scotland, 89–90, 92–5; Shetland, 211–13, 266–9, 271; Wales, 236–7, 245–8
Kopytoff, Igor, 3

lace knitting, *254*, 266–75, *267, pl 25*
laceweight yarn, 260–1, 267–8, 272–3, *pl 26*
Ladies of Llangollen, 250–1
land enclosures, 39–40
language: Channel Islands, 188, 195; woollen metaphors, 14–15; yarn and knitting vocabulary, 23–5
lanolin, 135
Latour Doyle, Phyllis, 81
Latvia, 162
Le Grand, Father Leon, 198
Le Grand, Maria, 198
Le Maistre, Frank, 192
Lee, Hermione, 72
Lee, William, 108
Leeds, 13, 166–7, 174–5
Leicester, 109
Leicestershire, 244–5
Leighton-White, Sue, 19, 20
Lennox, Gavin, 111
Leominster, 248
Lerwick, 207–11, *208*, 214–19, 225
Lesueur, Jean-Baptiste, pictures by, 76, 77
Léttlopi yarn, 160, *160, pl 15*
Levengle, Madame, 80–1
Levenson, Lawrence, 207
Lewis, 258
Lewis, Eliza, 243–4, *pl 24*
lichen, 97
Lightfoot, Amy, 99–100
linkers, 116, 119
Liskeard, 183
The Little Knittery, 67
Llanrwst, 245–6
Loch Broom, 93
Locker, Steve, 55
Long, Rob Harvey, 138
Longbottom, Peter, 173–4
Looe, 183
Loop, 74
Lorenzetti, Ambrogio, 163
Lothian, 110
Loudon, Alice, 126–7

Louis XVI, king of France, 75
Lucca, 163
Luddite movement, 113
Lyle, William, 116–17
Lyle & Scott, 116–17, 117–18, 119

Macaulay Land Use Research Institute, 98
Macdonald, Finlay J., 96, 97
Macdonald, Gordon, 119
MacDougall, Robert, 196
machine-knitting, 108–21, 166–70, 196–201
McKellan, Ian, 241
Mackenzie, Sir Francis, 91
Mackenzie, Sir Hector, 90–1
Mackenzie, Dr John, 91–2
Mackenzie, Sir Kenneth, 91–2
Mackenzie, Lady Mary, 91–3
Mackenzie clan, 90–3, 101
madder, 226, 227, 239, *pl 20*
Madonnas of Humility, 163–4
Magnus Barelegs Saga, 297
Man, Isle of, 57–8
Man of Aran (film), 151–2
Mantua, 163
Marie-Antoinette, queen of France, 75
Maritime Heritage Centre, 50–2
Markham, Albert Hastings, 243
marriage lines pattern, 50
Martin, Jeanne, 75
Martin, Richard, 139
Mary, Virgin, 163–4
Mary I, queen of England, 194–5
Mary Queen of Scots, 185
Massachusetts Bay Company, 240
matinee jackets, 261
Mathers, Emma, 148
Melrose, 105, 106
mental health, and knitting, 27–9, 70–3
Metcalfe, Kit and Betty, 31
micron counts, 131
midwifery, and knitting, 274
Milan, 163
Milton, 180

Moar, James, 268–9
Monmouth, 235, 239, 241
Monmouth caps, 238–42, 248,
    251–3, *pl 22*
monokinis, 122–3
Moray Firth, 48
mordant, 226
More, John, 239
Moreton-in-Marsh, 139
Morrell, Lady Ottoline, 72
Mouat, Betty, 219–22
Mrs Hunter's Shawl, 261–2, 263
Murray brothers, *51*
Murrell, Elly, 134–8, *pl 14*
Murrell, Suzanne, 28–9, 65
Musselburgh, 50

nålebinding, *154*, 155–7, 158–62,
    164–5, 170, 175, *pl 15*; needles,
    158–9, *160*, 170; pattern
    abbreviations, 161; yarn, 159–60
Naples, 163
nappy wrappers, 261
Nares, Sir George, 242–3
National Football Museum, 280–1
Natural Fibre Company, 66, 251,
    259
needle guards, 21–2, 47
needles, *276*; dialect words for,
    30, 53; for ganseys, 36, 47;
    for knit-frocks, 182; latched,
    166, *168*; mediaeval, 162; for
    nålebinding, 158–9, *160*, 170;
    types and sizes, 24
Neeson, Liam, 241
Nelson Museum and Local
    History Centre, 241
Netherdale Mill, 114–16
Netherlands, 228
New Mills Cloth Manufactory, 110
Newtonmore, 85–90
Niccolò di Buonaccorso, 163–4
niddy-noddies, 137, *137*
Norbury, James, 262, 263
Norman, Greg, 118
Norns, 14
Northcott, John, 182

Northleach, 139–42, *141*
Northumberland, 40, 50, 127, *pl 12*
Norway, 99–100
Nottingham, 109, 113
Norwich, 132, 143
Novita, 173–4

Odent, Michel, 274
Okumura, Sayaka, 73
Old Shale pattern, 272–3, 274–5
Ollaberry, 264–6, *pl 25*
organic yarn, 251–2
Orkney, 257, 259–60
OXO motif, 213

Padua, 163
papier timbre, Revolt of the (1675),
    79
Parmenter, Jack, 147, 153
Parmenter, Pip, 278
parramatta, 13, 294
Paton, John, 262
Patons & Baldwins, 215, 261–4
patterns: history of circulation,
    256–7; vintage, 256–7, 261–4,
    272; written instructions for
    ganseys, 5
peat fires, 220
Penelope (Homeric character), 14,
    27
Pennant, Thomas, 250
Penzance, 177, 179
Pepper, William H., 166
Pergolotti family, 139
Peter, Sister, 199
Peter Scott Knitwear, 117
philabegs, 86–7
Philpott, Robin, 56
Phrygian caps, 79–80
pilch knickers, 261
Piperell, Colonel, 196
Pipps & Co., 285
plaids, 86
plying, 137
Plymley, Joseph, 145
Plymouth, 183
Poingdestre, Jean, 184, 187, 191

Poland, 162
Polperro, 178, 181–3, *181*
Pope, Alexander, 12–13
post-traumatic stress, 70–1
Potato Blight (1846), 92
presents *see* gift knitting
Preston North End fans, 280–1, *281*
Priaulx, T. F., 194, 195
pricks, 30
princetta, 13, 294
Pringle, 116, 118, 119
purl stitch, 25
Pussyhats, *60*, 67–8, 73–4, 82, *pl 3*

Queen of the South, 282, 283–4

R. H. Barker yarn company, 262
Rae, James, 89
raepin string, 266
railroad patterns, 58, *pl 27*
Raith Rovers, 282, 283–4
Raleigh, Sir Walter, 185
Ramsay, Mrs (Woolf character), 72–3
rationing, 123
Rawnsley, Eleanor, 18–19
Réard, Louis, 122
retting, 129
Richard I, the Lionheart, king of England, 140
Rigg, Diana, 241
Rinker, Molly, 80
Ripon, 239
Rob Roy tartan, 89
Roberts, Brian, 144
Roberts, Dunja, 143–5, 235–6
Robertson, James, 224
Robertson family, *43*
Robin Hood's Bay, 49
Rodger, Andrew, 99
Rodger, Meg, 98–100
Rogers, Penelope Walton, 159
Romans, 10–11, 157–8, 251
rooing, 23
Rosebery, Countess of, 94
Rosher, Lucia, 253
Roslin, 258

Ross, James Clark, 242
Ross, John, 242
Rovers, Wimpje and Cor (Dutch knitters), 228
Ruddington, 111–12, 113, 169, *pl 11*
runrig system, 39
Russell Beale, Simon, 241
Rutt, Richard, 151–2
Rutter, Esther, *pl 3*, *pl 12*, *pl 14*; childhood, 9–10; first meeting with future husband, 282–3; knitting skills, 15, 126–7, 290; pregnancy, 260–1, 270, 273–4
Rutter, Gabrielle, 63, 131, 133–7
Rutter, Michael, 45–7, 58, 288, *pl 28*

sails, 99–100
St Blazey, 179–80
St Chad's Home Stocking Industry, 166–7
St Fagans National Museum of History, 242–3, 248, *pl 24*
St Helier, 185, *186*, 198–201
St Kilda, 23, 257–8
St Kilda Laceweight yarn, 260–1, 271–2, *pl 26*
St Peter Port, 194, 196, 197
Salt, Titus, 172–3, 175
Saltaire, 172–3
Sandness, 218
Sangan, Louis Jules, 198
Sangan, Robert, 199
Sara (Swedish knitter), 222, 231
Sarnicoll (Thomas Jacob Thomas), 246
sarples, 142
Scarborough, 49, 50–2
Scarborough Cricket Club, 148–52, *149*
scarves, *204*, 219, 227; football scarves, 278–85, *281*; temperature scarves, 66–7, *pl 5*
Schmitt, Larry, 161
Scotland: ganseys, 43–5, 48, 50; history of farming and fishing, 38–43, 52; history of wool, 13;

knitting and textiles, 85–103; machine-knitting industry, 108–11, 113–21; spinning industry, 97–8, 215–16, 218, 268; *see also* the Borders; Shetland islands
Scott, Irene, 119–20
Scott, Walter (businessman), 116–17
Scott, Sir Walter (author), 210, 223
Scottish Fisheries Museum, 38
Scottish flag (kilt pleat) pattern, 44
Scottish Home Industry Association (SHIA), 94–5
scouring, 135
sea, early names for, 53–4
Searle, Richard, 182
Second World War (1939–45), 81, 199–200, 213
Sedgwick, Adam, 32
Selkirk, Alexander, 223
Shackleton, Ernest, 38
Shakespeare, William, 238
shawls, 210, 237–8, *254*, 261, 263–75, *267*, *pl 25–6*; etymology, 264–5; yarn, 271
sheep: line-breeding, 107; moulting, 23; Shetland names for markings, 23–4
sheep breeds and types: Badger Face Black Mountain, 236; Balwen, 236; Black Welsh Mountain, 236; Blackface, 40, 107, 258; Border Leicester ('Great Improver'), 107–8; Borders, 89–90; Boreray, 257–60; Bowmont, 98; Brecknock Hill Cheviot, 236; broad classifications, 133; Channel Islands, 191; Cheviot, 40, 100, 107; Clun Forest, 145; Cotswold, *128*, 138; Cotswold Longwool, 252; Cretan type, 11; Galloway, 40; Hebridean, 98–9, 100; Hebridean Blackface, 258; Herdwick, 4, 26, 130, 131; Highland, 39, 40, 90, 95; Hill Radnor, 236; Icelandic, 159–60; Jersey, 191; Kerry, 95–6; Kerry Hill, 236; Lammermoor, 40; Linton, 40; Llandovery White Face, 236; Llanwenog, 236; Manx Loaghtan, 192–3; Masham, 133; Merino, 130, 131, 133; Ryeland, *234*, 248–9, 252–3; Scottish Dunface (Shortwool), 106–7; Shetland, 4–5, 6, 22, 23–4, 26, 64, 96, 209; Soay, 23; Suffolk, 134; Teeswater, 133; Tweeddale, 40; Viking, 159; *villsau*, 99–100, 159; Wensleydale, 108, 133; Wiltshire Horn, 11
sheep farming: Borders, 105–8; Channel Islands, 191–3; Cumbria, 4; history of, 22, 131–2, 139–40; Orkney, 257, 259; St Kilda, 257–8; Scotland, 39–40, 101; Shetland, 209; Suffolk, 9–10; Wales, 235–6, 251–2
Sheepscombe, 139
Sheffield FC, 279–80
Sheila (crafter), 63
Sherborne, 138–9
Shetland caps, 206–7, 209–10, *pl 21*
Shetland Handspun yarn, 64
Shetland Heritage yarn, 217
Shetland islands, 23–4, 205–32, 264–72
Shetland knitting, *204*, 210, 211–19, 222, 227–8, *pl 18–21*; haps, *254*, 263–75, *267*; patterns 213–14; yarn, 4–5, 214–18, 227, 271, 272–3
Shetland Museum, 208–11, *pl 18*, *pl 21*
Shetland Wool Week, 205–32, 264–6, 270–2, *pl 19–20*, *pl 25*
SHIA *see* Scottish Home Industry Association
Shima knitting machines, 114–15
Shipley, 171
Shipton, 139

Shirreff, John, 209
shows *see* festivals and shows
shrouds, 12
silk yarn, 65–6, 109, 130
Sinclair, Sir John, 107
Sitwell, Dame Edith, 71
Skene, Bailie Alexander, 89
Slater, Mary, 213–14
smirlset, 24
Smith, Brian, 207
Smith, Donna, 270–2
Smith, George Campbell, 92
Smith, John 'Sheepie', 215
Soay (island), 23
socks, *154*, 155–62, 164–75, *pl 15*;
    etymology, 157; knitting two
    at a time, 165; second sock
    syndrome, 165; sock knitting
    machines, 166–70, *168*
sokket, 24
sound, and knitting, 229–30
Southey, Robert, 17
Spain, 162, 225
Speedo, 122
Spence, James R., 225
spencers, 195, 304
spinning: in general, 129–38, 144;
    in the grease, 135; handspun
    vs machine-spun, 266; in
    mythology and folk tale, 13–14;
    tools, *137*; worsted vs woollen
    spun, 144
spinning industry: Channel
    Islands, *176*, 184, 189; Cornwall,
    251, 259; Fair Isle, 224;
    Scotland, 97–8, 215–16, 218,
    268; Yorkshire, 151, 171–5
spinning jennies, 171
spinning wheels, 136, *176*, 189,
    pl 16
spit-splicing, 159
sprangwork, 157–8
Sprott, Walter, 72
stag's head pattern, 90, 102
Staithes, 49, 50
staple length, 133
staple towns, 132

Starmore, Alice, 214
stash, 62
Stead, J., 187, 188–9
Stephen, Adrian, 71
Stephen, Julia, 72
Stephen, Vanessa *see* Bell, Vanessa
Stewart Brothers, 215–16
stitch counting, 32
stocking stitch, 88
stockings: Channel Islands, 185–7,
    190, 195–6; etymology, 87;
    footless, 246; funeral stockings,
    243–5, *pl 24*; Gairloch, *84*,
    90–3, 95–103, *pl 6*; history
    of, 87–8, 157–8; Italian, 163;
    machine-knit, 109–13, 116,
    166–7; military, 87, 88–9, *pl
    9*; sailors', 30–1; Scotland, *84*,
    87–93, 95–103, *pl 6*; Shetland,
    207, 210; Wales, 238, 243–8
Storm family patterns, 49
Stout, Jerome, 222
Stow, John, 239
Stow-on-the-Wold, 139, 140
Strachey, Lytton, 71–2
stranded colourwork: Scotland,
    84, 88–90, 93, 95–6, 102, *pl 6*;
    Shetland, *204*, 210, 211–19, 222,
    227–8, *pl 18–21*; Yorkshire, *8*,
    17–22, *17*, 26–7, 33–4, *pl 1*
Strathpeffer, 93
Stubbes, Philip, 88
Suffolk, 9–10, 131
Suh, Krista, 67
suint, 135
Sumburgh, 219
Summerland, 198–201
Sutcliffe Gallery, 58
Sutherland, David, 269
swastikas, 213
swatching, 20
swaving, 19
sweater curse, 285–6
swimwear, *104*, 121–7, *124*, *pl 12*
Swiss Cottage Workshops for the
    Blind, 168–9
Sykes, Sir Christopher, 246

T. M. Adie, 216
tacksmen, 39, 40
Talbot, Lord Gilbert, 238
tartan, 86–7, 89
Taylor, Rita, 54
television, and knitwear, 241
temperature scarves, 66–7, *pl 5*
tension maintenance, 266
tension squares, 20
textiles industry *see* knitwear
    industry; weaving and textiles
theatre, and knitwear, 241
Thomas, Thomas Jacob *see*
    Sarnicoll
Thomas Ramsden yarns, 47
Thompson, Gladys, 50–1
thropples, 25
Thurso, 48
Thurso flag pattern, 44
Thwaite, Margaret, 27–8
Tibbot, S. Minwel, 250
Tindall, Hazel, 182
Tingwall, 230
Titus yarn, 175, *pl 15*
Todenham, 139
tods, 142
Tolkien, J. R. R., 30
Tomlin, Stephen, 72
Tommaso da Modena, 164
Tømmervik Textile Trust, 99–100
tops, 143
Torbuck, John, 249
Torridon, 101–2
Town End Yarns, 282–3
tradition, and knitting, 288–90
Trefeca, 237
Tregaron, 245–6
Trevelyan, Marie, 249
Le Tricoteur, 196–7
tricoteuses, 68–70, 76–80, 77
Trondenes, 99
truck system, 212–13
Trump, Donald, 67–8, 73–4, 82,
    pl 3
turmeric, 226
tweed, 93–4
twinsets, 118

Uist, 96–8
Uist Wool, 97–8, 216, *pl 7–8*
underwear, 108, 116–18
Underwood, Michael, 261
Unst, 266–9
Uyeasound, 268–9

Val (crafter), 63
Vatersay Raiders, 97
Verona, 163
Victoria, queen of Great Britain
    and Ireland, 87, 210
Victoria and Albert Museum, 155,
    256, 261, 272
Vikings, 98–100, 156–7, 223, 290,
    297; *see also* Coppergate Sock
Vindolanda, 158
Vitale da Bologna, 163

wadmal, 99–100, 209
Waifs and Strays Society, 166–7
Wales, 235–43, *pl 22*, *pl 24*; border
    with England, 235; traditional
    costume, 237–8
weaving and textiles, 11, 13, 14,
    93–4, 107; *see also* knitwear
    industry
wedding-ring shawls, 268
Wedigh family, 239
weirs, 53
Weisz, Otto, 118
Welsh wigs, 242–3
Wendy Ascot yarn, 150
West Yorkshire Spinners, 151, 171,
    173–5, *pl 13*
Westermann, Karie, 16
Westminster Abbey, 139
Whistlebare, 66
Whitby, 50, 54–7, 58
whuskers, 53
wigs, Welsh, 242–3
Wild, J. P., 23
Williamson, Betty, 265–6;
    items knitted by, *267*, *pl 25*
Williamson, Gilbert, 269
Williamson, Linda, 265–6
Willey, Marsha, 66–7

Winchcombe, 140
woad, 226
Women's March, Washington, DC
    (2017), 67–8
woodruff, 226
wool: history of British, 10–13,
    22; laceweight yarn, 260–1,
    267–8, 272–3, *pl 26*; measuring,
    130–1; mediaeval wool trade,
    131–2, 139–42; its memory, 287;
    organic, 216, 251–2; price, 216;
    in production, *pl 8*; structure
    and characteristics, 6, 130;
    vintage yarn weights, 271;
    washing, 137–8
wool types *see* sheep breeds
Woolcraft, 262, *pl 23*
Woolf, Virginia, 70, 71, 72–3, *pl 4*
the Woolsack, 11–12, 82
Wordsworth, Dora, 264
Wordsworth Museum, 16–19, *17*,
    264, 282
Worstead, 26

worsted, 26, 144, 294
Wright, Mary, 178–9, 182
wusset, 53

Y-fronts, 117–18
Yarmouth, 132, *pl 2*
Yarn (film), 287
yarn: ethical, 65–6; organic, 251–2;
    see also alpaca; dog hair; silk;
    wool
yolk, 135
York, 27–8, 156–8, 239; *see also*
    Coppergate Sock
Yorkshire: Dales knitting, *8, 17*,
    16–22, *17*, 26–34; ganseys,
    48–50, 54–7, 58; and St Blaise,
    193–4; spinning industry, 151,
    171–5; textiles industry, 13;
    yarn companies, 151, 171, 173–5,
    262–4, *pl 13*

Zweiman, Jayna, 67